BizB Press

New York London

First published by BizB Press 2019

Copyright © 2019 by John J. Cousins

ISBN 9781795149617

MBA ASAP

Master the Game of Business

John Cousins

BizB Press

New York   London

About the Author

John Cousins is an independent business advisor. He helps people explore opportunities so they accelerate success, transition to what they love doing, and have more fun. Before creating MBA-ASAP.com, he was a systems engineer for ABC Television, launched seven startups, took two companies public, and was a public company CFO and CEO for 15 years. John has his MBA from Wharton and undergrad degrees from Boston University and MIT. He lives in New Mexico.

Sign up for my Newsletter and get free books. Sign up at www.mba-asap.com and receive **Reading and Understanding Financial Statements** absolutely free.

Receive announcements of free and discounted books and courses.

MBA ASAP
Master the Game of Business

Table of Contents

7

13

15

Introduction

You are a business

You already know all you need to know about running a business. You just haven't convinced yourself of this fact. Once you read through this book you will gain the confidence to move forward and eliminate the self-doubt that holds you back.

"People always overestimate how complex business is. This isn't rocket science—we've chosen one of the world's most simple professions."
    Jack Welch former CEO of GE

Business is a Game

You need to know the rules in order to play. And you need to know how to play well in order to succeed. This book is designed to help you become the chess player, not the chess piece.

Most of business knowledge is common sense. Practitioners, professionals, and academics wrap business fundamentals in jargon. The fundamentals are common sense and the further one strays from business fundamentals the more mistakes are made.

You already have plenty of experience operating a business called "your life".

You are a business. I'm not referring to your job, or your company. I mean you. Your quotidian, everyday existence is a business. Every day you run the business that is your life. From when you get up until you go to sleep. And actually while you are sleeping, because you have a bed and pillow and pajamas (or not) and a dark place and an alarm clock. It's all planned and maintained.

You also have lots of marketing experience. You have been marketed to since you were a child. You know good advertising from bad as far as what appeals to you and grabs your attention. You have also developed a finely tuned bullshit detector that goes off when someone is trying to sell you crap.

You know how to treat customers because you have been on the customer end of every transaction, purchase, and product and service experience in your life. We gravitate toward products and services that deliver what they promise and meet our expectations.

You perform all the basic business functions in your daily life. How you dress, speak, the car you drive, and how you present yourself is marketing. Dreaming, developing goals and planning is strategy. Managing relationships with your family, friends, and lovers, that's management and communications. Managing your phone, tablet, computer, TV, and other electronic devices is IT.

Getting, spending, saving and managing money is finance and accounting.

And everything else you do during the day: from making meals and getting ready for work, to preparing for bed, doing the laundry and dishes, falls into the category of operations.

Some people take this to the extreme like celebrities where personal branding and self-promotion actually are their business. Think of the Kardashians.

I like Jay Z's great quote: "I'm not a businessman I'm a business, man." He gets it.

Well, we all are a business, man (and woman). And by thinking of all you do and already know as business categories and skills can help transfer that knowledge and experience to any commercial or professional endeavor you choose to do.

You already run a complex enterprise.

It's called your life, and it's about getting, spending and saving. In business it's called Revenues, Expenses and Retained Earnings. You have a job where you make your money, it gets deposited in your checking account, and you use it to pay your bills, buy groceries and clothes, go out to eat or a movie; and hopefully there is some left over at the end of the month that you can put aside for a rainy day.

You manage bank accounts, checkbooks, debit and credit cards, electronic transfer, PayPal, a mortgage or rent, car payments, insurance, healthcare, utilities… It's complicated! But its common sense.

Sometimes (most of the time) you must make hard decisions about what you can and can't purchase or afford to do. Everything we do has an opportunity cost related to time and our budget. If we decide to do one thing, we can't do the other stuff that is appealing as well.

You have plenty of hard-won experience running an enterprise. Every household is an enterprise and have earned your Domestic MBA.

You also have your work experience to draw on to form opinions about how best to operate a business. In any job, we are thrown together with a bunch of people for a large part of each day and we have to figure out their personalities and how to navigate working with them. There are bosses, colleagues, clients and customers you like, and ones you don't like (not all of them have heard of the No Asshole Rule).

There are stupid processes that don't make sense and annoy you with their inefficiency. But there are also things that make you feel good about the work you do and give you a sense of accomplishment and self worth. And then there are the things that make you feel less than good.

These experiences and knowledge, from both your personal and working life, form the basis and context for what you already know about business and management. This knowledge base should form the touchstone against which you test anything you read or study about business and management to see if it rings true to your experience.

To get the most out of this book, read it in this manner. Challenge and measure each concept against your experience. Integrate your learning into what you already have experienced. At the end of the day, it's all elaborations and nuance of common sense.

The core concepts of business are basic common sense:
• Create something of Value
• Make People Aware of it
• Sell it for more than it costs you to make

The only way to create value for yourself is to create value for others. Figure out what the market needs and turn that objective into a daily practice, step by step.

As Seth Godin eloquently and succinctly puts it, "Do work that matters for people who care."

When it comes to competition, ultimately, we are competing against the best version of ourselves.

Think of this book as an antidote to intimidation

It is good to take a moment to take stock of what you already know, and have experience in, when looking at a new subject with intimidating buzzwords like business, finance, accounting, marketing, and strategy.

It reminds me of the fellow who wanted to be wise and traveled and studied only to realize, when he fell ill with cancer, that he was already wise. He just didn't understand the language of his wisdom.

This realization also reminds me of the character, Mr. Jourdain, from the Molière play, The Bourgeois Gentleman. While taking lessons to become cultivated, Mr. Jourdain is delighted to realize that he has been talking prose his whole life without knowing it.

It comes as a surprising revelation to him, "My faith! For more than forty years I have been speaking prose while knowing nothing of it, and I am the most obliged person in the world to you for telling me so."

Moliere is making fun of someone who has pretense and is desperate to become an aristocrat. Mr. Jourdain pursues his dream in the most superficial ways, but the situation is revealing.

Sometimes the language used obscures from us our own hard earned knowledge. Sometimes impenetrable language is intentionally used to keep people out of "the know".

My intent in this book is to get you over the hurdle that the skills and disciplines of business are difficult to learn. You already know them.

Even Plato thought that we already know everything and philosophy is a study and discipline that helps us remember.

This book will help you trust yourself and be authentic. Your business persona and leadership style should be an extension of your existing personality

Be yourself only more so.

In many ways running a business is simply a special case of the set of activities you perform regularly in your private life. Many parts of the business equation have to do with interactions you have been continuously involved in, but from the other side as a customer or someone who is advertised or marketed to.

How these activities have impacted you and how you react to them, and interact with them, provide you with a deep understanding and context about what is effective and important to you, and what is not.

By taking stock of your personality and predispositions in this manner, you can develop a business persona and set of operating principles that are in line with your innate strengths, interests and preferences. Model this extension of your behavior on what you already know about yourself and not on some abstract idea of a business executive.

Look at developing these skills and knowledge base as a way to impress your personal stamp on the world in an effective and beneficial way, not as an oblique strategy to impress others with your success.

This is a journey of self-discovery. C'mon let's go.

About this Handbook

This Handbook is a distilled version of the spectrum of business disciplines in an MBA program. You will learn skillsets that will make you more valuable at your job, help you start something on the side, or let you quit your job and start your own business.

We will cover entrepreneurship and startups, accounting, understanding financial statements, corporate finance, decision making tools, becoming a better negotiator, management and leadership, digital marketing and growth hacking, intellectual property, human resource management, operations and supply chain management, and statistics, among other subjects.

I focus on giving you what you need to get to work now. This book will help you overcome any fear and intimidation of diving into subject matter that is usually embedded with arcane buzzwords and overly sophisticated concepts.

By applying concepts of accelerated learning I break down business subjects and disciplines and give you the core 20% knowledge that gets you 80% of the practical skills and knowledge ASAP.

About My Approach

Seeing the Forest Through the Trees

I have created this program and materials with my students, undergrads and grad students, the companies I consult, and the entrepreneurs I mentor and the startups I advise, in mind.

The book is organized in topics that relate to MBA courses and also provides a general sense of how all these various disciplines fit together and how we can orchestrate and bring them to bear on meeting goals and getting things done.

Fundamentals that you will encounter most of the time are emphasized. We won't spend a lot of time going over lots of contingent information about things you will rarely, if ever, encounter.

MBA ASAP takes the approach of using the Pareto Principle. The Pareto principle states that, for many events, roughly 80% of the effects come from 20% of the causes.

20% of the information in a traditional MBA program represents 80% of the information you need. We focus on the 20% so you can get going. This knowledge is functional and emphasizes useable skills. You can fill in the rare information when needed.

Business skills can be applied in a wide variety of scenarios to pursue and actualize goals and dreams.

This book is an alternative where people who don't choose to pursue a traditional MBA, whether for cost, time, geography or luck of the admission process, can pick up the business skills that will advance their careers and open opportunities.

These materials are also great for refreshing business knowledge or complementary to other curriculum you pursue. It can also function as a preparation curriculum for a traditional MBA or business undergraduate degree, so you can crush it and perform at your highest level by already being familiar with the material.

C'mon, let's go!

Here is a summary of the various disciplines and the sequence in which they are presented:

Entrepreneurship and Startups

Value creation is the first general topic we will explore. At the core of every business is a value proposition. It is made of products and services that people want, need, or desire.

Value creation is the essence of entrepreneurship and the playbook of how to do it, while managing risks and increasing the probability of success, has been codified in Silicon Valley in the past few decades.

Many of us aspire to create something new; do original work; make an impact and help people solve their pressing needs. We have all heard of the entrepreneurial heroes like Steve Jobs, Bill Gates, and Elon Musk and their achievements. We use and benefit from the tools, products and services that they created.

If you harbor hopes of doing something similar, making your own dent in the universe, here is where you can get a quick handle on the latest thinking and processes for turning your dreams into reality and creating sustainable profitable businesses.

I'm starting this overview of business administration with a study of entrepreneurship because entrepreneurs are searching for product/market fit.

What you want to sell has to fit a customer need. The sum total of those potential customers is the market.

A Startup is a temporary organization in search of a sustainable business model.

That is the essence of every business enterprise: a business model that works and a fit between your product and customers.

In this rapidly changing and evolving business landscape, driven by technology and customer expectations, every company needs to be constantly re-evaluating their position and offerings and thinking entrepreneurially.
We, and our enterprises, need to be adaptable. As Reid Hoffman said, "In times of change and uncertainty adaptability creates stability.'

For these reasons, the tools and techniques of entrepreneurship are a sensible launching platform for gaining context and intuition into all business activities.

Ethics

Business ethics examines moral or ethical principles and problems that arise in a business environment. It applies to all aspects of business conduct and is relevant to the conduct of individuals and entire organizations.

Ethics is about how we conduct ourselves. It's about being honest and trustworthy. When money is involved it is easy to have your ethics become compromised.

Most MBA programs bolt on some obligatory talk about ethics. Here I put it front and center. It's critically important. It provides our "why" we do things and expend the effort. With a "why" we can figure out the "how".

Marketing in the Digital Age

Once we know about how to **create value** for customers, the next step is making them **aware** of our offering.

Every aspect of business has a marketing and sales aspect to it. Besides convincing customers of the value proposition of your products and services, you must convince employees and investors of the value of your vision and strategy.

We will go over the timeless aspects of marketing and then explore the recent emerging world of digital marketing.

The Internet and Web 2.0 have transformed marketing. This course will introduce you to traditional marketing principles and get you familiar with the new landscape.

There was a time when television and magazines ruled, and marketing meant advertising campaigns. This was the Mad Men era. Now marketing means an entire suite of activities based on product/market fit, customer engagement and awareness. It's no longer about manufacturing desire for a fait accompli product. Customer needs and feedback are baked into the product and the customer experience is integrated into every aspect of the company. Marketing activities pervade the enterprise.

Customers are segmented and micro targeted, results are measured with Analytics, and campaigns are designed to go viral through growth hacking. Growth Hacking is about customer participation in the marketing process and turbocharging awareness campaigns by creating viral products and content.

Growth Hacking resides at the intersection of Marketing, Engineering, and Programming. It takes advantage of all the new tools of websites, mobile, analytics, email and social media available to us that help us reach and communicate with customers and measure their behavior in order to provide the best user experience possible. It has gone from one-way advertising to two-way engagement

Welcome to your new world.

Financial Literacy: Understanding Financial Statements

The next focus, after value creation and awareness campaigns, is selling things for less than they cost to make. We need to know how to measure our efforts in terms of money.

We need to know how to read and understand financial statements.

Financial Statements are the end product of Accounting and the gateway to Corporate Finance. Understanding and being able to read them is a critical business skill. We will explore:

- Balance Sheet
- Income Statement
- Cash Flow Statement
- Financial Statement interconnection and Flow

Accounting

Accounting is the most fundamental part of any business. You need to have a grasp of its concepts and workings. This section provides that knowledge quickly, clearly, and directly.

With this information, and the inexpensive and accessible accounting software now available, you can keep your own business accounting records. And, when you hire an accountant, you will be able to effectively communicate with them.

Accounting knowledge is critical for interacting with investors, bankers, and taxing authorities.

We will also discuss financial projections and budgets. We will go through the accounting process and how financial statements are prepared for reporting purposes. We will look at who the users of accounting information are both inside an enterprise and external.

If your dream is to start a business, take this practical step and draw it closer. If you are running a business, read this section and get familiar with the accounting ASAP!

There are also lots of careers in accounting and this section will give you the basic knowledge to apply for bookkeeping and accounting related jobs.

Management & Leadership

Let's examine interpersonal skills. You will need the help of others in order to fulfill your dreams.

We have covered enough of the basic components of business and we can move into how to conduct the orchestra.

- Leadership is the art of accomplishing more than the science of management says is possible.

- The manager asks how and when; the leader asks what and why.

- The manager operates within the status quo; the leader challenges it.

- The manager has his eye on the bottom line; the leader has his eye on the horizon.

These sayings describe the symbiotic relationship between management and leadership. A healthy organization needs both. Leadership is Vision. Management is Implementation. They are the yin and yang of business.

"Vision without execution is just hallucination." Thomas Edison

Learn both management and leadership skills. Become a student of the possible

Become a Better Negotiator

Negotiation is a learn-able skill that you can develop and hone to resolve conflicts, build agreements, and get deals done.

Being a capable negotiator is also a key management skill.

In this new world where direct lines of authority have transformed into networks of collaboration, negotiation has become the primary form of decision-making and a key to management and leadership.

Gain the skills and confidence you need to negotiate well and achieve better outcomes

Operations and Supply Chain Management

How do you make and deliver things in the most cost effective and efficient ways and also maintain the highest quality?   There are always tradeoffs between quality and cost.

Operations management is about how you optimize and balance those tradeoffs to make the best product at the best price for your customers. Sometimes the highest quality product is what people need, sometimes "good enough" and cheap is what is required. Market Research helps understand customer needs, operations has to make it and deliver it.

Operations and Supply Chain Management (OSCM) is defined as the design, operation and improvement of the systems that create and deliver the products and services of an enterprise. OSCM involves a series of steps and processes where inputs are transformed into finished goods.

Operations refers to the process steps used to transform the resources employed by the company such as raw materials, labor, machines and scheduling, into products that are desired by customers. It can be a physical or digital product, or a service, or some combination of both.

Supply Chain Management refers to the processes that move information and material to and from manufacturing and then on to customers.   It also includes dealing with follow on customer support and returns.

We will also talk about Project Management and inventory control in this section.

Corporate Finance

Corporate Finance is about how companies make decisions about what projects to pursue, and how to value those projects. This section will provide a framework for how financial professionals make decisions about how, when, and where to invest money.

Corporate Finance comprises a set of skills that interact with all the aspects of running a business. It is also extremely helpful in our personal lives when making decisions about buying or leasing, borrowing money, and making big purchases. It provides analytic tools to think about getting, spending, and saving.

We will analyze financial statements using Ratio Analysis. We will explore the time value of money and develop a set of tools, , like Net Present Value and Internal Rate of Return, for making good financial   decisions.

We will explore the trade off between risk and return, how to create financial projections, and how to value income producing assets.

Economics

Economics is the big picture.

Economics can be thought of as the study and understanding of the contexts in which an enterprise operates. A stable, safe and predictable environment where we are able to confidently forecast a future is critical for companies to flourish. This is the realm of economic policy.

The study of economics provides us an analytical sense so we can explain what is going on and make rational predictions about the near future. Economics can be separated into three fields: Macro, Micro and managerial, each with different emphasis and focus. We will explore all three.

Understanding the Financial Markets

Now that you have studied the Time Value of Money and Economics, you are ready to examine Financial Markets such as the Stock and Bond Markets. We will review Value Investing. This is the way Warren Buffet does it!

Business Law

All businesses operate in a legal environment and you need to know the basics. We will look at:

Entity formation: LLC or Corporation

Corporate Law and board governance
Contracts
Intellectual Property Law
Liability protection
Securities Law and Fundraising
Regulatory institutions
Legal counsel
Litigation

Human Resource Management

Human Resource Management (HRM) refers to the functions in an organization that designs the job descriptions, recruits, hires, creates and administers the rules of employee conduct and the relationship between employer and employee, and manages termination through firing, severance, or retirement.

HRM has become more sophisticated in the last several decades as a greater appreciation of the strategic importance of leveraging an organization's talent pools has developed.

Statistics for Business

Statistics is a set of power tools for gathering and analyzing data for decision making.

We aren't going to become statisticians here but an appreciation of statistics is important.

Statistics is the study of the collection, organization, analysis, interpretation and presentation of data. It deals with all aspects of data, including the planning of data collection in terms of the design of surveys and experiments.

Business statistics is the science of good decision making in the face of uncertainty and is used in many disciplines such as financial analysis, econometrics, auditing, production and operations including six sigma, and marketing research

More and more data is collected as a by-product of doing business and by government agencies. This section provides some basic knowledge and skills to interpret and use statistical techniques in a variety of business applications.

Business statistics covers descriptive statistics (collection, description, analysis, and summary of data), probability, normal distributions, test of hypotheses and confidence intervals, linear regression, and correlation.

Statistics is used in marketing in helping understand customers and purchasing behavior. It is also used in operations in manufacturing processes and eliminating defects with programs like Six Sigma.

Intellectual Property

Patents, Trademarks, Copyright
How to file you own patent

Here I will help you understand how to:

- Protect and monetize your inventions and ideas
- Create value for your startup
- Attract Investors
- Create a multi-million dollar IP portfolio

In the past decade the patent research, drafting, and filing process has evolved and the tools are now in place that makes it feasible for you to perform all the steps and file your own patent.

The process hasn't gotten easier but the tools of word processing and the database on the United States Patent and Trademark Office website create an environment that empowers all of us to protect and commercialize our ideas and creativity.

This section looks at the patent application process from the standpoint of U.S. patent and filing procedures.

You can file your patent for under $500 and the average value of an issued patent is $1 million. This is lucrative work and well worth your time to learn.

Drafting a patent application is a surprisingly straightforward process. The hard part is having the idea of an invention. If you have ideas of things you think could be patented you owe it to yourself to understand the process and draft an application.

Even if you decide not to file it, this knowledge will come in handy for the next big idea you have. Then you will be ready to draft the application and won't be intimidated because you have already familiar with it.

Strategic Planning and Implementation
Put it all together

In this section we will synthesize the various disciplines we have studied into a conceptual picture of how they work together in a functioning enterprise.

This will give you insight into the thinking that takes place in the C level suite among the CEO, CFO, COO and the Board of Directors of a corporation.

Orchestrating all these elements we have covered into a plan is the realm of **Strategy**. Strategic thinking can be broken into long term planning (5 year plan), short term tactical planning and budgeting for the coming year.

We will address such issues as planning to grow your business and deal with competitors and alternative products.

The challenges arise in how to keep planning as part of an organic, continual process and how to implement strategy and manage strategic momentum.

It is so easy to get complacent and start to drift or lose focus and become diluted in your efforts by chasing too many goals. We will discuss focus, discipline and mindset as we bring it all together.

The Big Picture

In this section we will get a feel for business dynamics as a whole before we look into each discipline separately.

Remember as we discussed in the introduction, this is nothing new. You already run a complex enterprise.

Overview

"There Are Two Classes of People in the World; Those Who Divide People into Two Classes and Those Who Do Not."

- Robert Benchley

In running a business you interact with people and have processes and money to deal with, getting and spending, just like in your everyday life.

We can split business activities into two parts: internal and external. Internal are operations and external is marketing. Lets break it down in more detail below.

Fundamental Aspects of a Business

- Develop and deliver products and services that meet the needs of customers you have identified.

- Make potential customers aware of what you are providing and the value it represents to them.

- Make and deliver in efficient and effective ways so you create sustainable profits.

- Develop goals and measure how effective you are in achieving them.

- Keep track of the money coming in and going out of the business.

Let's bunch these functions into some general categories.

People

There are customers, employees, partners, vendors and suppliers, investors, contractors, the media, government, lawyers, accountants, your significant other, parents, friends… you get the idea. There are lots of different stakeholders and relationships and dynamics and personalities that you will have to assess, navigate, motivate, and negotiate.

You must learn to love dealing with people and develop a refined set of social and negotiation skills. These interactions and skill sets are the basis of:

- **Management**
- **Leadership**
- **Negotiations**
- **Human Resource Management**
- **Organizational Design**
- **Conflict Resolution**

These are all topics we will cover in more detail.

Awareness

Making people *aware* of what you have to offer and convincing them of its value is the realm of **Marketing**.

We are all marketers and marketing is all around us.

If you need to persuade someone to take action, you're doing marketing. If you're looking for votes, or a promotion, you're marketing. If you're writing copy on your website, or posting to your social media profile, you're marketing.

We are constantly being marketed to for a piece of our attention, our trust and our action. It helps to know what they're doing right and wrong.

Marketing drives our culture. Marketers drive the links we click on, the shows we watch, and the people we vote for.

You have lots of marketing experience. You have been marketed to since you were a child. You know good advertising from bad as far as what appeals to you and grabs your attention. And you know how to treat customers because you have been on the customer end of every transaction, purchase, and product and service experience in your life.

Funneling and converting marketing awareness into creating demand and purchases is what **Sales** is all about. Creating an identity to sustain those sales and leverage marketing through customer loyalty is **Branding**.

A business needs to be focused on Marketing and Sales. It needs to be focused on understanding customers and what their needs are. Understanding customer needs is half the job of fulfilling them. Make something people want.

What problem are you solving, or what benefit are you providing, and is it really relevant to the potential customer? How can you make your offering continually better suited to customer needs? Can you charge a premium for it based on the perceived value?

Feedback from customers on how they use your product should be analyzed early, often, and always. This external focus on delivering satisfaction to customers is crucial and it takes sustained continuous discipline to enact.

You have to deliver on your promises and meet or exceed their expectations.

There are so many incredible new ways to engage potential customers and market your offerings through the web, social media and mobile platforms. You can create awareness campaigns that target and reach on a global scale, and measure the effectiveness of your messaging, for relatively little cost. We will go through a lot of tips on platforms and practice.

Strategy
Another component of external focus is continuously monitoring and revising your understanding the competitive landscape. The speed of innovation is fast and constantly increasing. What works today will need to be re-imagined in order to be compelling tomorrow.

We all know lots of businesses and industries that have been disrupted out of existence like: videocassettes, cameras and film, rotary phones, and cathode ray TVs. **Strategy** is the field of knowing who your competitors are and where to position your offerings, what technologies are on the horizon, and converging together, that will change your industry.

It is also critical to assess how your industry is concentrated and segmented. This is the realm of **Economics**.

Strategy overlaps with **Marketing, Operations, Economics**, and all the other disciplines and attempts to focus and marshal all of these resources and initiatives toward well defined and stated goals to increase the performance of the enterprise. **Strategy** is the big picture.

Goods and Services

In general, producing Goods (products) and Services is the act of transforming raw materials into finished products that are delivered to customers. This is the realm of **Operations & Supply Chain Management**. As the world becomes more fluid and previous constraints are removed via mobile computing and communications, the differences and distinctions between a product and a service are becoming blurred.

Products used to be considered tangible and **Services** as intangible. This made for a nice clear distinction. Now, many goods are electronic copies like many games, music, movies and eBooks that are sold directly as digital downloads. A lot of content consumption is done completely virtually without any physical exchange. And in many cases now, even ownership of electronic copies is being replaced with a model of access on demand like streaming music and movie services.

A new broader definition of a **Product** is something that is uniform and homogeneous in its production and sale. Quality issues in goods usually center on concepts of achieving zero variability. Digital copies provide very high fidelity of reproduction and by definition, achieve this ideal goal of quality assurance.

Digital copies sold directly as downloads have three other advantages as a business model. First, they scale. Scale is a short hand term for economies of scope and scale. This means after you hit your breakeven point, it doesn't take much expense to produce and sell additional copies, so more money falls to the bottom line as profit.

Second is there is no working capital tied up in inventory. You don't have to estimate (guess) how many copies to produce (supply) to meet potential sales (demand). As many copies of a downloadable product can be sold as the market wants instantaneously.

Third is that distribution is virtually costless. Your market does not have to be concentrated or rely on physical stores or outlets or even mail delivery. A small percentage of a diffuse population of customers can add up to a big market.

Its important to take some time here and think about these concepts. These new digital business models should influence your thinking about what to develop and how to deliver it. Whether you are an entrepreneur or working in a large company, we always need to be thinking if there is a better, more efficient way to do things.

Services can be categorized as something that is customizable and molded to the needs of customers on a case-by-case basis usually scoped around subject matter or domain expertise. Consultants provide services. They also differ in the level of interaction with the customer. Service assets are more skewed towards human resources that go down in the elevator each evening.

Traditionally it has been difficult to scale service oriented companies and offerings. As Artificial Intelligence capabilities continue to develop, more ways of automating services are becoming feasible.

This is especially true in services that are rule based. Think of how Turbo Tax has automated and scaled a business in tax return preparation. Tax accounting used to be thought of as a white-collar profession not vulnerable to automation. Also think of the travel agent business. Most of us now make our own travel arrangements after consulting aggregators like Travelocity or matching engines like AirBnB.

Software as a Service SaaS is also a model that has revolutionized the delivery of what used to be thought of as a product by morphing it with service attributes.

Most product offerings and strong business models are based on a combination of products and services.

Product offerings that are primarily at core Goods can create more customer engagement and loyalty by adding service components.

Think of Apple Computer and their network of retail stores. Those stores help brand Apple with high profile visibility and provide Apple with the ability to capture the retail markup of their products. The retail stores also help Apple understand its customers and what they like and dislike about their products. This information is extremely valuable in helping to continuously improve their products and identify what to work on and roll out next. These stores also act as forums to help users understand and better utilize their products. This creates loyal customers by providing more value.

Apple's type of business model of controlling the entire chain from raw materials through design and manufacturing and marketing and sales is called **Vertical Integration**. Companies can improve their strategic position by integrating either upstream or downstream of their initial offering or competency. These are powerful concepts to keep in mind.

Business models based on Core Service Providers can gain advantages and achieve additional revenue streams by providing complementary Goods that enhance their services. They can create businesses that scale rapidly and hugely by providing a uniform goods component, especially an electronic product component that can be marketed on line and through social media and sold as a download or app. These goods can be priced very attractively as they cost little to reproduce and covering the development costs can be spread across the volume of units sold.

It can even make good business sense to provide a basic initial good or service for free in order to get potential customers engaged and familiar with your offering. This is a marketing approach called a Freemium model. I am sure you are familiar with and use many products of this type especially on your mobile device where there is a free version and if you want more capacity or additional features there is a paid version.

Processes

In some way, you are proposing to add value with what you are selling and providing. It might be a product or a service, or some cool and exciting combination of both.

How you make and deliver your product/service (let's call it product for short) determines your costs. Managing those costs is crucial. That means measuring costs in an accurate and timely manner, and continually looking for ways to reduce them. This is the realm of **Accounting.** Internal to an organization we use **Cost Accounting** and **Management Information Systems (MIS)** to accurately measure costs and provide reporting.

Production and distribution is the realm of **Operations Management** and **Supply Chain**

Management. Making and delivering things as efficiently as possible is what makes a business sustainable.

Improving and documenting processes is a critical part of staying competitive and delivering the best value to customers. We will talk about systems like Six Sigma and Just In Time inventory control.

It is the world of Quality Control and Assurance; Inventory Management; continual improvement programs; and linear programming.

The details of optimizing Operations can get technical, analytical, and quantitative. It is all in the service of very graspable and sensible goals however, and that is what we will focus on: the ends that justify the geeky means.

Computers, bar code readers and scanners and information systems have been instrumental in transforming this area of business into a strategic advantage.

The discipline of Operations and Supply Chain Management has provided advantage to scale that has transformed the retail landscape from small local Mom and Pop operations to mega store chains like Walmart, and online retailer Amazon, with their global supply chains, dominating.

Money

Green grease makes the world go round. Money is how business transacts and sustains itself. It is the vehicle for how business operates and determines how needful your value proposition really is. Money is how we keep score in business.

Bills need to be paid, supplies purchased, funds raised, and salaries met. Running a business is all about Revenues (sales), Expenses (costs), and Net Income (profit/loss). These flow of money are organized and measured by accounting. The goal is to sell things for more than they cost you to make or procure. Its simple but not easy.

This simple statement can get complicated as operations grow and a business scales up. Even in a small business there are many costs that are not directly related to the product like: the building or workspace and the utilities and computers and receptionist and secretaries and travel.

Decisions need to be made as how to allocate those indirect costs to the units sold. This is the realm of **Accounting** and **Bookkeeping**, and as painful or boring as it may seem, it is the fundamental lifeblood of business.

Accounting is how you can tell how the business is performing: whether you are making money or not, and how much. Accounting is the measuring stick and, as the famous management guru Peter Drucker said, "what gets measured gets managed". So we need to measure what matters.

51

The difference between the price that you sell something for, and the costs it took to make it, is the Net Income. It can also be thought of as the value you have created.

Business operations are ultimately focused on value creation and **Marketing** and **Branding** is about making people aware of you value proposition, creating needs and desires for your product and enhancing the perceived value.

Marketing practices can devolve into cynical and duplicitous practices of creating psychological connections between a product and deep aspirations in order to move superficial goods. This touches on issues of a philosophical nature related to **Business Ethics.**

Our aspirations and goals should be to use business methods and models to create sustainable enterprises that actually help people and meet genuine needs. Make things of value for people who care.

It is easy to be seduced and get caught up in the desire to make lots of money, acquire the prestige and command the respect we seek. We are status-seeking animals.

Don't give into these less than virtuous motives and add to the consumer frenzy in less than meaningful ways. Keep this in mind as we study and implement these concepts and as we go about our career and making meaning in our lives and the lives of others. The section on Business Ethics delves into this area in more detail.

How do you get the money to start? When and how should you expand? Should you perform certain operations in-house or outsource? Should you lease or purchase? The tools and techniques of **Corporate Finance** will help you answer these questions.

Corporate Finance also provides us with tools for valuation and decision-making based on the concept of the **Time Value of Money**.

"The importance of money flows from it being a link between the present and the future."
– John Maynard Keynes

Past, Present and Future
The Numbers side of Business

Money is the denomination of the numbers side of business. At the end of the day business boils down to numbers. Here is a quick summary of the big picture of the numbers side.

Money in business is what we count and keep track of first and foremost. Its how we keep score. Money is what we measure and what gets measured gets managed.
If your output is more than your input, your upkeep is your downfall.

A successful business model is all about making more than you spend. Even if you are losing money with a strategy of gaining market share, the present value of that increased future market share needs to be more than the dollars you are spending today to capture it. That is the only rationale that makes economic sense.

Corporate Finance

Corporate Finance in its broadest sense encompasses everything that has to do with money in business. It includes accounting, funding, spending and investing in assets, and budgeting.

Accounting

Accounting produces Financial Statements. There are ten steps in the accounting process that starts by recording individual transactions and ends by aggregating all the transactions into Financial Statements.

Funding

Funding has to do with the right hand side of the balance sheet: debt and equity. Debt, also called a loan, is money you borrow with a contract to pay it back and collateralized by the assets. Equity, also called stock, is money invested in exchange for an ownership share in the company.

There is straight debt and equity and lots of hybrid finance instruments that mix the two. You can have senior and junior debt depending on the claims on the assets, you can have debt that is convertible into stock, and you can have common and preferred stock.

These instruments are all negotiated with investors and bankers and they are used to acquire the assets listed on the left hand side of the balance sheet.

Discounting Cash Flows

There is a time value to money. A dollar today is worth more than the promise of a dollar two years from now. The time value of money is described as interest rates.

Corporate Finance tools calculate the present value by discounting future cash flows. I'll talk a bit more about this in the Future section below.

Investing

In business you need to know which income producing assets to purchase and which projects to pursue. Financial decision making tools like NPV and IRR are used to analyze and choose.

Finance is all about the sources and uses of funds and keeping track of how those decisions are performing.

The Past

Accounting and Financial Reporting are retrospective activities. They provide a detailed account of what has happened. It's the equivalent of a rear view mirror.

Ratio Analysis

Ratios are a way to compare accounting information. It can be over time or across companies. Ratios are used to gauge performance by comparing if the numbers are getting better or worse. Ratios help you uncover the direction things are going.

Horizontal ratio analysis is over time. Vertical ratio analysis is comparing one company to another. Using ratios normalizes the numbers so you are comparing apples to apples. It eliminates size differences.

What gets measured gets managed.
So measure what matters.

The Present

Current financials represent a picture of where the company is today. It's a picture of how the company has performed in the most recent reporting period. This is how the present is connected to the past in business.

Financial Statements

There are three basic financial statements:

Balance Sheet

Income Statement
Cash Flow Statement

They are interconnected and financial data and information flows from one financial statement through the others.

The present is connected to the future in business through interest rates or discount rates. These take into account all the uncertainty and risks inherent in the business's future prospects.

"The importance of money flows from it being a link between the present and the future".
—John Maynard Keynes

The Future

Financial Projections are the best guesses about what the company is going to do and how it is going to perform going forward. This view equivalent to through the windshield.

Pro Formas

Financial projections are sometimes called pro formas because they are presented "in the form of" financial statements.

Valuation

We use discount rates in order to discount future cash flow projections back into today's dollars. The

Present Value of Future cash flows are essentially the valuation of the enterprise or the income-producing asset.

In publicly traded stocks, the present value of future cash flows is what is being guessed at by all the participants in the market for that stock. Stocks are bought and sold in an auction format based on investor's guesses of the present value of the future cash flows.

Budgets

Yesterday's tomorrow is today.

Budgets are the best guesses about how much money will come in to a company through sales and how much will go out via expenses. Budgets are created for the next year.

Budgets are then measured against the actual revenues and expenses and any differences (called variances) are then examined and explained.

Budgets, actuals and variance analysis comprise a basic management technique.

Putting it All Together

Orchestrating all these disciplines is the realm of the C-level executives: the CEO, COO, and CFO. It is also the skill set required of entrepreneur/founders.

Codifying these elements into a coordinated plan is the realm of **Strategy**. Strategic thinking can be broken into **long term planning** (5 year plan), short term **tactical planning,** and **budgeting** for the coming year.

How are you planning to grow your business and deal with competitors and alternative products? Challenges arise in how to keep planning as part of an organic, continual process and how to **implement strategy** and **manage strategic momentum** which means keeping employees and contractors on task and focused on the right actions. It's easy to get complacent and start to drift or lose focus and become diluted in your efforts by chasing too many goals.

According to Steve Jobs, "People think focus means saying yes to the thing you've got to focus on. But that's not what it means at all. It means saying no to the hundred other good ideas that there are. You have to pick carefully. I'm actually as proud of the things we haven't done as the things I have done. Innovation is saying 'no' to 1,000 things."

Communications is the skill set of clearly defining, articulating, and relating the goals of the organization so that people know precisely and explicitly what is expected of them, how their performance will be measured, and how to know if we are moving in the right direction at a satisfactory pace.

Communications is integral to the **leadership** skill of how to motivate people by aligning their aspirations with those of the enterprise.

Incentives are the systems and plans that motivate behavior and they must be aligned with the messaging. Rational beings will do what they perceive is best for them and we must make sure that their behavior is aligned with our targets and goals for the company. The only meaningful work in a company is work the contributes to the strategic goals.

Strategy and Leadership also includes a discussion of decisions relative to your **Business Model**. How do you make and market your products and services, and how do you protect and expand your markets and profit margins? What do you do in-house and what do you contract out?

Having a good handle on **Economics** will provide you with a context in which to analyze and explain what is going on in the larger world in which your enterprise operates and which surrounds our lives. It will also help provide the ability to make more accurate and reasoned predictions about future. This is important for planning, budgeting and strategy. And it will help you react quicker and smarter, in a reasoned fashion, to unforeseen changes in the environment.

Business economics can be divided into three disciplines:

- Micro Economics: the study of individual behavior and purchasing decision, the theory of the firm and production, and the study of competition and market structures.
- Managerial Economics: the study of applying Micro Economic theory to managerial decision-making.
- Macro Economics: the study of economies as a whole including: interest rates, monetary policy, banking, government regulation, and international trade.

Summary of Overview

Some of the topics introduced above spilled from one section into the next and may have seemed redundant or repetitive in places. The fact is, these subjects all overlap and knit together in an operation. A well functioning organization cannot have each discipline and division operating in a separate silo. It is the role of the senior executives, the "C" level executives, to have a vision and overview that incorporates all the elements in a smoothly running manner. This book is here to help you prepare for such a role and to understand the concerns of the big picture wherever you currently reside in an organization.

Occam's Razor is a principle from the Middle Ages that essentially states "the simpler the better." It is easy to get tied up in all the complications that can arise out of such a seeming large bunch of competing interests and concerns. You can end up suffering analysis paralysis. How can one keep all of this in one's head and make decisions taking it all into account on the fly in real time. That is where William Occam's advice always helps to clear the air—the fewer assumptions that are made, the better.

It is important to maintain a bias towards action. This means making calculated decisions in the face of incomplete information.

In the interest of keeping it simple and being concise, here is a short summary of the above section. There are four areas to keep in mind when you are analyzing a business proposal or business performance, or when questioning the direction of your personal destiny for that matter:

- Strategy: develop and articulate clear and compelling goals.
- Structure: are we organized to fulfill those goals?
- People: do we have the right people and capabilities to meet our goals?
- Process: do we have the operations and supply chains we need to meet our target goals. Can we improve them?

Keep it Simple. Keep it Clear.

Much of effective communication and leadership hinges on clarity.

Skill Sets

This section discusses important skills to be aware of and develop over time. These skill disciplines are more general and fundamental than the business disciplines and will help you in all aspects of your life including anything business oriented.

Focusing on developing these skills will make you a top performer; the best you can possibly be. The goal throughout this book is self-actualization, to reach your potential in all aspects of your life. This section addresses long-term development of the overall person to amplify your personality and become a powerful force for good in the world.

As an analogy let's look at yoga. Yoga is a great exercise regimen. It is a thorough full body routine that helps you assess your body's functionality top to bottom and side to side. Yoga can uncover interesting asymmetries as you realize you may be more flexible or stronger or have better balance on one side than the other. Yoga helps you uncover and focus on developing your weak spots and achieving a powerful balance.

These skill areas will help you identify and work on your weak spots and help you soar with your strengths. These are all lifetime long skills to develop. Some are as old as human interaction. Lots can be learned from the ancients as well as moderns. Some are extremely modern like computer skills that are constantly evolving and must be revised and updated on a constant basis.

There is a great website that you should check out and keep as a reference in skills development. Check out www.skillsyouneed.com

Some Skills to focus on are:
People skills; Social skills; Emotional intelligence; Communication Skills; Listening to Understand; Speaking to be Understood; Language learning and acquisition; Presentations; Public Speaking; Writing; Reading; Typing; Word Processing; Math Skills; Spreadsheets; Computer coding and programming; The Ability to Learn Quickly; Creativity; Dressing and appearance; Health; Fitness; Nutrition; Developing Good Habits

These are some of the dimensions that make up a well-rounded person. To be an inspirational business leader you must walk the walk and talk the talk.

Advice

Be good and work hard. Stay focused on creating and maintaining good habits so you can be focused and productive over the long haul. Running a business is not a sprint, it is an ultra marathon so it is imperative to be self disciplined and create a sustainable pace. You can't do everything in a day, a week or a month.

Try to be aware of developing a consistent cadence and rhythm to your work and progress.

You need a plan and you need routines. You need to know how to take breaks and refresh. There are diminishing returns to working 14-hour days, seven days a week. Creating a work/life balance so you don't feel torn and split by competing demands is crucial. It's about creating that sustainable cadence.

You also need strategies to deal with stress. Some stress is a good thing as a motivator and to create a sense of urgency. Some good stress can focus the mind to the tasks at hand. Too much stress is toxic and corrosive and will wear you down and wear you out. You want to work hard and smart and you want to enjoy the ride!

Another aspect of reducing work and stress levels lies in knowing how to delegate and develop systems that take you out of the information flow so you are not responsible for making all the trains run on time and putting out all the fires. It is ineffective for you to be a rate limiter on decision-making.

Dialing in the proper balance is a constant mindfulness exercise of priority setting and course correcting.

Get the Easy Things Right

We tend to spend a lot of time searching for the secrets to success. According to the Pareto Principle

20% of causes result in 80% of effects. Getting the easy stuff right is that 20%.

Here are two of those things:

Show up.

80 percent of success is showing up.
- Woody Allen

Show up. Don't be reluctant and don't be distracted. Show up and be present and mindful.

If you are reluctant, trust your instincts. Instead of committing to something half-heartedly, just say no. Don't agree out of a feeling of obligation and then sleep walk through things or sabotage them with passive aggression

Be punctual.

If you aren't early, you are late. Try to shoot for being ten minutes early to everything. Legendary football coach Vince Lombardi was even more aggressive, "If you are five minutes early, you are already ten minutes late."

Being late acknowledges that you find it acceptable to make others wait on you. Tardiness is an act of selfishness. If you are regularly early to events, you will notice that when things go wrong, you still are on time. Being early is a sign of respect and forethought.

Barack Obama said "My greatest strength? Probably that I'm always early." He famously likes to turn up early for every meeting. He has made a conscious commitment to being early. When I first heard about this I started to give it a try.

I find when I am early I can count on having my best conversations and networking. It gives me a sense of control. I also don't arrive stressed from trying to rush. And I started to realize how I consistently underestimate how long is takes to get somewhere.

Give it a try. Decide to show up. And show up early.

The Rules of the Game

Now we are going to take a more detailed look at the 16 topics I introduced up above. These make up the disciplines of Business Administration.

- Entrepreneurship and Startups
- Ethics
- Financial Literacy: Understanding Financial Statements
- Marketing in the Digital Age
- Accounting
- Management & Leadership

- Negotiations
- Operations and Supply Chain Management
- Corporate Finance
- Economics
- Understanding the Financial Markets
- Business Law
- Human Resource Management
- Statistics for Business
- Intellectual Property
- Strategic Planning and Implementation

These 16 subjects constitute an MBA program.
These are the Rules of the Game of Business. You become a Master of Business Administration when you understand these 16 subjects.

You have to learn the rules of the game, and then you have to play better than anyone else.
- Albert Einstein

Entrepreneurship and Startups

My rationale for starting with a study of entrepreneurship is because entrepreneurs are searching for a sustainable business model. They need to get the basics of an entire business up and running.

Successful entrepreneurs do this by initially focusing product/market fit. They are looking for customers that understand and are willing to pay for the value they are presenting. The goal is to do meaningful work for people that care.

A Startup is essentially a temporary organization in search of a sustainable business model.

That is the essence of every business enterprise: a business model that works day in and day out, and a fit between your product and customers.

Our rapidly changing and evolving business landscape is driven by technology, sophisticated customer expectations, and competition. Every company needs to be constantly re-evaluating their position and offerings and thinking entrepreneurially. The ones that are most adaptable survive.

For these reasons, the tools and techniques of entrepreneurship are a sensible launching platform for gaining context and intuition into all business activities.

Startup Methodology

We used to think of startups as mini versions of existing companies and entrepreneurs as mini versions of CEOs. Now we have better conceptions of what a startup is and what its goals are.

The process of creating successful startup companies has transformed over the past couple of decades as the reality of what works, and what is just an exercise, has sunk in.

Before the twenty first century entrepreneurial activities relied on brute force and luck. They were mostly intellectual exercises and not tested against customer requirements and expectations until late in the process. So it was lucky if what you thought customers wanted actually matched what the really did want.

The exercise always began with lots of top-down research into markets and elaborate detailing of products and services. All this work was codified into the Business Plan and it was the sacred document that encased how things were going to be executed. Its credibility was directly related to its heft. All of this work would be done at a desk and in a conference room and, amazingly, would usually not include interactions with potential customers.

Few read these plans and they crumbled in the face of the first customer interactions. As the famous Prussian military general Von Moltke said, "No plan survives contact with the enemy."

The famous boxer Mike Tyson said: "Everybody has a plan until they get punched in the face."

The same thing applies to Business Plans drafted without serious systematic customer involvement and feedback. They are delusional documents that are not grounded in reality.

Relatively recently, a generation of entrepreneurs, business leaders, investors and academics have created a method that addresses this fundamental flaw in prior thinking and execution of products and business models.

In the past ten years or so, thanks to the efforts of Steve Blank, Eric Ries, Alexander Osterwalder Tim Brown and others, an entirely new way of thinking about and planning and executing startups has emerged. It has been a paradigm shift in thinking about reducing risk and navigating a viable path toward making something customers want.

It applies the scientific method to proving up guesses about aspects of the business model. You write down and test your assumptions before doing a bunch of misdirected work. Working on the right thing is more important than working hard.

At the beginning all you have are guesses. Admitting that and dealing with it is the big discovery. We make our guesses, test them against customers, and double down or course correct based on the feedback we receive.

It seems simple and obvious now. All significant breakthroughs seem obvious after the fact.

In this section we will explore the different approaches to this new thinking. It is meant to jump start your understanding and awareness of these different strains and tools and point you toward further study. At the end of the book there is a list of additional resources and books.

This knowledge will also act as a way to step back and take stock of business fundamentals. We all sometimes get caught up in arcane details and eddies. We need context and perspective to see the forest through the trees. When in doubt, this can help get back into the mainstream and flow. Revisit this section when things seem overly complicated.

Entrepreneurship is an incredibly important subject and set of skills to develop, own, and implement. Besides helping individuals gain agency and control in their lives, the products and services created that help customers can make an immense beneficial impact on society.

Much of our best hope for the future lies in creative solutions to our most pressing problems. Entrepreneurs and their startups will create that future. We are all counting on you!

Entrepreneurial Thinking

We are in the midst of massive change. Post-Modern life and our economy are being reinvented. There is no longer such a thing as a stable career or job security. Industries are being eaten by software and devoured by robots. Companies are disrupted out of existence.

Think Kodak. They dominated the film industry creating and developing it. Then cameras dematerialized into smart phones and film become obsolete. Overnight. All the jobs associated with that industry   evaporated.

The age of corporate paternalism, where we can rely on a company to employ us and take care of us for an entire career, is past. We must adapt or be marginalized.

The flip side of this radically changing world and workplace is opportunity. There are no longer gatekeepers and barriers to entry in many traditional businesses and industries. And there are new industries being invented and rapidly developed. Legacy experts no longer dominate fields. Access to markets is widespread. There has never been a more opportune time to dream big, be creative, and fashion lives   well   suited   to   our   deep   needs.

Farsighted individuals are using these tools and techniques to adapt to a rapidly world. Robotics,

Artificial Intelligence, Automation, Machines, and Algorithms are changing how we do everything.

As Darwin put it: "It is not the strongest of the species that survives, nor the most intelligent; it is the one most adaptable to change."

Entrepreneurial thinking is about taking ideas and making them into products or services that meet the needs and wants of customers. Lets call the product/service mix P/S for short. The incubation of ideas into concrete P/S is performed in a startup.
The key criterion of the P/S is that it meets some need or want of a group of potential customers. The pool of potential customers is referred to as the market. The function of a startup is the search for **product/market fit**.

A startup is *not* a mini version of an existing enterprise. Startup is a temporary organization in search of a repeatable, sustainable, scalable Business Model. The goal of a startup is to evolve itself out of existence and into a company. A startup is a caterpillar and the resulting company is the butterfly.

Ex Nihilo

Ex nihilo is a Latin phrase meaning "out of nothing". It often appears in conjunction with the concept of creation, as in creatio ex nihilo, meaning "creation out of nothing"

That is what entrepreneurship and startups deal with: creating something out of nothing. We are looking to create something that fits a need, something of value. We do it for a profit so that the process is scalable, meaning it can grow.

Peter Thiel, the co-founder of PayPal and the first outside investor in Facebook, wrote a book about entrepreneurship called Zero to One based on this premise of going from nothing to something; that the act of creation is singular and incredibly worthwhile.

Entrepreneurs help nudge innovation forward, accelerate the most disruptive technologies, or shape a simpler or better way to do something. It is all in the service of solving problems.

Business Model Canvas

The Business Model Canvas (BMC) is a simple and quick way to think about and grasp the major parts of any business. The BMC is a template used to organize our thinking around developing business models.

A Business Model outlines how a company creates value for itself by delivering products and services to customers for revenue and profit.

The Business Model Canvas is a visual chart with elements describing a firm's offering, customers, infrastructure and finances. It is comprised of nine interrelated elements:

- Offering
  - o Value Proposition
- Customers
  - o Customer Segments
  - o Channels
  - o Customer Relationships
- Infrastructure
  - o Key Resources
  - o Key Activities
  - o Partner Network
- Finances
  - o Cost Structure
  - o Revenue Streams

Thinking about an enterprise, whether it is one you want to start or an existing one, can get complicated. We need a tool that can overlay any business situation and ask the basic questions about how it is structured, what is being offered and to whom.

This tool is the Business Model Canvas. It helps us keep the whole picture of the business enterprise in our mind so we can evaluate it, test it, and make productive changes.

The Business Model Canvas is where we capture our best guesses about the key business elements and turn them into facts by testing them against potential customers in our search for a viable Business Model. We will look at this testing and searching process in the next section **Lean Startup Methodology**. But first lets look at the nine elements of the Business Model Canvas in more detail.

BMC: The Nine Elements

Value Proposition: What are you building and for whom? Here we need to be careful not to be overly product or technology focused. It's all about perceived value to customers. In order to be in business, we have to be solving a customer problem or satisfying a customer need.

Customer Segments: You exist for them and you need to understand them in detail: who they are and why they would buy.

Channels: How you deliver your Value Proposition to your Customer Segments. Its about logistics, distribution and communication; how do you sell and deliver. Pre 1990s channels were all physical: stores, sales people, and warehouses. Now there are virtual channels as well: Web, Mobile, Cloud and digital downloads and streaming services.

Customer Relationships: How do you get, keep and grow customers. This is the role of Marketing and, as we will see in the **Growth Hacking** section, these customer engagement attributes are becoming baked-in to products and services. The first stage is Customer Acquisition where we activate customers to do something through calls-to-action. Next we want to keep them and not lose them to competitors. Then we want to grow them by giving them compelling reasons to spend or use more of what we offer.

Key Resources: What do you need to make the Business Model work? What are the working capital requirements? What physical resources are required for fulfillment: manufacturing, machines, inventory, and delivery trucks. What Intellectual Property is needed: patents, customer lists. What are the Human Resources needed?

Key Partners: Strategic alliances, joint ventures, and suppliers.

Key Activities: What are the most important things the company must do to make the Business Model work? Is it Production, making something or Problem Solving like consulting or engineering, or Supply Chain Management? What do you need to become expert at?

Costs: What are the costs and expenses to operate the

business? What is the cost structure of the product/service? What are the fixed and variable costs? Are there economies of scale and scope? What are the most expensive resources and activities as a percent of the budget?

Revenue Streams/Models: How do you make money from your product/service being sold to customers? What value are customers paying for? What is your strategy to capture value: direct sales, subscription, or freemium? What are you pricing tactics?

The Lean Startup Method

The Lean Startup Methodology is a way to bring analytical rigor and a systematic process to understanding and refining a new venture or growing enterprise and making it successful. Lean Startup reduces the risk of failure and ups the odds of success. Lean startup has become incredibly popular because of how effective it is. It was developed and promulgated by Steve Blank and Eric Ries.

The Lean Startup Methodology applies the Scientific Method to venture development. It starts with a set of hypothesis (guesses) about the various elements of the business model, tests them against customer expectations, and revises and refines them based on the feedback.

There are three basic components of Lean Startup methodology:

- Business Model Design
- Customer Discovery
- Agile Development

Lean Startup is an iterative process searching for a Business Model that is stable, reproducible and sustainable. The goal is to develop a Business Model that works over and over, each and every day and that is scalable. This means that there is a profit or net income relative to sales. If you put one dollar in, you get two out. This is the mechanism and model that allows a business to thrive and grow. This is the mechanism of scale.

The first step is to fill out the Business Model Canvas. As you fill out the Business Model Canvas you end up with a series of thoughtful first guesses about:

- Who do we think our customers are?
- What are we making for them?
- How much to charge?

Odds are these initial guesses are wrong but it's a great first step. Next we will change those guesses into facts through the Customer Development process.

Lean Startup Process

Crafting a viable Business Model is an iterative process of exploring the relationship and engagement between your core product/service features and feedback from potential customers.

Don't be dejected if you get negative feedback. This is incredibly valuable and can save you from squandering resources building things nobody wants.

The goal of this process is to achieve Product/Market Fit. This is where your product or service offering resonates deeply with a customer base and they can't get enough of it even in its limited prototype configuration.

The two components of this process of moving towards product market fit are a **Minimum Viable Product** (MVP) and **Customer Discovery** based around that product.

We want to perform this process Lean, meaning we want to conserve our limited resources in this exploration and discovery phase. We need lean discipline in order to deploy our resources in a way that allows us to refine our offering in the face of customer feedback until we hit on a truly compelling match.

We need to conserve our money so we can go back to the drawing board and implement the feedback we get from customers. Most startups fail because they run out of money. We want to limit that risk.

In order to run lean, we develop our prototypes with just the core essential features and present that to customers ASAP in order to get feedback. This is the MVP idea. Get something meaningful in front of potential customers and start the learning and refining process.

The MVP can be a website splash page, a PowerPoint slide, a wireframe or cardboard mockup, or a working prototype. It needs to embody a feature set that customers can respond to, but little more, so it can be changed, tuned and calibrated to meet customer needs.

This type of development process is called **Agile Development**. It's a set of engineering principles designed to quickly iterate around feedback from customers. Also check out other development frameworks like TRIZ, Scrum, and Six Sigma.

Customer Development is about by getting out and talking with potential customers, partners, and vendors centered on presenting the MVP and getting feedback. We do this, not in a random way, but with some rigor and a process:

1. Design Experiments
2. Get Data
3. Get Insights
4. Rinse and Repeat

By keeping the development costs low and lean and focusing on learning from customers we can course correct, iterate, pivot, persevere, or double-down in search of the holy grail of Product/Market Fit and a viable, scalable Business Model.

When you have achieved this goal, then you are ready to write a business plan, negotiate funding, and build a company!

OODA Loop

The OODA Loop is a tool for better decision-making. The OODA Loop refers to the decision cycle of **observe, orient, decide, and act**, developed by military strategist and U.S. Air Force Colonel John Boyd. Entrepreneurs have adopted it as a learning tool and method for dealing with uncertainty. The OODA loop concept complements the Lean Startup methodology in customer discovery, assessing MVP feature sets, and product/market convergence. Use the OODA Loop approach to course correct as you iterate forward.

Design Thinking

The Lean Startup methodology came out of business and engineering thinking about how to create a standardized process for developing startups that limits risk and ups the odds of success. Design

Thinking is a methodology evolved out of the design field. It is more creative and aesthetic in its approach and concept and entrepreneurs have adopted it.

Like Lean Startup, Design Thinking is also an iterative process that focuses on understanding the needs of potential customers, testing ideas, and searching for product/market fit. It is a user-centered way to conceive and create successful products.

Designers use this approach to solve complex problems and find optimal solutions. A design mindset is solution focused and action oriented. Design Thinking draws upon logic, imagination, intuition, and systemic reasoning, to explore possibilities and to create desired outcomes that benefit the end user, the customer.

Design thinking is inquiry-based and open-ended. It forces you to put yourself in the customer's shoes. It is initially about generating empathy with the customer and their needs and wants.
There are a number of variations, but the basic steps in the Design Thinking process are:
- Empathy
- Define
- Ideate
- Prototype
- Test

Like Lean Startup, Design Thinking is based on building a **Minimal Viable Product**, a product with enough features to gather meaningful feedback in order to see what's working, and double down on those features that really moved the needle.

Design Thinking is a systematic innovation process for gaining deep customer understanding and deciding which features and which products to design and launch.

In the world of startup incubation, Design Thinking is often compared and contrasted with the Lean Startup approach, which is more engineering-based and quantitative. The two methods are far from mutually exclusive as both seek to effectively serve customers' needs through a systematic, low-risk path to innovating in the face of uncertainty.

"Design thinking can be described as a discipline that uses the designer's sensibility and methods to match people's needs with what is technologically feasible and what a viable business strategy can convert into customer value and market opportunity."

Tim Brown CEO, IDEO

Growth Hacking

There was a time when television and magazines ruled and marketing meant advertising campaigns. This was the Mad Men era. Now marketing means an entire suite of activities based on product/market fit and customer engagement. It's no longer about manufacturing desire for a fait accompli product. Customer needs and feedback are baked into the product and the customer experience is integrated into the company.

Growth Hacking is about customer participation in the marketing process and turbocharging awareness campaigns by creating viral products and content.

Growth Hacking resides at the intersection of Marketing, Engineering, and Programming. It takes advantage of all the new tools of websites, mobile, analytics, email and social media available to us that help us reach and communicate with customers and measure their behavior in order to provide the best user experience possible. It has gone from one-way advertising to two-way engagement.

Growth Hacking is a process of rapid experimentation across marketing channels, like email and social media, and also product development focused on enhancing the user experience. The goal is to identify the most effective, efficient ways to grow a business by understanding what is most compelling to customers both in messaging and product feature sets.

Growth Hacking refers to a set of marketing experiments that leads to the rapid growth of a business. The experiments are run by A/B testing features and messaging, and measuring which aspects customers respond to best. Measurement tools like

Google Analytics provide the measurement metrics and feedback that help refine awareness campaigns and product features.

It's about how you get, keep and grow customers. The first stage is Customer Acquisition where we activate customers to do something through Calls-to-Action. Calls-to-Action are designed to activate lead generation and sales. Initially it could be a sign up or download of valuable content and ultimately leading to becoming a paying customer.

Next we want to keep them and not lose them to competitors. Then we want to grow them by giving them compelling reasons to spend more or use more of what we offer.

Marketing funnels are developed to measure how many people respond and then convert to being customers. This process is obsessively measured and continually refined and optimized.

Customer Acquisition Costs (CAC) are calculated and compared to the Lifetime Value (LTV) of a customer. We obviously are looking to optimize CAC<LTV. Conversion Rates are tracked and optimized along the customer journey.

Growth Hacking includes engagement with customers through delivering content like blogs, digital downloads, and social media posts. **Viral Marketing** is a method where customers are encouraged to share information about products or services via various Internet channels especially social media.

Startup Funding

The whole process of funding and developing startups has become more widespread because the cost of getting a product to market has dropped so precipitously in the past couple of decades from millions of dollars to typically anywhere from under $20,000 to around $500,000.

The funding levels are relatively manageable by investors and the potential returns are huge. Potential. The risks are very high of any return, but the few startups that break out create legendary fortunes. That is why there are startup founders and startup investors.

A startup goes through a series of funding rounds on its journey from founder's idea, through developing an MVP and customer discover, to finding Product/Market Fit, and scaling up operations and sales.

There are a lot of terms tossed around to describe the various rounds of funding that a startup can potentially receive.

These are the typical rounds encountered in an Angel and Venture-Backed Startup and not all startups receive all these rounds. Most small businesses don't plan on scaling to become Unicorns and don't pursue this funding journey.

Startup Funding Stages

The following funding stages are presented in their evolutionary order relative to the development of a startup.

Sweat Equity
In the beginning of most startups, the founders will work on the idea for free. This is where things start. All the ownership resides with the founders at this point and they figure out how to develop the business concept using their own resources. This is where hustlers and builders push the development of their company forward without outside funding.

Like Teddy Roosevelt said: "Do what you can, where you are, with what you have."

If your idea is compelling enough, you can enlist the talents of others to work for sweat equity. This may take the form of paying a computer coder to help develop an MVP in exchange for stock in the company instead of cash.

Bootstrapping
Bootstrapping is taking early revenues from products and services developed with sweat equity and plowing it back into more development work. There is some outside money from early adopter customers, but not

from investors. This is an important milestone because it signals that there is a need for what the company is creating. It is a signal that the founders are resourceful and committed to finding a way forward. This is the kind of grit investors look for in founders.

The 3 Fs

This is usually referred to as: Friends, Family, and Fools but I like to replace the last one with Fans. Once a fledgling startup has developed the concept and identified some preliminary customer interest and has a clearer idea of what the next steps should be then it is time to tap the founders' personal network. This is personally risky because raising money from your grandmother or uncle and then throwing in the towel in six months can make for an uncomfortable Thanksgiving get-together. You want to be sure that you are on to something before hitting up loved ones and old college roommates. The first two stages move the idea along and also help develop discipline about how to parsimoniously deploy these precious funds in the most effective and efficient manner

Here you want to have a plan to get to clear milestones and deliverables that will be inflection points of added value and reduced risk. This plan needs to include a detailed budget of how to get from here to there. An entrepreneur needs to be scrappy and capital efficient.

Self-Funding

This is a select group that has the resources to fund the initial development. A serial entrepreneur who has sold previous startups are in this category. These are founders that want to focus on building an MVP without having the distractions of pitching investors before knowing whether the idea is feasible and customer interest is reasonably there.

These seasoned folks also realize that the further along the business is, the higher the valuation for the company and the less equity they need to give up in order to raise capital.

Incubators and Accelerators

Incubators and Accelerators are formal programs that accept startups and put them through a program to help develop their idea and then present the graduates to an investment community during a presentation day.

Founders can get a modest amount of funding from these programs. They also get credibility because they have been scrutinized, vetted and accepted by the incubator program.

Y Combinator is one of the most popular incubators and they have had some great success stories come through their program like Dropbox and Airbnb.

Crowd Funding

Kickstarter, Indiegogo and others have made crowd funding a viable option for taking projects from ideation to execution and prove market validation.

These website driven funding sites are attractive because the represent a funding vehicle that is non-dilutive. This means that the money raised is not in exchange for equity (ownership) in the company. Other incentives besides equity are offered such as exclusive access to the founders or early access to the product.

A crowd-funding project can also act as a way to gauge demand and generate interest in a concept early on.

Angel Investing

This funding round is also called Seed Funding and represents the first professional outside investment. Most founders get their seed round after successfully going through two or three of the early-stage funding strategies discussed above.

Angel investors are individuals who scout for great startup opportunities and generally make a lot of relatively small money investments in early-stage high-risk ventures. They are essentially buying lottery tickets on the character of the founder and the potential upside of a company breaking out into a huge success. They look to make 100 times their money back if a company "exits" successfully by being acquired or going public.

Angels represent varying degrees of professional investor and they must be convinced of the potential of a startup to really scale and become hugely valuable. After looking at many such deals, their greed needs to overcome their skepticism in order for them to invest.

Series A

The Series A is the funding round where the company becomes a professionally organized entity: a corporation. Professional venture capital firms who as part of the deal join the board and create proper "governance" do this funding round. Proper governance means that the company is legally incorporated and holds regular board meetings and keeps a detailed record of board resolutions all designed to increase the share price of the company.

Prior to the Series A, founders run the show and answer to no one. Focus is on trying to find product/market fit. After Series A the CEO will spend a significant amount of time (25%) managing the board and the legal requirements of running a corporation.

Series B,C,D etc.

These are the follow-on rounds once a company makes the transition to being a professionally managed operating entity.

Cap Table

The cap table is short for the capitalization table. It is the official list of all the shareholders in a company and how much they paid for their shares. The above funding rounds represent the people that populate the cap table.

Exit

This is the event that represents the big payday for early investors and founders. An exit is either an acquisition or an IPO Initial Public Offering. An IPO is where a company gets listed and traded on a stock exchange and sells shares to the general public.

IPOs are relatively rare. The more usual exit is an acquisition where the startup is bought by an established company to add to its portfolio of offerings or for some other strategic reason.

The purchase price of the company is split among the various shareholders and the value of their pro rata portion is what determines their return on their original investment. The exit is the end game goal of venture-backed startups.

Summary

The methodologies described in this section are not mutually exclusive approaches. Apply design thinking, lean and agile methodologies, and growth hacking together. Integrate them in your ideation and development process. The interplay is valuable. Keep it lean and experimental. Lather, Rinse, Repeat.

The goal is to get to know the customer well. Put in the minimum amount of effort and resources to get the maximum learning ASAP. One way is to build a web page to see if people will click on it. Another way is to place keyword ads around your core feature or value proposition. As an entrepreneur, repeat this process again and again. Doing it cheaply allows you to do more iterations.

An element of lean startup is the notion of the pivot. If the data invalidates your hypothesis, you keep some elements fixed and change other elements. But how do you know what to pivot to? The guiding principle is deeper customer understanding. This scenario is an example of how Design Thinking and Lean Startup can interact: The empathy you gain through Design Thinking helps you identify possible pivots.

A startup venture is a series of hypotheses about who's a customer, what makes your product or service attractive to these customers, and so on. Lean startup provides a rigorous framework that you use to prove or disprove as many of these hypotheses as possible at as low a cost as possible. An interesting question is how do you generate the hypothesis? If you have not already identified the user need through your own experience of a pain point, having experienced the need firsthand, how would you discover that need?

Again Design Thinking can help. In Design Thinking you develop a prototype that is used to get feedback that's very qualitative and Lean Startup makes the process more rigorous. In this way you don't delude yourself that the feedback is necessarily positive.

These approaches complement each other and can be used to converge on insanely great products and services that meet customer needs and wants. When features are baked in that facilitate Growth Hacking, you are on your way to a very promising Startup Venture!

Business Ethics

Now we have a comprehensive set of ideas about how business functions in a capitalist society from studying entrepreneurship and startups. The next fundamental concept is how we conduct ourselves and treat others when pursuing opportunity. This is business ethics.

Ethics is foundational to good management and leadership practice.

Business ethics examines ethical principles and problems that arise in a business environment. It applies to business conduct. Ethics is relevant to the conduct of individuals and organizations.

Ethics is not simply a business concern, it is a human concern.

Ethics is the study of how to live a good life. We want our lives to be meaningful and as such we want our business activities and the way we make our living be meaningful. Look at developing business skills and knowledge as a way to impress your personal stamp on the world in an effective and beneficial way, not as an oblique strategy to become successful as a way to impress others with your success.

I chose the word "meaningful" purposefully because that is the center-piece of thinking about ethics in relation to business. Our goal should be to make a positive impact on people's lives, including our own.

We live in a time of increased latitude about creating our careers and of interacting directly with customers. Our responsibilities in such situations require us to have a firm grasp of ethical behavior. People and brands must deliver on their promise.

Ethical issues arise in business settings as a result of the tension between profit maximizing behavior of capitalism and non-economic concerns. The profit maximizing behavior may derive from the perspective of the individual, a group, a corporation or country.

There are many questionable business practices and we must all decide how we behave and promote our business activities, and what business activities we decide to pursue and participate in.

Business ethics seems to be taught primarily as a reaction to highly publicized lapses of basic ethical conduct by stewards of corporations like Enron, WorldComm, Bernie Madoff, Arthur Andersen, the savings and loan scandals of the late 1980s, the banking and financial crises of 2008, and FIFA. We are confronted with many cautionary tales of personal greed perverting the decisions and behavior of people in positions of responsibility and power.

Power is not only abused for financial gain. Sexual misconduct is another example of abusing power.

Business ethics has been added to MBA programs in recent years ostensibly as an antidote and preventative measure to this kind of behavior. Businesses have also added Codes of Ethics and Social Responsibility to their mission statements as ways of acknowledging the dilemma. It is questionable whether these efforts actually address the issue at large in any effective way. People have an innate sense of right and wrong. Yet this innate ethical sense is challenged when right decisions fly contrary to personal gain.

There are obvious issues to address such as "don't steal and don't lie." These are often quoted without any context and so everyone readily agrees with and likes to stand for them. Yet these basic tenets often dissolve into grey areas and it is easy to devise a rationalization for bending the rules when the outcome can be personally favorable.

Ethical concerns about the business world are not new. Industrialists have exploited workers with long hours in unsafe environments for little pay and there have always been tensions between wages and workers rights, and the profits flowing to owners. There is also industrial pollution and the use of public property for private gain.

We have gained more agency in making decisions for ourselves and the people which our careers and businesses impact. The following are some examples of the kinds of questions that currently arise.

The oil and gas industries are very lucrative, but they are also contributing to pollution through contaminating groundwater, carbonization of the atmosphere, and acidification of the oceans. These large-scale impacts are reducing the biodiversity of the planet by driving species of flora and fauna into extinction and by changing the climate to a point where the Earth is no longer habitable for humans. Should you work for these companies? Should you hold their stock in your portfolio? Should their stocks be in the portfolio of your retirement fund? Should you drive a car that uses gas?

Tobacco companies sell cigarettes even though we know they contribute to all sorts of diseases. Alcoholic beverages are sold even though we know they are detrimental to our health and lead to bad decision making while under the influence. Manufactured foods contain salt, sugar and fats in unhealthy amounts in order to get us to buy more and eat more. Advertising appeals to us in ways that have little to do with the products being sold and in many instances misrepresent what is being sold.

Many business models would not be profitable if the broader impact of what they do to the environment or social orders is taken into account. There are lobbyists and politicians and scientists and business people who have much to gain by the status quo and by maintaining and promoting these ways of doing business. Not surprisingly, they are very artful at obscuring the issues and misdirecting sympathies in order to protect their markets, business models, and revenue streams.

There are also ethical decisions in career choices relative to the opportunity costs to society at large.

There has been much recent debate over the relative merit and contributions of bright, talented and highly educated people who have opted to take jobs in financial firms designing financial instruments and predictive models of ultimately questionable long-term societal value instead of pursuing less immediately lucrative careers in solving pressing environmental issues and addressing other social concerns.

We all wrestle with these challenges. I am by no means above these issues I am outlining. I have a car and I drive and I buy gas and I am responsible for adding to the carbon exhaust problem. I try to be aware and avoid problematic issues, but we live in a society that makes some choices difficult to avoid.

Acting ethically takes continual vigilance and commitment. It is about being aware of the choices we make and acting intentionally. We need to be mindful of where our self-interest and societal common interests align and diverge.

It is important to understand the difference between self-interest and selfishness. Here are the definitions of the words from the Cambridge Dictionary:

Self-Interest is the consideration of advantages for yourself in making a decision, usually without worrying about its effect on others.
Selfishness is caring only about what you want or need without any thought for the needs or wishes of other people.

Selfishness promotes a petty and small-minded perspective. In order to combat this narrow perspective we need to expand our view to see how our actions affect others, especially those relying on us. Also, in order to negotiate effectively we need to be able to step into the other side's shoes and understand their point of view.

Self-interest, on the other hand, is something we all need to cultivate. Practicing self-care is extremely important. We are of little use to others if we are depleted. It's like in a plane emergency: we are instructed to place the mask over our face first before helping others.

The purpose of life is not happiness. It is usefulness. As managers and leaders we must first be self-possessed and aware of how we are, and want to be, in order to consider ourselves worthy prime movers.

Ethics and the Law

Governmental institutions implement laws and regulations to limit and direct business behavior in what they consider to be beneficial or benign ways and away from what is perceived as detrimental behavior. Regulations can have pernicious effects and unintended consequences and there will always be smart people who are prepared to devise ingenious work-arounds and loopholes to any well meaning regulations and laws.

Business Ethics first and foremost is about making decisions about career, and products and services, that positively impact people, places and things. The Hippocratic oath that physicians take says "first do no harm". This is a proper initial criterion for business decisions also.

Unethical Behavior

We read about it and hear it on the news. Corporate corruption is widespread: fraud, exploitation, cheating, stealing...

It rarely is organized from the top however. A few leaders are crooks no doubt. Managers can become involved in institutionalized breaking of rules and ethical standards in order to meet aggressive targets and goals in order to keep their jobs. The motivations can be fear of loss or downright greed and sociopathic insanity.

But that is the exception. The intention of the majority of managers and leaders is to run ethical organizations and make a beneficial impact on customers and society.

Sometimes individual incentives are not aligned with those lofty goals. Usually employees end up bending or breaking ethics rules for personal gain and because those in charge are lax in oversight and unwittingly encourage skirting ethical guardrails with aggressive mantras like "Move fast and break things". If controls are loose, temptation can be overwhelming.

In many cases ethics is not even taken into consideration in business situations. Companies are in business to maximize profits and create shareholder value. Ethical considerations are not embedded in Corporate Bylaws and Articles in Incorporation.

Correcting mistakes takes time and resources and that translates into additional costs. This type of scenario cascades into lost revenues and reduced profits and that could mean losing one's job and the security it offers.

Admitting problems and attempting to remedy them can also hurt a brand's reputation and erode market share. These are all business issues that incentivize not dealing with problems from a strictly ethical standpoint. Delaying or covering up issues may seem like the expedient way to deal with a problem. Kick the can down the road and hope for a miracle.

We need an ethical framework to rely on when tough situations arise. It's easy to behave well when things are going well. Everybody's good when its easy to be good. A person isn't judged under such circumstances. It's how we act when things aren't going well that tells us who we really are. It's best to be prepared so we don't fail the test.

"Live one day at a time emphasizing ethics rather than rules."

- Wayne Dyer

Case Study: Consider the Pinto

Consider how the Ford Motor Company dealt with safety issues surrounding the Ford Pinto. The Pinto was a cheap ill-conceived compact car. It was a product of the 1970s; a time when the American auto industry took its eye off the ball.

The Pinto gained infamy for its tendency to leak fuel and explode into flames if rear-ended. Not necessarily a feature drivers look for in a car and not something, in retrospect, Ford would want to be known for. It's a big ding to the brand when you are known for "safety last".

Close to thirty people were killed or maimed in exploding Pintos before Ford reluctantly issued a recall. Subsequent investigations into the decision process behind the company's "damn the torpedoes" launch revealed a cascade of incredibly poor judgment. Ford at the time was feeling the heat of competition from domestic and international car manufacturers. Under a sense of competitive urgency, Ford had rushed and cut corners to produce the Pinto.

In preproduction crash tests, engineers uncovered the danger of the fuel tanks rupturing, but with the

104

assembly line ready and Ford executives decided to move forward.

When this all was exposed, people were shocked and viewed the decision as evidence of callousness, carelessness and greed. Now, removed by decades, we can look at this and other cases through a more nuanced lens.

Behavioral economics has given us a growing body of research and literature and a better understanding of cognitive biases and how they pervert the application of ethical criteria in decision-making.

Ford and the Pinto is a case of groupthink blinding decision makers to ethical issues. Now its considered doubtful any of those responsible for the Pinto decision believed they were acting unethically. The reason is that ethics didn't enter the picture. They thought of it as purely a business decision.

In business school, one is trained to make rational decisions based on numbers. This is considered objective. One of the tools is cost-benefit analysis to see if the potential revenues are bigger than the costs. In the case of the Pinto they calculated costs for redesign, lawsuits, and even lost lives. They calculated it would be more cost effective to pay off lawsuit awards from deaths than to recall and repair the cars.

That methodology abstracted the situation and influenced how they viewed and made their subsequent decisions. The ethical dimension was not part of the calculus. This is called "ethical fading".

Ethical fading is a self-deceptive, unconscious psychological mechanism by which even the morally competent are lead to disregard the ethical consequences of a particular choice.
It is a phenomenon that results in taking ethics out of consideration and increases the tendency for unaware unethical behavior. It results in a cognitive blindness.

Lee Iacocca was then a Ford executive. Iacocca is an iconic American automobile executive. He is best known for the development of Ford Mustang while at Ford in the 1960s, and then later for spearheading the turnaround of the Chrysler Corporation as its CEO during the 1980s. He was a corporate rock star.

Lee was involved in the Pinto launch as a top executive. When the design flaw was discovered during testing, no one dared tell him. In a 1977 article in Mother Jones magazine a company official who worked on the Pinto recounted why. "That person would have been fired. Safety wasn't a popular subject around Ford in those days. With Lee it was taboo. Whenever a problem was raised that meant a delay on the Pinto, Lee would chomp on his cigar, look out the window and say 'Read the product objectives and get back to work.'"

The pressure to perform from shareholders, analysts, investors, and senior management can be intense. No one's job is secure in the face of perceived failure.

Iacocca and the team in charge of the Pinto were probably not conscious of acting unethically. They didn't intentionally perform or explicitly sanctioned unethical behavior. Psychological, analytical and organizational factors conspired to distract attention from the ethical dimensions of the problem.

The same delusional forces today influence executives and few are self aware of how cognitive biases impact behavior in less than virtuous, or widely beneficial, ways.

Recognizing and understanding how these blind spots influence decision-making can help leaders create the ethical organizations they aspire to run.

Protecting the franchise and the brand is paramount. Any ethical lapse that endangers customers or society can severely damage a company.

"It takes twenty years to build a reputation and five minutes to ruin it. If you think about that you'll do things differently."
- Warren Buffett

Ethical Caveats of Goals and Incentives

Managers and leaders need to be aware of the pernicious effects of goals and incentives that are not well formed. Be on the lookout for unintended actions.

When employees behave in ways other than what we think we are motivating, we need to examine what we are measuring and the behavior we are rewarding. We need to evaluate what we are actually encouraging them to do.

In the 1990s, management at Sears wanted to increase the speed of repairs being done by the mechanics in their automotive shops. They set a sales goal of $150 an hour. But rather than work faster the mechanics attempted to meet the aggressive goal by overcharging and fabricating repairs. The new goal institutionalized ripping off customers.

This type of unethical behavior emerges in service firms that keep score of performance based on billable hours. Professionals at accounting, consulting, and law firms are under severe pressure to maximize billable hours. This creates pernicious incentives similar to that of the Sears mechanics. And systems designed to be more transparent and promote ethical behavior end up requiring a huge reporting burden and backfire.

Unintended Consequences

What gets measured gets managed so measure what matters. And be on the lookout for incentives with pernicious effects. Be vigilant.

A failure to examine the potential pernicious effects of incentive systems can lead to the unintended consequence of inspiring or motivating unethical behavior.

Employees and organizations require specific, moderately challenging goals in order to perform at a high level. There is a compensating need to create a broad index to measure results, or we risk incentivizing them to neglect other areas that impact stakeholders.

We especially don't want to alienate customers or place then at risk through poorly designed goals and incentives. The ends do not justify the means and we don't want to inadvertently create an environment where employees end up engaging in unethical behavior.

When setting goals, we need to adopt the perspective of those whose behavior we are trying to influence and think through their potential responses. This is the responsibility of managers and leaders. Not thinking through the consequences of goals and exhortations is tantamount to blindly engaging in unethical behavior.

Motivated Blindness

"A man sees what he wants to see, and disregards the rest."

- Paul Simon "The Boxer"

People see what they want to see and disregard information that contradicts their opinions, especially when it's in their interest to do so. This is a psychological bias known as motivated blindness.

This bias applies to unethical behavior where there are conflicts of interest. This happened to accountants at Arthur Andersen who worked as outside auditors for Enron. Enron paid them. Arthur Andersen also had big consulting engagements with Enron. The lowly audit accountants were pressured to overlook accounting discrepancies.

There were similar conflicts of interest between the rating agencies Standard & Poor's, Moody's, and Fitch and the investment banks who paid them to provide AAA ratings to mortgage securities that were much more risky. This behavior ended up triggering the 2008 financial crisis.

These powerful conflicts of interest blinded the perpetrators to their unethical behavior. Those with a stake to benefit financially have a powerful motivation to look the other way.

Motivated blindness shows that awareness of conflicts of interest isn't enough to remove them. And it's not just a matter of integrity. Honesty is not an antidote for motivated blindness. Executives need to be vigilant and aware that conflicts of interest may be obscured and easily rationalized away. Work to remove them from your organization. Begin by examining incentive systems.

Indirect Blindness

"I'm a fool to do your dirty work." - Steely Dan

This is a situation where the unethical behavior is outsourced.

Managers may tell subordinates, or agents such as lawyers and accountants, to "do whatever it takes" to achieve some goal, which ends up sanctioning bad actions. This is delegating unethical behaviors to others.

Slippery Slope

If you place a frog in a pot of boiling water, the frog will jump out. But if you put it in a pot of warm water and raise the temperature gradually, the frog will tolerate the slow change and will cook to death.

This is analogous to our failure to notice the gradual erosion of ethical standards. If we are OK with minor infractions we are more likely to accept major infractions so long as a sequence of violations are only incrementally more serious.

This has a corollary in criminal justice. The Broken window policing theory became popular in the 1990s.

The broken windows theory says that visible signs of crime, like broken windows and graffiti, create an environment that encourages further crime and disorder, including serious crimes. The solution is policing methods that target minor crimes, such as vandalism. This helps create an atmosphere of order and lawfulness that prevents more serious crimes.

In order to avoid the slow and subtle creep of unethical behavior, managers need to address even trivial-seeming infractions immediately. A zero tolerance policy is in order.

The ends do not justify the means

Many managers and incentive systems overlook bad decisions by rewarding results rather than high-quality decisions. An employee may act unethically but, if things turn out well, be rewarded for it. This undermines the ethics of the organization. Reward quality decisions, not just results.

Ethics and Philosophy

A well-developed sense of ethics requires a well-developed personal philosophy. And that requires a basic understanding of philosophy.

Most lapses of ethical behavior derive from fear. We fear loss of comfort and safety. We fear pain and death. Philosophy can help us better deal with these fears and the behavior they engender.

Philosophy can appear as an abstract and arcane field of study that has little to do with our daily lives. There is a branch of philosophy that can provide us with a sense of a basic support structure for operating in the world. It is called Stoicism.

The following is adapted and excerpted from a great piece by Ryan Holiday and Tim Ferriss called "Stoicism 101." Here is a link to their blog post: http://fourhourworkweek.com/2009/04/13/stoicism-101-a-practical-guide-for-entrepreneurs/

The central teachings of Stoicism are intended to illustrate to us how best to prepare to deal with the unpredictable nature of life. Life is uncertain. Often we feel tossed and turned by events and anxious about what the future holds. Stoicism's project is to help inoculate us from the distractions and paralysis of misplaced worry.

Stoicism teaches us how to be disciplined and free. It illuminates the sources of our dissatisfaction and how to combat our impulsive dependency on our reflexive reactions.

The lessons of Stoicism are practical and meant to be practiced and applied in life. It is not simply a theoretical endeavor. It is a set of attitudes we can use to become better managers, leaders, entrepreneurs, better friends, partners, lovers, and better people. Worry and fear are contagious and debilitating; we want to learn how to control those tendencies so we nurture perspective and spread a sense of calm.

There are three main Stoic philosophers.
Marcus Aurelius was the emperor of the Roman Empire during its golden age in the second century A.D. He was the most powerful man on earth. He was

also one of the wisest ever to live. He was well aware of the potential for ethical distortions that power and wealth can produce. His writings are called the Meditations and are about restraint, compassion and humility. Get a copy.

The writings of Marcus Aurelius are the only intimate reflections we have of someone in such a role of ultimate power and wealth. Many emperors gave into temptations and became debouched, depraved and dissipated. Marcus Aurelius was famously **different**. Marcus observed that: "it is difficult but not **impossible, to live** well **even in a palace**. He led a life that is well worth modeling: that of a true philosopher king.

Epictetus grew up at the opposite end of the social spectrum. He was a Roman slave and endured the degradations of slavery and ended up founding a school where he taught and influenced many of the great Romans.

Seneca was tutor and advisor to the Roman emperor Nero. Nero ultimately turned on him and demanded his suicide. Seneca comforted his wife and friends and obliged the emperor. His philosophy taught him how to live well and how to die well.

Reading the Stoics can have similar benefits as a yoga session or listening to a coach's pre-game speech. It's a philosophical preparation for the life of action – and will remind you that the right state of mind is crucial to making good decisions and maintaining one's poise and focus.

Stoics practiced exercises designed to give them the psychological strength and confidence to act in the face of uncertainty. Here are three important Stoic exercises:

Practice What You Fear

"It is in times of security that the spirit should be preparing itself for difficult times; while fortune is bestowing favors, it is then the time to be strengthened against her rebuffs." -Seneca

Dig your well before you are thirsty. Inure yourself to hardships by preparing and renouncing luxuries now and again: fast; exercise hard; sleep outside.

In Hermann Hesse's book, when asked what he could do Siddhartha answered, "I can think. I can wait. I can fast."

Seneca enjoyed wealth and prestige as the adviser of Nero. But he also knew that his cushy circumstances were tenuous and could change. To prepare for such contingency he said that we ought to take time on a regular basis to practice living in poverty. Take little food, wear crappy clothes, and remove yourself from the comforts of your home and bed. Place yourself in circumstances of want, and ask yourself "Is this what I fear?"

In this situation you may become more comfortable in the knowledge that "deprivation" isn't so bad. In fact, you may begin to understand that luxury and excess is a distraction that keeps you from doing more important things.

The message here is: Live simply and keep distractions to a minimum so that you can focus time and energy on important things you have always wanted to do but never seemed to have the time for.

For the Stoics this is a daily exercise, not a thought experiment. Seneca doesn't instruct us to "think about" adversity, he means *live* it. Comfort can be the most abject kind of slavery if you are always worrying that circumstance might take it away. If you *practice* misfortune, then fate, chance, and circumstances lose their ability to cloud and disrupt your life.

Anxiety and fear have their roots in uncertainty and are rarely based on our experience. Mark Twain said: "I am an old man and have known a great many troubles, but most of them never happened."

The solution is to become intimately familiar with the scenarios that worry you. Then you can confidently take risks and act ethically because you will realize that the downside is almost always reversible and transient. Practice what you fear, and you can act fearlessly.

Treat Obstacles as Opportunities

"Choose not to be harmed and you won't feel harmed. Don't feel harmed and you haven't been."
-Marcus Aurelius

The Stoics practiced their philosophy by understanding how to turn a perceived problem into an opportunity. To the Stoic, everything is opportunity. Similarly, entrepreneurs and leaders have the ability to take advantage of, and even create, opportunities.

Stoics don't make judgments relative to good or bad luck. They understand it is simply a perception and you control how you perceive a situation. From that vantage point one can make clear decisions about opportunity and the path forward.

The space between something happening and your reaction to it becomes the leverage point. Developing that space is also a goal of meditation and mindfulness practice. By developing your ability to tie your initial response to dispassion, by viewing events with some emotional distance and disinterest, you will notice opportunities.

There is an interesting trope in motivational speaking that is based on a mistranslation of a Chinese character. It goes like this: "In the Chinese language, the word "crisis" is composed of two characters, one representing danger and the other, opportunity." Even though it is based on a misunderstanding, it is insightful; kind of like the phenomena of mishearing lyrics to a song and the wrong lyrics being more meaningful than the true lyrics.

Instead of looking at problems as making your life more difficult, Stoic practice regards them as opportunities to direct you towards developing virtues like patience, understanding and creativity.

Marcus Aurelius described it like this: "The impediment to action advances action. What stands in the way becomes the way."

All Things Must Pass

"Alexander the Great and his mule driver both died and the same thing happened to both."
    -Marcus Aurelius

Death is the great equalizer. Alexander the Great was one of the most powerful men of all time. He conquered and ruled much of the known world. He had great cities named after him. His tutor was Aristotle. He had everything: power, glory, wealth, and knowledge.

Once while intoxicated, Alexander got into an argument with his dearest friend, Cleitus. It escalated into a fight and Alexander accidentally killed Cleitus.

118

When he came to his senses, he was inconsolable, and rightly so, he had made the kind of grave mistake for which there is no remedy.

This episode leads one to question what it means to lead a successful life. From a personal perspective, what do all riches and accomplishments matter if you lose perspective and hurt those dear to you?

Don't lose sight of why you aspire to do great things. A sense of pride can take control of you and make you vulnerable. Achievements are ephemeral. Practice humility and be honest and aware. Learn from Alexander the Great and his mistake.

When you study martial arts you are taught that power is a responsibility and that you should never use your skills for less than virtuous ends.

Parting thought on Ethics

Learning about business can be like learning karate. We must use our knowledge in the pursuit of beneficial ends and not for the advancement of indiscriminate personal gain and aggrandizement without regard for how our actions affect others. That, in a nutshell, characterizes ethical behavior.

Financial Literacy: Reading and Understanding Financial Statements

Being able to read and understand financial statements is a fundamental skill to understanding how businesses function. Since financial statements are the end product of accounting, understanding them provides the context for understanding accounting. Mastering this skill will help you become a better manager.

Being able to read financial statements will also help you make better investment decisions in the stock market because you will be able to get meaningful information out of an Annual Report or a 10K.

If you are an entrepreneur planning a start up then understanding financial statements is critical for your credibility as you meet with angel investors, bankers, and VCs.

Financial Statements

Accounting information is prepared, organized, and conveyed is in Financial Statements. Financial statements are reports in which accounting information is organized so *users* of financial information have a consistent, quick, and thorough means of reading and understanding what is going on in the business.

There are two basic financial statements: the **Balance Sheet** and the **Income Statement**.
Interested parties need to understand the financial and accounting activities of a business. The Balance Sheet and Income Statement are a formal record of

the financial activities of a business. They are presented in a structured manner and in a form that is consistent and easy to understand once you understand the format.

Financial Statements provide a high level view of accounting and a summary of how a business is performing. They provide a quick picture that can be easily compared across businesses and industries. Understanding how to read and analyze a Balance Sheet and Income Statement is a great place to start understanding accounting and finance.

Financial statements are the end product of bookkeeping. Think of financial statements as the destination or goal of bookkeeping and accounting. When you know where you are going and who the audience is, it is easier to make good bookkeeping decisions. When you understand the liquidity, solvency and capital structure of a company you can make good financing and investment decisions.

Financial Statements contain information required to quickly analyze and assess the relative health of a business. A basic understanding of financial statements also provides the high level perspective on the goals of the bookkeeping work and accounting entries. The daily operations of a business are measured in the money that comes in as revenues, the money that goes out as expenses, the money that is retained as profit, the money that is invested in operational assets, and the money that is owed. It's all about the money. Financial statements let you follow the money.

The report that measures these daily operations, of money in and money out over a period of time, is the Income Statement.

The Income Statement

The Income Statement can be summarized as: Revenues less Expenses equals Net Income. The term Net Income simply means Income (Revenues) *net* (less) of Expenses. Net Income is also called Profit or Earnings. Revenues are sometimes called Sales.

You understand this concept intuitively. We always strive to sell things for more than they cost us to make. When you buy a house you hope that it will appreciate in value so you can sell it in the future for more than you paid for it. In order to have a sustainable business model in the long run, the same logic applies. You can't sell things for less than they cost you to make and stay in business for long.

Think of the Income Statement in relation to your monthly personal finances. You have your monthly revenues: in most cases a salary from your job. You apply that monthly income to your monthly expenses: rent or mortgage, car loan, food, gas, utilities, clothes, phone, entertainment, etc. Our goal is to have our expenses be less than our income.

Over time, and with experience, we become better managers of our personal finances and begin to realize that we shouldn't spend more that we make. We strive to have some money left over at the end of the month that we can set aside and save. What we set aside and save is called **Retained Earnings**.

Some of what we set aside we may **invest** with an eye toward future benefits. We may invest in stocks and bonds or mutual funds, or we may invest in education to expand our future earning and working prospects. This is the same type of money management discipline that is applied in business. It's just a matter of scale. There are a few additional zeros after the numbers on a large company's Income Statement but the idea is the same.

This concept applies to all businesses. **Revenues** are usually from Sales of products or services. **Expenses** are what you spend to support the operations: Salaries, raw materials, manufacturing processes and equipment, offices and factories, consultants, lawyers, advertising, shipping, utilities etc. What is left over is the Net Income or Profit. Again: Revenues – Expenses = Net Income. "Your Income needs to be more than your Outflow or your Upkeep is your Downfall." My Mom used to say that. :)

Net income is either saved in order to smooth out future operations and deal with unforeseen events; or invested in new facilities, equipment, and technology. Or part of the profits can be paid out to the company owners, sometimes called **shareholders** or stockholders, as a **dividend**.

Sample Income Statement

On the next page is a sample Income Statement to give you a sense of the format and presentation of the numbers.

JJC Corporation
Income Statement
For the Year Ended
December 31, 2018
(In Millions of Dollars)

Revenues	
Sales Revenues	2306
Service Revenues	1066
Total Revenues	3372
Expenses	
Cost of Goods Sold Expense	1492
Selling, General, and Administrative Expense	983
Research & Development Expense	505
Interest Expense	54
Total Expenses	3034
Pre Tax Income	338
Income Tax Expense @ 22%	74
Net Income	264

The Income Statement is also known as the "profit and loss statement" or "statement of revenue and expense." Business people sometimes use the shorthand term "**P&L**," which stands for profit and loss statement. A manager is said to have "P&L responsibilities" if they run an autonomous division where they make the decisions about marketing, sales, staffing, products, expenses, and strategy. **P & L**

responsibility is one of the most important responsibilities of any executive position and involves monitoring the net income after expenses for a department or entire organization, with direct influence on how company resources are allocated.

The terms "profits," "earnings" and "net income" all mean the same thing and are used interchangeably.

Remember: Income (revenue or sales) – Expenses = Net Income or profit.

Google the term "income statement" and you will see lots of examples of formats and presentations. You will see there is variety depending on the industry and nature of the business but they all follow these basic principles.

The Balance Sheet

The Balance Sheet can be summarized as: **Assets = Liabilities + Equity**. This is called the accounting equation; memorize it. These three *balance sheet* segments give the interested reader an idea as to what a company owns (**assets**) and owes (**liabilities**), and the amount invested and accumulated by the owners or shareholders (**equity**).

The Balance Sheet is a snapshot of the financial position of a company at a particular point in time. It is compiled at the end of the year or quarter. It is a summary of the Assets, Liabilities and Equity.

Think of how your home is financed as simple balance sheet. The **asset** is the value of the house. This is determined by an appraisal or sale. The value of your home varies as the market varies. An appraiser takes into account recent sales in the area and adjusts for differences like an extra bedroom or bathroom. An appraisal also takes into account replacement value; how much would it cost to recreate the house with the current costs for materials and labor. The **liability** is the **mortgage** balance and the **equity** (in this case we call it the homeowner's equity) is the difference between the two.

If the house is worth more than you owe, then you have positive equity. If the mortgage balance is more than the value of the home, then you have negative equity, sometimes called being "upside down" or "underwater".

The same concepts apply to a corporate balance sheet. If the assets are greater than the liabilities then there is positive shareholder's equity. If the liabilities are more than the assets, the company is considered **insolvent**. In this case a company declares bankruptcy.

Balance Sheet Presentation

A Balance Sheet is constructed of two basic parts. Assets are listed in a column and totaled at the bottom of the column. Liabilities and Equity are listed in another column with the liabilities section listed above the equity section. Liabilities and Equity are each totaled separately and then together at the bottom. Sometimes these columns are presented in a stacked form with the Asset column on top. And sometimes these columns are presented side by side with the Assets on the left hand side and both Liabilities and Equity on the right hand side.

The Liabilities and Equity show how the Assets are financed. Liabilities and Equity totals in the right hand column must exactly equal the Asset total at the bottom of the left hand column.

When someone talks about the left hand side of the balance sheet, they are referring to assets; if they talk about the right hand side of the balance sheet, they mean liabilities and equity.

For comparison purposes, the Balance Sheet numbers of the previous year are also usually presented next to this year's numbers. Remember the goal of these Financial Statements is to present the financial information in a clear and meaningful way so interested parties can quickly grasp the performance and status of the enterprise.

According to GAAP, the U.S. accounting standard, assets and liabilities are listed in the order of their liquidity, from short term to long term, as you go down the items listed in each column. Cash is the most liquid asset so it is listed on the top left of the Balance Sheet. Long term debt comes after short term debts in the Liability column and Equity is listed below the Liabilities. Equity is listed below Liabilities because shareholders have a junior claim on the assets of the corporation. In case of a bankruptcy or liquidation of the company, the money collected from the sale of assets goes first to pay the lenders. Any residual money after the lenders are paid off is distributed to the shareholders.

Outsides the United States, the rest of the world presents balance sheet items in the reverse order, from least liquid on top to most liquid at the bottom. The International Accounting Standards are referred to as IAS.

Sample Balance Sheet

On the following page you find an example of a Balance Sheet. Since they vary in their contents and presentation it is a good idea to take a quick look at a bunch of examples. Google the term "balance sheet" and you will see lots of examples in various formats and presentations.

Balance Sheet
For Years Ended December 31
(In Millions of Dollars)

		2017	2018
Assets			
Current			
Cash	$	500	771
Accounts Receivable		232	307
Inventory		420	420
Pre Paid Expenses		123	123
Total Current Assets		1275	1621
Property, Plant, & Equipment		747	747
Patents		711	711
Total Assets	$	2733	3079
Liabilities and Stockholder's			
Current			
Accounts Payable	$	101	183
Accrued Liabilities		92	92
Notes Payable, Short Term		71	71
Total Current Liabilities		264	346
Bonds Payable		973	973
Total		1237	1319
Shareholder's Equity			
Common Stock		840	840
Retained Earnings		656	920
Total Shareholder's Equity		1496	1760
Total Liabilities & Stockholder's Equity	$	2733	3079

Assets and Depreciation

Assets are listed on the left hand side of the balance sheet. There are liquid assets such as cash, marketable securities, and Accounts Receivable. These are called **Current Assets**. Many assets are long-lived items like equipment, vehicles, factories, and machines. These are called **Fixed Assets**.

A significant amount of money is spent when fixed assets are purchased. Fixed assets have a shelf life that is significantly longer than the year in which they are purchased. For these reasons fixed assets are **capitalized** at their cost and each year of their proposed useful life a portion of the price is expensed to show how much of the asset was "used" in that year. This concept is called **Depreciation**. It provides a more accurate picture of how the operating assets of a company are contributing to the operations and spreads the expense through the years of its useful life when the asset is contributing to generating revenues.

For example if we buy a machine that is assumed to last five years for $50,000 we would record this transaction and list the machine on the Balance Sheet at $50,000 as a Fixed Asset. Each year we would reduce that number by $10,000 of depreciation ($50,000/5). So in the second year the asset would show up as being worth $40,000; $30,000 in the third year and so on. The number shown on the balance sheet is the original asset at cost, less (net of) depreciation. Assets are not listed individually on the

Balance Sheet but are aggregated together and shown as a total number.

This is one reason why we need a Cash Flow Statement. The $50,000 would reduce our cash position in the first year and that would show up in the Investment section of the Cash Flow Statement. Each subsequent year, the $10,000 depreciation expense listed in the Income Statement would be added back in the Cash Flow Statement because it was not a cash expense in that year. It was just an accounting expense to keep track of the amount we are allocating to the "use" of the machine.

Amortization is similar to depreciation. Depreciation is used for tangible assets and amortization is used for intangible assets such as intellectual property like patents and trademarks. Amortization roughly matches an asset's expense with the revenue it generates. Amortization can also refer to the paying off of debt with a fixed repayment schedule that included both interest and principal, in regular installments over a period of time.

These types of non-cash events are what are compensated for in the Operations section of the Cash Flow Statement in order to accurately reconcile the financial statements to how much cash is in the bank. We will discuss the Cash Flow Statement in more detail after we finish talking about the right side of the Balance Sheet: Liabilities and Equity.

Liabilities

Liabilities are claims against the company's assets. These claims are categorized as current or noncurrent. Current liabilities are ones that will come due within the year. Liabilities consist of obligations the enterprise owes to others. Along with Equity, they are how assets are funded. The debt can be to an unrelated third party, such as a bank, or to employees for wages earned but not yet paid. Accounts payable, payroll liabilities, and notes payable are examples of Liabilities.

Both assets and liabilities are categorized as current and noncurrent. This distinction is essential for the user of the financial statements to perform ratio analysis. We will discuss ratio and other financial statement analysis techniques later in this book.

Current Liabilities

Current liabilities are ones the company expects to settle within 12 months of the date on the balance sheet. Income and Assets are used to pay these liabilities. The money can come from revenues generated from sales, or from current assets such as cash in the bank account.

The most common Current Liabilities are accounts payable. Any money a company owes its vendors for supplies or services, or to employees in the form of wages, or the government for taxes is considered a current liability. Most companies accrue payroll and related payroll taxes, which means the company owes them but has not yet paid them. All these types of obligations are acknowledged by the company and are intended to be settled in the relative near term.

Loans due in less than 12 months after the balance sheet date are also current liabilities. For example, a business may need a brief bridge loan in order to meet a payroll expense. Often this is structured as a line of credit (LOC) with the expectation that the LOC will be paid off from the collection of accounts receivable or the sale of inventory.

Current portion of long-term notes payable is also considered a current liability. A long-term note will be paid back in full after that 12-month period. However, you must show the current portion, that which will be paid back in the current operating period, as a current liability.

Unearned revenue is a category that includes money the company has collected from customers but hasn't yet earned by performing the work. The company anticipates completing the tasks and earning the income within 12 months of the date of the balance sheet.

Long Term Liabilities

Noncurrent or long-term liabilities are ones the company doesn't expect to be liquidating or settling within 12 months of the balance sheet date. Businesses use debt to finance a portion of their activities and assets. These are structured as loans, notes, or bonds with interest and principal payments over the term. A business is financed by a mixture of debt and equity. This mix is called the capital structure of the company.

There are different types of Long Term Debt. They differ primarily by their claim on the assets of the company. This becomes important when a company becomes insolvent and declares bankruptcy. Senior debt is first in line to get paid from the proceeds of the sale of assets. Junior debt has to wait until the senior debt is paid off before it can get its money back. As you can see this makes junior debt more risky because it has a greater chance of not getting paid back in the event of bankruptcy. Because there is more risk, junior debt positions demand a higher interest rate to compensate for taking more risk.

Another financing instrument is Convertible Debt which can be converted into stock.

Stockholders' Equity

Stockholder's Equity, along with liabilities, can be thought of as the funding sources of the company's assets. The stockholders are the owners of the company. The ownership of a corporation is divided into **stock** or shares. There is an amount of shares authorized for the company when is created. This amount of authorized shares can be increased by a vote of the existing shareholders. A corporation raises money by selling shares of stock. The amount of shares issued and sold is called the Shares

Outstanding. This represents 100% of the ownership of the corporation. The amount of money raised and the amount of shares issued is tabulated and displayed in the Equity section of the Balance Sheet.

Stockholder's equity is equal to the asset amounts reported on the balance sheet minus the reported liability amounts. Or put another way, Equity is the residual of assets minus liabilities. In order to understand this think of the basic accounting equation:
Assets = Liabilities + Equity
And rearrange it to solve for Equity
Equity = Assets – Liabilities

In a corporation there may be more than one type of stock issued. These classes of stock will have different rights relative to voting and claims on assets and as such will have different values. In simple terms we can classify stock into two types: Common and Preferred.

Common Stock is the type of stock that forms the ownership of every corporation. Shares of common stock provide evidence of ownership in a corporation. Holders of common stock elect the corporation's directors and share in the distribution of profits of the company via dividends. If the corporation goes bankrupt and liquidates, the secured, or senior, lenders are paid first, followed by unsecured, or junior, lenders, then the preferred stockholders, and lastly the common stockholders.

Another financing instrument that corporations can issue in addition to their common stock is preferred stock. **Preferred Stock** is a class of stock that provides for preferential treatment of dividends. The preferred dividend can be thought of like interest on a loan. Preferred stockholders will be paid dividends before the common stockholders receive dividends. These dividends are sometimes paid in stock instead of money.

Both the common and preferred stock accounts are separated into two categories: Par Value and Additional Paid-in Capital or APIC. The bulk of the money is allocated to APIC.

The Par Value account is simply a nominal value like one cent and a way to keep track of the amount of shares outstanding. The par value is a small monetary value attributed to each share. It is an arbitrary number, usually $.01. So if the company has 1,000 shares outstanding there would be $100.00 in the par value account. Par Value may also be $0.001. Par Value has no connection to the market value of the share of stock. Think of it as a placeholder.

The Additional Paid-in Capital (APIC) account is where the amount paid for a share of stock, less the par value, is recorded. When a share of common stock having a par value of $0.01 is issued for $15, the account Common Stock will be credited for $0.01 and the corresponding Additional Paid-in Capital or APIC account will be credited for $14.99 (and Cash will be debited for $15.00).

Retained Earnings is the stockholders' equity account that records and reports the net income of a corporation from its inception until the balance sheet date less the dividends declared from its inception to the date of the balance sheet. This account tracks the profits or losses accumulated since a business was opened. The profits and losses accrue to the shareholders. At the end of each year, the profit or loss calculated on the income statement is used to adjust the value of this account. In an analogy from your personal life, think of Retained Earnings as your savings left over after you have paid all your expenses.

Contra Accounts

A contra account offsets the balance in another, related account with which it is paired. If the related account is an asset account, then a contra asset account is used to offset it with a credit balance. If the related account is a liability or equity account, then a contra liability or equity account is used to offset it with a debit balance. Stockholders' equity accounts normally have credit balances.

Contra equity accounts are a category of equity accounts with debit balances. A debit balance in an owner's equity account is contrary (contra) to an equity account's usual credit balance. An example of a contra stockholders' equity account is **Treasury Stock**. Treasury stock is a corporation's own stock that has been repurchased from stockholders and is being held by the corporation. Because it is stock that is outstanding but not in the hands of shareholders, it needs to be subtracted from the value of the outstanding stockholder's shares in order to properly value the equity. This is the purpose of a contra account. Depreciation is an asset contra account that reduces the value of an asset in a similar way.

We have now discussed the major accounts equity accounts. Some may be named differently but these synonyms represent the same functions. The stockholders' equity section of a corporation's balance sheet will look like this:

Stockholder's Equity
    Paid-in capital
        Common Stock
        Preferred Stock
        Additional Paid-in Capital – Common Stock
        Additional Paid-in Capital – Preferred Stock
        Additional Paid-in Capital – Treasury Stock
    Retained Earnings
    Less: Treasury Stock
        Total Stockholder's Equity

Cash Flow Statement

Besides the Income Statement and the Balance Sheet, there is a third financial statement called the **Cash Flow Statement**. The Cash Flow Statement reconciles the Income Statement with the actual cash position of the company (the balance in the bank account) by adding and subtracting revenues and expenses that were properly recorded on the Income Statement, but are non-cash events. Depreciation and changes in Accounts Receivable are examples of non-cash events. This reconciled bank account balance is the number that then is used for the Cash account at the top of the asset column on the Balance Sheet. This is important. This is how the financial statements are interconnected.

The need for a Cash Flow Statement arises from Accrual Accounting where we book items like Receivables and Payables and Depreciation in order to provide a more accurate picture of the operations of a company by matching revenues and expenses. These "non-cash" transactions distort the Income Statement relative to how much cash actually came in and went out of the company and how much is actually in the bank. The Operations portion of the Cash Flow Statement reconciles these differences.

Besides **Operations**, there are two other parts of the Cash Flow Statement that follow the Operations portion: **Investing** and **Financing**. The Investing section shows the money that was spent on capital equipment items that don't show up as expenses on the Income Statement because they have been capitalized as Assets. The Financing section primarily shows money that has come into the company through the sale of stock or the proceeds of a loan.

The concepts behind the Cash Flow Statement are relatively nuanced and may seem a bit confusing to someone familiarizing themselves with the basic principles of accounting for the first time. As you read and work with financial statements, the different aspects of the Cash Flow Statement will become clear.

Sample Cash Flow Statement

On the following page you find an example of a simple Cash Flow Statement. Since they vary in their contents and presentation it is a good idea to take a quick look at a bunch of examples. Google the term "Cash Flow Statement" and you will see lots of examples in various formats and presentations.

Statement of Cash Flows
For the Year Ended December 31, 2018
(In Millions of Dollars)
Operating Activities

Net Income from Operations	$10,000
Add: Depreciation Expense	100
Total Operating Activities	$10,100
Investing Activities	
Purchase of Equipment	(1,000)
Sale of Equipment	500
Total Investing Activities	(500)
Financing Activities	
Increase in Long Term Debt	$2,500
Issuance of Stock	5,000
Dividends Paid	(3,000)
Total Financing Activities	$4,500
Net Change in Cash Flow	**$14,100**

Financial Statement Interconnections and Flow

The three Financial Statements are interconnected and the numbers flow through them. Basically you start a year with a Balance Sheet showing the financial position at the beginning of the period; next you have the Income Statement that shows the operations during the year period, and then a balance Sheet at the end of the year. The Cash Flow reconciles the cash position starting from the Net Income number at the bottom of the Income Statement.

The cash number calculated from the Cash Flow Statement is added to the cash from the beginning Balance Sheet. This number needs to match the actual cash in the bank and is used as the Cash account balance at the top right (Asset column) of the end of year (EOY) Balance Sheet. The Net Income number from the Income Statement is then added to the Retained Earnings number in the Equity section (left hand side) of the end of year (EOY) Balance Sheet. If this is done correctly, all the numbers should reconcile and the Assets will be equal to the Liabilities and Equity of the EOY Balance Sheet.

Think of it as a system of two Balance Sheets acting as book-ends for the Income Statement. And the Cash Flow Statement used to reconcile the Net Income (or Loss) at the bottom of the Income Statement with the amount of cash actually in the bank. This process accounts for every penny that has come in and gone out of a company during the period. Understanding these three financial statements will allow you to assess the financial health, viability and prospects of any company, and make rational fact based investment decisions.

This section, though short, ties together the functionality of the financial statements. This might be an "aha" moment for you. It was for me when I finally realized how this all fit and worked together. Understanding this conceptual big picture of accounting will provide a context to keep you from ever getting lost in the details.

The Role of Auditors

As per the SEC requirements and regulations, in order to be eligible to be traded on a stock exchange, a publicly traded company's financials must be prepared by the company and then reviewed and audited by an outside Certified Public Accountant (CPA).

Many investors in private companies also require audited financials in order to ensure that the accounting practices and the financial statement presentation is prepared fairly and transparently.

What is an auditor?

The auditing process entails reviewing the financial statements prepared and drafted by the company to make sure they conform to GAAP and other rules. The auditors also "test" the numbers by requesting and reviewing supporting documentation such as invoices, checks, bills, and contracts. They send letters to the company's banks to confirm bank balances and contact lawyers the company has worked with to confirm that there are no latent liabilities or lawsuits pending that have not been disclosed.

The Auditing Process

In any company there are strong temptations to commit fraud. People who run companies have the power to exploit financial information for personal gain. For publicly traded companies annual auditing is a legal requirement and investors of many privately held companies, including their bankers, also require annual audited financial statements.

The audit process is designed to protect against misrepresenting financial information to improve results, avoid taxation, hide fraud, or not report latent liabilities. Audits are a process of gaining information about the financial systems and the financial records of a company.

Financial audits are performed to ascertain the validity and reliability of accounting processes and information, as well as to provide an assessment of the company's internal control system. Audits are carried out by a third party impartial accounting team led by an accountant that is certified as a CPA.

To work on other company's financials you must be a CPA. In the United States a CPA will have passed the Uniform Certified Public Accountant Examination and met additional state education and experience requirements for membership in their state's professional accounting body. You don't have to be a CPA to work for a company internally as an employee in accounting or finance.

Since the auditor cannot feasibly know or discover everything about a company, an audit seeks to provide reasonable assurance that the financial statements are free from material error. Test work and sampling of documents is performed in audits as a way to statistically confirm the likelihood that the accounting has been done properly by the company.

A set of financial statements are understood to be 'true and fair' when they are deemed free of material misstatements. The auditor confirms this in their opinion letter that precedes the financials in the final and finished presentation. The opinion given on financial statements depends on the audit evidence obtained. You find the opinion letter at the beginning of the audited financial statements.

GAAP and IFSR

GAAP is short for Generally Accepted Accounting Principles. These are the rules and accounting principles that have been adopted by the accounting profession in the United States. The rest of the world has adopted a different set of standards called IFSR. IFSR stands for International Financial Reporting Standards. It is the accounting standard used in more than 110 countries, but not in the United States. Both standards intend to capture and represent the economics of accounting transactions as accurately and clearly as possible.

The fact that there are two different accounting frameworks in the world creates complexities that are a problem for users of accounting information and a burden to international companies. International companies must keep two sets of accounting records and provide two completely different sets of audited financial statements. That ends up being a cumbersome and expensive amount of extra work. Although there has been an effort to harmonize the two standards into one universal standard, they have not arrived at one yet.

Users of Accounting Information

Management needs to know how the overall company is performing or how their division is doing. Managers may need feedback ASAP on how a new marketing campaign or pricing strategy is working. When and how transactions are booked is very important to users of accounting information. Users need timely information about how the business is doing in order to make decisions.

Besides the internal interests of management, there are external users of accounting information such as:

- Bankers who are interested in your credit worthiness and ability to repay loans,

- Vendors who are interested in your ability to pay and your credit worthiness,
- Investors who want to know whether to invest or how their investment is performing,
- Stock Analysts who research companies and opine on whether or not they are good investments for their clients,
- Potential customers, especially of big ticket items or services, who want to know that the company is sound and will be around to offer support and spare parts, and
- Taxing authorities who want to know how much money the business has made or lost.

Reporting the results of business activity on an accrual basis is important to these parties that have a stake in the company's performance and health. Accrual provides a much more accurate picture of the operations to those who are not intimately involved in the day-to-day operations but need to know the operational details.

The way this kind of reporting of the accounting information is prepared, organized, and conveyed is in Financial Statements.

I hope you have found this section helpful and informative. Now let's move on to Marketing. We will return to the numbers side of business in the Finance section.

Marketing 2.0

Principles and Practice in the Digital Age

Marketing is probably the most important part of any enterprise. Nothing happens until something gets sold.

Many people equate marketing with advertising. Advertising is certainly a key component of marketing. Advertising can create awareness, enhance perceptions of value, build brand equity, and ultimately help make the sale.

But Marketing is much more than just advertising.

Here's the definition of Marketing on dictionary.com:

"The total of activities involved in the transfer of goods from the producer or seller to the consumer or buyer, including advertising, shipping, storing, and selling."

Marketing basically encompasses all of the outward facing activities of a business.

You Already Are a Sophisticated and Experienced Marketer

For most all of your life, from when you were first cognizant of your surroundings, you have been exposed to the shrewdest marketing campaigns. Ever since you first wanted a particular toy or breakfast cereal or candy bar or to watch a favorite TV show, you have been on the business end of marketing campaigns.

We are all bombarded by marketing messages all day long and have become very astute at quickly assessing if we are interested or not, if they are trustworthy or not, is their proposition of value to us or not.

Like it or not, most of our desires are manufactured and manipulated (certainly the attempts are made) by marketing. We know some of what works and what doesn't on ourselves. And some marketing gets in past our conscious discretionary barriers and manipulates us in more subliminal ways.

Draw on your reservoir of personal experience and opinion as you work your way through this book. And be more aware as you go through your day as to what marketing campaigns you find tasteful and effective and which you find stupid, tasteless, offensive or ineffective. And realize that some of the worst ones are also quite memorable. Its not just good marketing that is sticky.

The Times They Are A Changin'

Of all the business disciplines and skills, Marketing has changed the most dramatically over the past couple of decades.

The folks that inhabited the world of Mad Men, the TV show about the advertising business centered along Madison Avenue in Manhattan, at mid century wouldn't recognize the business. Their world was about generating demand by creating desire through crafting artful images and messages; and broadcasting those messages in print, radio and television.

It was mostly Advertising. The effectiveness of the ad campaigns was taken on faith to a degree. If you got your ads in front of enough people enough times on billboards, magazines, radio and TV, they would remember to buy your products at the supermarket. But there was no way to directly measure the impact, efficiency or effectiveness of campaigns.

It was also a self-fulfilling practice. If you could convince a client of the worthiness of a campaign and get them to commit to a large budget for media buys like radio, print and especially TV, you were pretty much guaranteed a spike in demand and sales. But then again, how effective and efficient was the entire campaign relative to other ones that weren't tried. You picked an agency and campaign and hoped for the best.

As the pioneering marketer John Wanamaker said in the late 1800s: "Half the money I spend on advertising is wasted; the trouble is, I don't know which half."

Mr. Wanamaker would be blown away by the tools we now have to craft marketing campaigns and funnels and finesse all the touch points along the customer journey.

When we think about marketing, images of sleazy car salesmen often pop into our heads. Those folks are still around and I'm sure you have run into hard sell messages all over the Internet. If you ever go to the mall they are like carnival barkers.

Counter to that, there is also a new movement underway based on social proof and word of mouth where your friends share something with you that they have found interesting or valuable. There is also a big move toward permission marketing and content marketing where marketers share things of value and interest only after you have agreed to take a look and be involved in co-creating the experience. This is the kind of marketing interaction with customers we are going to explore in this book; where we build a relationship based on trust and value.

Non Linear Marketing

A career in marketing has not been linear over the past 50 years. By this I mean that the ways marketing and advertising and sales were done transformed with the advent of the Internet, web, and mobile.

The underlying skill sets of art direction and copywriting are still paramount, but added to that mix is now required a facility with a wide range of digital tools applied across owned, earned and paid channels.

Now content is distributed and leveraged through techniques of Growth Hacking and one of the goals is the Viral sharing of content. These techniques rely on customers and evangelists becoming involved in the marketing process.

Awareness campaigns and customer journeys are monitored, and their effectiveness measured through analytics tools and metrics, and optimized through split A/B testing.

This is a rapidly evolving field where new tools and innovative techniques are being constantly developed and refined. Legacy expertise still applies in the fundamental concepts and ultimate purpose of marketing. But the ways that content gets distributed and consumed has transformed and continues to rapidly evolve.

Digital marketing is disrupting most industries and keeping up can feel like surfing a tsunami, but attempting to protect old-line businesses by creating competitive barriers while disregarding the new landscape will not end well.

Adapt to the changes, get excited about the potentials, and thrive in this new environment. Hop on this rocket!

We will look at digital marketing later in this book but first we will examine the basic concepts and fundamental principles of marketing

Marketing Basics

An enterprise can be thought of as divided into two parts: internal and external. The internal is focused on how to most efficiently make and deliver the product or service. It includes management, accounting, and operations activities.

Marketing is the outward facing activities of a company. Marketing is the set of functions related to customer-focused and customer-facing activities. Marketing deals with reaching and convincing customers of the value of your product, differentiating it from competitor's offerings and creating loyalty to your brand.

Marketing communicates the fit between your offering and the customer's needs and desires. Marketing also analyzes the market for your goods: how big it is, what share of the market you may achieve, who the competitors are and how to differentiate your offering from theirs.

Marketing is about how you reach your customers and how you deliver your products and services. These are called Marketing Channels and distribution.

Marketing also looks at the product/market fit and models the demand and how pricing affects the quantity demanded.

The Value Proposition Canvas

The Value Proposition Canvas (VPC) is a useful conceptual framework for thinking about the relationship between the Value Proposition and Customers. The goal is achieving a fit between what you are offering, the value proposition, and what customers want and need. We call this Product/Market Fit.

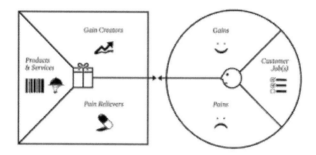

The VPC helps you create the value your customers want by organizing, mapping, and matching the dimensions of your customer's needs and your product's feature set.

The VPC is a tool to help you to understand your customer's needs, and develop products and services they want and are willing to pay for. It works in conjunction with the Business Model Canvas we looked at in the Entrepreneurship section.

Frameworks for Marketing

Let's look at some of the most popular and best frameworks that have been developed for understanding what we are trying to do when we talk about marketing. These frameworks help us organize our ideas and marketing strategy. They also insure we are talking about the same things in brainstorming sessions or meetings.

Basically in business we need to create something people need or want, and then get them to buy it from us. And in so doing, we want them to pay more than it cost us to make and sell.

Sounds simple right? But it can be disheartening how challenging it can be to get people interested in and buying what you are offering. You need enough people to really make it worth your while. You need enough customers to overcome fixed costs and at least break even.

This can be challenging and we risk throwing in the towel before our business idea has a chance to succeed. Different frameworks and approaches can provide us with alternatives so we don't give up too soon.

It can be challenging to get a handle on a big and varied concept like Marketing at first. For us to understand complex concepts like marketing, it helps to break them down into various parts so we have context and differentiating factors.

Marketers are very good at messaging so it is not surprising that there are a bunch of analytic frameworks with catchy acronyms related to the ins and outs of Marketing. They have names like:

AIDA
The 4 P's
STP
The 7 S's

The acronyms help us remember the different steps and the steps help us get a handle on the whole field. And each one gives us a different perspective on Marketing and that provides insight. The goal is insight, context, and intuition about marketing. Its like the old series of landscape prints by the Japanese artist Hokusai: 36 views of Mount Fuji. Each one shows a different aspect of Mount Fuji and together they provide an idea of the mountain.

The nice thing about these conceptual frameworks is they provide a simple way to think about a complex set of issues. As Kenneth Boulding said:

"There are two kinds of people in this world: those who divide everything into two groups, and those who don't."

Parsing and separating into groups can be helpful especially when first approaching a topic.

As with any simplification or abstraction though, they reduce out a lot of details. It's like a map and a map is not the territory.

In my presentation here, I will try my best to balance between clarity and simplicity on the one hand, and providing enough detail so as to make it meaningful and useful.

Let's check out a few of these so we can get a good sense for Marketing; what it does and how it does it.

AIDA

AIDA is   an acronym that   stands for Attention, Interest, Desire and Action. The AIDA model describes the customer journey in stages from the moment a consumer first becomes aware of a product or brand through to when they make a purchase decision.

This process is called the Customer Journey.   In Digital Marketing, with analytics tools we can measure the progress along this AIDA path, and which messages can be attributed to the actions we want to evoke.

We measure success with conversion rates: how many people that see the ads or messaging convert to paying customers.

Consumers become aware of products, services, and brands   through   advertising   and   marketing communications. We call this front-end activity Awareness Campaigns.

AIDA principle (Attention, Interest, Desire, Action) is an acronym for a principle coined by the American sales and advertisement legend Elias St. Elmo Lewis in the late 1880s.

The AIDA model is insightful in explaining how an advertisement or marketing message engages and involves consumers in awareness and choosing one brand over another. Each of the steps represents "touch points" with the potential customer where we engage with them.

A great way to engage potential customers is by providing informative and useful information or content. Content marketing has become a very effective vehicle for creating customer engagement and building trust.

Content marketing involves the creation and sharing of material online such as videos, blogs, and social media posts that do not explicitly promote a brand but are intended to stimulate interest in its products or services or draw attention to the problem being addressed and solved.

All products and services are geared toward either solving a problem for the customer or providing enjoyment.

The AIDA model describes the arc of actions that the messaging needs to accomplish in order to move a potential customer through a series of sequential steps from brand awareness through calls-to-action (**CTA**) to conversions such as purchase and consumption, and repurchase.

The sequential steps of AIDA are:

- **Attention** - The potential customer becomes aware of a category, product or brand through advertising, social media, or word of mouth referral.
  ↓
- **Interest** - The consumer becomes interested and engaged by learning about brand benefits and how the brand fits with their lifestyle, interests and needs. This is where blog posts, videos, email marketing, and other content play a major role. Depending on the type and size of purchase, this is usually a phase of multiple engagements.
  ↓
- **Desire** - The consumer develops a favorable disposition towards the brand. Here is where testimonials and other social proof are critical.
  ↓

- **Action** - The consumer forms a purchase intention, after shopping around, and makes a purchase. After the sale you want to maintain engagement, get feedback and look for opportunities for repeat sales and referrals.

The AIDA model was developed in the 1880s. I begin with this model to show that even with all the technological advancements, the core principles of marketing haven't changed drastically. What works is pretty much timeless and constant and you can always refer back to the basics when things get too complicated and convoluted.

There are lots of modified versions since its first appearance, but it is still valid in the current web and mobile-based platform environment.

Cognitive, Emotional, Behavioral

There are many variations on the AIDA model that you can check out and explore. The basic idea is one of a hierarchy of effects, where one stage leads to the next in a linear, sequential fashion. The idea is that consumers move through a series of steps or stages. The variations all incorporate three broad stages: Cognitive→ Emotional →Behavioral.

Cognitive is the awareness stage where we first come in contact with a product and learn about a brand. This is where awareness campaigns and content marketing come in. The content that you provide helps your potential customer understand what you are about. The more helpful and valuable the content the more understanding and trust develop.

The **Emotional** stage is where feeling, interest and desire are developed around the brand, products and services offered. Developing an emotional engagement with a brand is based on a continued development of trust.

Finally the **Behavior** or Action stage is where the potential customer becomes a real customer and purchases. This stage is initiated with Call to Action **CTA** and is fulfilled in a Conversion, a purchase event.

This is the basic arc of the customer journey. There are calls to action and conversions along the way for example when a customer joins a mailing list in exchange for free content. This step is called **Permission Marketing** where you offer something of value in order to gain the permission to continue and deepen the dialogue.

Though AIDA breaks the process into discreet and sequential steps, this process may take place very rapidly as a customer makes the assessments and decides to buy. The purchase cycle could be collapsed or extended over time depending on the size and consequences of the purchase. If it is a small ticket item, it could be an impulse buy. If it is a large ticket item then several iterations of interaction and comparison will probably take place before the purchase decision is made.

AIDA describes the front end of the **marketing funnel**. After the initial conversion or purchase we want to continue to engage the customer and make sure they are satisfied and convert them into a loyal return customer. This idea of purchasing more products and services over time is calculated and quantified as the Lifetime Value **LTV** of the customer.

The 4Ps

Alliterating Ps is a popular way to create a memorable acronym. There are the 5Ps of planning: Proper Preparation Prevents Poor Performance. This saying comes from the British army and is a shortcut of the original, cruder, 7Ps which mean Proper Planning and Preparation Prevent Piss Poor Performance.

Marketing is all about creating messages that are memorable. This section is about the main Ps of marketing.

Marketing is about delivering the right message about the right product, at the right price, at the right place, at the right time, and to the right person. The 4Ps detail this approach.

The four Ps is probably the most popular way to organize and analyze the marketing efforts of any brand, product or service. The four Ps are:

- Product
- Place
- Promotion
- Price

The 4 Ps are a way to think about and execute the marketing mix.

It is a great framework to use internally in any marketing department or effort because it provides a clear and concise way of talking about the basic elements of a marketing campaign. This helps coordinate efforts and gets everyone on the same page in planning and executing a successful offering.

Product

The first P is product. This stands for the offering or value proposition. It is what a company is selling. It can be a product or a service or some mix of both like a product and a service contract. We'll call it product for short here.

A product offering only really makes sense in relation to the needs and wants of customers.

Lets think of Product as the relationship between our
Value Proposition, which is the feature set of our
product/service, and the needs and desires of our
target customers. It is this Product/Market Fit that we
are trying to assess and optimize.

The Value Proposition Canvas is a concept that has
been developed to help entrepreneurs assess and
develop Product/Market Fit.

It can help to evaluate existing products and look to
optimize or rethink alignments of features and
customers to optimize perceived value. Perceived
value is the customer's perception of the value of your
offering. How big of a problem are you solving or
how much delight are you generating. This is critical
because it is the basis of a sustainable competitive
advantage, which translates into higher prices that the
offering can command and higher profit margins.

The Value Proposition Canvas (VPC) expands on the
relationship between the Value Proposition and
Customers. The goal is achieving the optimal fit
between what you are offering, the value proposition,
and what customers want and need. This fit needs to
be evaluated and tweaked for every customer
segment. Different customer segments have different
needs and wants. We will talk more about this
relationship in the STP section.

The VPC helps you move your product towards what
your customers want by organizing, mapping, and

matching the dimensions of your customer's needs and your product's proposed feature set.

The VPC is a clear way to organize and understand your customer's needs, and design products and services that meet those needs and customers will pay for. It works in conjunction with the Business Model Canvas. It basically refines the right hand side of the BMC. Both were developed by Alexander Oesterwalder to help entrepreneurs organize their ideas and test them against feedback from customers and the market.

Product Life Cycle

The product or service (or mix of the two) is a good that meets a specific customer need or desire. Products tend to follow a life cycle and marketers need to understand the product life cycle sequence and arc. You can then anticipate the various stages and plan to address the unique challenges of each phase.

A product progresses through a sequence of stages from introduction to growth, maturity, and decline. The changes this sequence represents, impacts marketing strategy and the marketing mix.

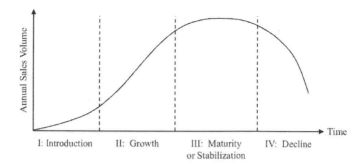

I: Introduction   II: Growth   III: Maturity   IV: Decline
                                   or Stabilization

Marketing management is involved with assessing where in the product life cycle an offering is, and employing a succession of marketing strategies that best address the situation. The markets in which a product is sold evolve over time as do the customer segments. These dynamics must be addressed and managed relative to the offering as it moves through the succession of stages.

Extending the product life cycle

Sales can be improved and optimized by attempting to extend the product life cycle. This can be achieved by:

- Boosting and recalibrating Advertising to reach additional audience and potential customers.
- Exploring and expanding to new markets to acquire more customers in different segments.
- Pricing changes: a reduction or discount in price can motivate potential customers that are on the fence to purchase.

167

- New features that add value to the product can capture new customers or fans looking to upgrade.
- Design and Packaging: Updated design and attractive packaging can influence purchases positively.

Price

Price is fairly self-explanatory. It is the amount the end user is expected to pay. But at what price to sell in order to maximize sales is tricky. The price of a product directly affects how well and how many sell.

Other things being equal, if the price of something goes down, the more of it will be sold, if the price goes up, the less units will be sold. In Economics this is called the **Law of Demand**.

Law of Demand

The law of demand is a concept in microeconomics that states, as the price of a good or service decreases, consumer demand for it will increase, and vice versa. If the price of pizza goes down during a sale, more pizza will be sold.

We graph this along dimensions of Price and Quantity. The demand curve is downward sloping which means as price goes down, quantity increases. You know this intuitively and have purchased things in this way your whole life. Don't get confused by the abstraction into a graph. The graph makes it easier to visualize and talk about.

Here is a simple graph of a demand curve with a supply curve. Where the two meet determines the price and quantity sold.

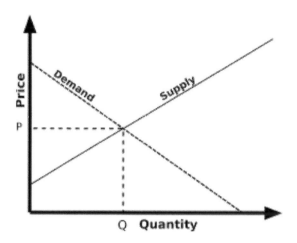

The quantity that will sell is related to the price along the demand curve. The relationship between how the quantity sold is affected by changes in price is called **the Elasticity of Demand**.

There is no objective costing criteria. The price is related to the perceived value of the product in the customer's mind.. Marketing and Branding are critical in creating an aura of prestige and desire around the product and enhancing perceived value. Educating potential customers about the utility of an offering through content marketing communicates the

169

functional value. These techniques support premium pricing, which translates into superior profit margins and a sustainable business model.

You need to understand how a customer values what you are selling. Feedback through customer engagement and social media listening provides vital information about how your products are being used and perceived by customers. Customers can be made aware of different use cases through content marketing.

Price may also be affected by how competitors price rival products. Differentiating you product offering from competitors helps you sustain your profit margins. Don't compete on price alone. Price wars are destructive. It's a race to the bottom where nobody wins; unless it serves a strategic goal.

It can work in the short term if it is part of a strategy that looks at the losses as an investment in driving out competitors and capturing market share and dominance. Think Amazon for its first ten years.

Pricing is one of the most critical decisions in the marketing mix. It influences consumers image of the brand and what the firm has to offer. There are a variety of pricing strategies depending on what you are trying to achieve or avoid. The price can be set to maximize profitability or to draw in customers. Pricing can be used as a defensive strategy to protect an existing market from new entrants. It can be used to increase market share or rapidly enter a new market.

Consumers are very selective regarding the purchases they make. Decisions on pricing strategy impact potential customer's decision on whether or not to purchase.

Another important factor is the competition within the market. Be attentive to the competition's actions and responses to price changes in order to gain or maintain a comparative advantage in the market. With Internet connected mobile devices customers can perform price comparisons quickly and with little effort.

Pricing Strategies and Models

Here are some examples of Pricing Strategies and Models:

- Freemium
- Premium
- Auction
- Subscription
- Bundling
- Two fer
- Loss Leader
- Service Contract
- Warranty

Consumer Perceptions and Price Sensitivity

In the book, The Strategy and Tactics of Pricing, the authors discuss customer perceptions relative to price and price sensitivity. These factors are related to different purchasing decisions and how available information is about alternatives and the ability to comparison shop.

Reference Price Effect –sensitivity to price increases for products depending on how high the price is relative to substitutes.

Difficult Comparison Effect – purchasers are less sensitive to the price of a known brand when it is difficult to comparison shop.

Switching Costs Effect – if there are costs associated with switching, like a new learning curve, there is less price sensitivity. Buyers are committed.

Price-Quality Effect – There is less price sensitivity for brands that are perceived higher quality.

Expenditure Effect – The larger the purchase relative to the available budget, the more sensitive buyers are to price.

Shared-cost Effect – buyers are less sensitive to price the smaller the portion of the purchase price the must pay for out of pocket. Think health insurance and prescription prices.

Fairness Effect – buyers have an idea in mind of what is a reasonable cost for a given item; the farther the price is outside this range, the more price sensitive the buyer.

The Framing Effect – buyers are less price sensitive for bundled goods. In this case it is difficult to separate out the cost for each good.

A couple of other great books that dive deep into pricing and value are:

- Priceless by William Poundstone
- The Price of Everything by Eduardo Porter

Now that we have spent some time analyzing price, think of this:

Price is dumb, value endures.

Promotion

Promotion covers the methods of communication and creating awareness that marketers use. It can include content delivered via audio like podcasts, video via YouTube, photos on Instagram and Pinterest, textual via blogs, social media posts, email, text, and others. There are new channels being constantly launched and adopted.

Promotion includes advertising, sales promotions, special offers and public relations.

Promotion channels can be broken into three categories:

- **Owned**: websites and email lists
- **Earned**: social media shares and likes
- **Paid**: advertising

Promotion is the communication aspect of marketing. Channels for communication and promotion have proliferated with the advent of the Internet, web, and mobile.

Whatever the channel used, it should suit the product, the price and the end user.

A promotion plan details the amount resources allocated to each of the elements in the promotional mix. These elements of the mix include personal selling, advertising, sales promotion, direct marketing, publicity as well as event marketing, exhibitions, trade shows and presentations.

Place

Place has to do with how the product is delivered to customers. Supply Chain Management and Distribution are key elements of Place or placement.

The strategic elements of placement are which mix of distribution channels are best suited to delivering a product or service. Purchasing, access and use patterns by end users are placement concerns that need to compliment and integrate with the rest of the product strategy.

We are looking for the ideal locations to convert potential clients into actual clients. Today the initial place potential clients are engaged and converted is most likely online. Engagement and the customer journey usually begin with permission and content marketing.

SaaS Software as a Service models have become very popular. This is where software is no longer purchased and loaded onto a personal computer, but accessed online and paid for with a monthly subscription. This is a revolutionary placement strategy and reduces some barriers to purchase in the customer's mind by reducing front end costs and commitments.

Place decisions detail where products are sold and how they are delivered to the market.

Fifth P: Positioning

Positioning could be considered a fifth P. Positioning refers to the place that a brand occupies in the minds of customers and how it is differentiated from competitor's offerings and messaging.

175

We will cover Positioning in depth in the next section on STP.

STP

STP in marketing stands for Segmentation, Targeting, and Positioning.

The STP model helps marketers craft their messaging and develop and deliver tailored and relevant messages that engage segmented, target audiences.

This approach is helpful in developing a digital strategy for content marketing. You can use STP to apply marketing personas and archetypes that help develop relevant and targeted digital communications.

This is an audience and customer approach to marketing. The goal is to deliver relevant messages to commercially attractive audience segments.

STP focuses on identifying the most valuable segments and then creating the right marketing mix and product positioning strategy (think 4Ps) for those segments.

Segmentation

In marketing we want to identify potential customers and convince them to buy. We also are interested in convincing past customers to be repeat customers.

We do this by providing products and services they need and want. It's all about making the right people aware of our value proposition.

Everyone is unique but we also tend to have interests in common with others. We want to identify those commonalities in the most refined and granular ways possible. These are called niches.

We use segmentation to identify niches with specific needs and desires that we can articulate clearly. In mature markets we use segmentation to find new customers. Segmentation allows us to focus our messaging and deliver it more effectively.

Marketing messages should be designed to address and inform each segment of the benefits and features that are most relevant to that segment. This is a different approach from mass marketing where one size fits all for all customer types. This approach is more efficient and affective, as it delivers the right mix to the right group of people, rather than a spray-and-pray shotgun approach.

Markets can be sliced and diced based on any variable, as long as it's clearly definable and measurable. Here are some examples:

Demographics

This is the most well known way of classifying people into groups. It can be done by: geography, age, gender, income, education, ethnicity, marital status, profession or occupation. Demographics explain 'who' your buyer is.

Psychographics

Psychographics delve into 'why' your customer makes a purchase. This is a way of classifying behavior based on personality and emotional traits linked to purchasing decisions. Psychographics include: attitudes, lifestyle, hobbies, personality and leadership traits and attitudes toward risk.

Gather data to help form psychographic profiles for your typical customers through interviews, surveys, questionnaires, customer data and feedback. This is the kind of information that Facebook gathers based on "likes".

Create archetypes of your customer segments based on their psychographic profile.

You can purchase and access massive troves of data on the interests and attitudes of potential customers from Internet, web and mobile sources. We will explore this more when we discuss analytics tools and sources later in the book.

Lifestyle

Lifestyle refers to non-work time endeavors like hobbies, recreational activities, entertainment, vacations, and other. Keywords and search terms used in such tools as Google Adwords can help you locate and address potential customers by their lifestyle interests and preferences. More on this later when we get into digital marketing.

An effective way to research these behavioral niches is Reddit, where like-minded people create subReddits about a given interest or hobby. The information that gets shared can be very valuable in understanding customer segments.

Belief and Values

This refers to Religious, political, nationalistic and cultural beliefs and values. Social media platforms like Facebook are Twitter good sources.

Life Stages

People change and prefer different activities and have different interests based on their age. A twenty something falls into different categories than a 60 year old. Life Stages is the benchmarking of people's lives at different chronological stages. Check out the book "Passages" for a great primer on this approach.

Geography

This is where you locate people by country, region, area, zip codes, metropolitan or rural location, climate or mountains etc.

Language

With translation tools freely available like Google and Bing we can think about targeting language groups relatively easily.

Behavior

Behavioral economics studies the effects of psychological, cognitive, emotional, cultural and social factors on the economic decisions of individuals. In segmenting it refers to how a customer relates to the nature of the purchase, brand loyalty, usage level, benefits sought, distribution channels used, and the reaction to marketing messages. Amazon has mastered accumulating this data to create profiles of purchasers.

Usage level

Usage is an interesting variable. Many companies recognize that they have "power users" that are responsible for an outsize portion of sales. Coca Cola for example has a club for their power users because they estimate that 20 percent of their customers are responsible for 80 percent of their sales. Identity and cultivate your power users.

Targeting

The list below relates to various criteria for evaluating the potential commercial viability of each segment.

- Size: The market must be large enough to justify segmenting. Market potential size has expanded as **Long Tail** markets have emerged. Long tail refers to markets that can be reached via the Web where there is no concentration geographically but there is enthusiastic interest diffused across the globe. Add up all those loners and they can represent significant markets. The more idiosyncratic your offering the more you will be marketing across geographic zones.

- Difference: Segments need to be distinct and identifiable. Measurable differences must exist between segments. Measuring tools and techniques have proliferated with digital marketing. Google Analytics is a major tool.

- Money: It has to be worth it economically. The anticipated incremental profits must exceed the additional marketing costs. The cost of acquisition of a customer (CAC) must be less than their lifetime value of purchases (LTV). CAC<LTV

- Accessibility: The potential customers in each segment must have the ability to receive your marketing messages and distribution networks must be able to reach them. Accessibility has increased dramatically with the advent of web and mobile messaging, digital downloads, SaaS models, and overnight shipping.

Different segments respond to different benefits so focus on communicating the different benefits.

Positioning

Positioning maps the variables discussed in the Segmenting and Targeting steps and defines the space where your offering resides relative to competitors in the view of your customers.

Thoughtful positioning is critical in staking out a competitive advantage in the market.

Positioning is a component of Branding, which we will discuss next. Customer perceptions and feedback influence a brand's positioning in the market.

Three types of positioning impact a brand and its competitive advantage:

- Functional
- Symbolic
- Experiential

Functional Positioning has to do with feature sets and user experience.

It is focused on the aspects of the value proposition that speak to meeting and fulfilling customers' needs and desires.

Symbolic Positioning Luxury and prestige brands operate in this realm. These are the aspirational elements of your offering; the characteristics of the brand that fulfill customers' self-esteem.

Experiential positioning focuses on the elements of a brand that address emotional connection with customers.

These three elements combine to position the brand. Positioning is a conceptual tool to help tailor your value proposition and communicate it to customers. You want to highlight your advantages relative to competitors and communicate this distinction in a compelling way to customers.

Branding

Branding is the focal point of any marketing strategy. Your enterprise value is deeply intertwined with your brand.

Your brand is your social contract with your customers. A brand conveys what can be expected from your products and services. It distinguishes your offerings and value proposition from your competitors. Customer loyalty is to your brand. Its what you aspire to deliver and what people perceive you to be.

Brand equity is the added value brought to your company's products and services that sustain your profit margins and influence repeat sales. Brands have cache and evoke emotional responses and aspirational intent.

Popular brands include Coca-Cola, Nike, Apple, and BMW. They have built powerful brand equity and can charge more for their products. Protecting the brand is a strategic imperative. Damage done to the brand through some misstep can have very long lasting, and costly, effects.

How you promote your brand is largely based on who your target customers want and need you to be. These are the positioning issues we discussed in the STP section.

You need to define your niche. You can't be all things to all people. Are you promoting innovation or the user experience and reliability? Does your perceived value lie in being the high-quality or the low-cost option?

Your messaging communicates what your brand stands for.

Design is a critical component. The look and feel of you offering creates the user experience. This is industrial design. The focal point of your brand is your logo. This is graphic design. Design thinking is a discipline that has emerged out of the design field and incorporates design principles into product development and branding.

What you communicate visually and verbally are crucial to your brand strategy. Your brand strategy is your plan for effectively delivering on your brand messages.

Brand strategy also includes how, where and when you deliver your message and what channels you use to distribute your product. These are the touch points for the customer and each touch point needs to be analyzed, refined, and finessed.

The added value of brand equity is derived from perceived quality and emotional attachment. Many sports brands associate their products with big time athletes via big time contracts. This is done in hopes that customers will transfer their emotional attachment from the athlete to the product. It's not just the product's features that sell but the aspirational linkage to super stars.

Defining your brand requires being very clear and precise about the following:
- Your company's mission
- The benefits of your products or services
- The features of your products or services
- What your customers and prospects already think of your company
- The qualities do you want them to associate with your company

- What are their aspirations and dreams and can they be actualized or rehearsed through association with you brand.

When you have a clearly defined brand, the next step is to build awareness (the first A in AIDA) Here are a few simple, time-tested tips:

- Create a powerful logo and integrate it into your brand image.
- Compose and craft your brand messaging which includes the key attributes you want to communicate about your brand.
- Create a "voice" that reflects your brand image and attributes and use it consistently.
- Develop a tagline that is memorable, meaningful and concise. It's a statement that captures the essence of your brand. The tagline appears under or alongside the logo. A lot of the messaging will flow from the tag line and the tag line should be a distillation of your messaging.
- Branding extends to all aspects of your business and must be coherent and consistent.
- Deliver on your brand promise.

The Customer Journey

In order to improve sales and build your brand, think more like a consumer. Keep your customer in mind every step of the way.

The customer journey is the term for all the interactions a potential customer has with your company, product, or service along the path to making a purchase. The purchase transaction is the endpoint of all the engagements leading up to the purchasing decision and including the follow on.

Any weak link in this chain could result in an abandoned shopping cart or a customer lost to a competitor.

Conceptualizing customer engagement as a journey helps you to focus on the entire experience of doing business with your company. It starts with becoming aware of your product, to comparing it to alternatives and substitutes, to making an initial purchase, to returning for repeat business.

The goal is to smooth out the process by identifying, creating and controlling these customer touchpoints.

A customer touchpoint is any time a customer comes in contact with your brand. This is your sales funnel and includes interactions before, during, and after the purchase. Your goal is to ensure your customers are satisfied every step along the way.

The best way to identify these touchpoints is by thinking like a potential customer. You want to put yourself in the shoes of someone who has never heard of your brand and is moving through the process of analyzing your offering and considering purchasing all the way through purchase and delivery, set up and use and support.

Touchpoints along the journey include:

Before the transaction:

This includes marketing efforts like ads, testimonials or social media activity. Customer impressions are also formed through product reviews and word of mouth. Monitor social media channels and listen to what is being said about your brand. Set up Google Alerts to be notified when your brand is mentioned.

During the transaction:

Your point of sale environment could be a physical store, a website or a printed catalog. You might sell physical items, digital downloads or SaaS. Your customers will interact with your paywall, sales team or call center.

It was reported to Jeff Bezos in a meeting that Amazon's average wait time on the phone was very low. Bezos put the phone on speaker and called. As the minutes painfully passed with hold music and "your call is important to us", Jeff became furious. Don't be that guy.

After the transaction:

This includes product support, answering questions and addressing returns. Customer feedback surveys can provide valuable product and customer journey information to help refine your offering and touchpoints.

Touchpoints create the experience

After detailing the sequence of the customer journey, take some time to analyze how all the touchpoints flow and fit together.

- Seek to remove any obstacles the customer might experience.
- Add any missing or underserved touchpoints.
- Make sure it's easy for customers to resolve any issues in the transaction.

Continuously monitor and evaluate your customer journey map and seek to make improvements.

Remember, the customer's needs always come first. The goal is to improve customer satisfaction and loyalty.

Permission Marketing

Permission marketing is a concept first articulated by Seth Godin. Seth has written a bunch of great books that are well worth reading and he has a very popular blog that you should subscribe to.

This is from Seth Godin:

"Permission marketing is the privilege (not the right) of delivering anticipated, personal and relevant messages to people who actually want to get them. It recognizes the new power of the best consumers to ignore marketing. It realizes that treating people with respect is the best way to earn their attention."

You need permission to provide relevant content to potential customers. One of your most valuable marketing assets is your email list. Members of your email community need to opt in and if you don't provide relevant interesting useful information to them, they will opt out.

The content you provide is how you build trust along the customer journey.

Marketing and the Business Model Canvas

The Business Model Canvas is a tool for strategic management and entrepreneurial startup development. It helps you see the big picture of your business. The discipline of describing your current thinking about the major aspects of your business helps facilitate brainstorming new ideas and designing and optimal business model.

"A business model describes the rationale of how an organization creates, delivers, and captures value."

–*Business Model Generation* by Alexander Osterwalder and Yves Pigneur

Using this conceptual tool aids in challenging your assumptions, inventing new approaches to try and test, and pivoting if some idea works better than how you are currently organized and what you are currently delivering as your value proposition. The BMC enables envisioning and re-envisioning business models. It helps you hit on the optimal one.

Marketing is concerned with the right half of the BMC, the customer facing side. Become familiar with the categories and how they fit together and interact. Think of them in terms of the 4Ps and the other systems we went over earlier.

Go back and review the Business Model Canvas section in the Entrepreneurship section. It is a powerful tool and widely adopted and used. Knowing about it is an essential part of your business literacy.

Growth Hacking

There was a time when television and magazines ruled and marketing meant advertising campaigns. This was the Mad Men era. Now marketing means an entire suite of activities based on product/market fit and customer engagement. It's no longer about manufacturing desire for a fait accompli product. Customer needs and feedback are baked into the product and the customer experience is integrated into the company.

Growth Hacking is about customer participation in the marketing process and turbocharging awareness campaigns by creating viral products and content.

Growth Hacking resides at the intersection of Marketing, Engineering, and Programming. It takes advantage of all the new tools of websites, mobile, analytics, email and social media available to us that help us reach and communicate with customers and measure their behavior in order to provide the best user experience possible. It has gone from one-way advertising to two-way engagement.

Growth Hacking is a process of rapid experimentation across marketing channels, like email and social media, and also product development focused on enhancing the user experience. The goal is to identify the most effective, efficient ways to grow a business by understanding what is most compelling to customers both in messaging and product feature sets.

Growth Hacking refers to a set of marketing experiments that leads to the rapid growth of a business. The experiments are run by A/B testing features and messaging, and measuring which aspects customers respond to best. Measurement tools like Google Analytics provide the measurement metrics and feedback that help refine awareness campaigns and product features.

It's about how you get, keep and grow customers. The first stage is Customer Acquisition where we activate customers to do something through Calls-to-Action. Calls-to-Action are designed to activate lead generation and sales. Initially it could be a sign up or download of valuable content and ultimately leading to becoming a paying customer.

Next we want to keep them and not lose them to competitors. Then we want to grow them by giving them compelling reasons to spend more or use more of what we offer.

Marketing funnels are developed to measure how many people respond and then convert to being customers. This process is obsessively measured and continually refined and optimized.

Customer Acquisition Costs (CAC) are calculated and compared to the Lifetime Value (LTV) of a customer. We obviously are looking to optimize CAC<LTV. Conversion Rates are tracked and optimized along the customer journey.
Growth Hacking includes engagement with customers through delivering content like blogs, digital downloads, and social media posts. **Viral Marketing** is a method where customers are encouraged to share information about products or services via various Internet channels especially social media.

This is where we segue into Digital Marketing.

Digital Marketing

Online marketing comprises a set of tools and skills that can be used by any size enterprise. These tools can be leveraged for any size business and are especially helpful if you are running a small entrepreneurial enterprise. The skills you need to connect with your customers online are the same regardless of the size of your enterprise. The difference is in the scale of the campaigns.

Digital marketing relies on the time tested methods of customer engagement we have previously discussed. Online there is more refinement of targeting and much better ability to measure the effectiveness of your messaging.

Digital marketing is about creating messaging, getting it in front of your target audience, measuring the effectiveness in terms of conversions or sales, and revising and optimizing your campaigns based on the feedback.

This includes: evaluating your website with analytics and SEO, creating text and display ads, social media and video marketing, email marketing, content marketing and mobile marketing.

Online Marketing Fundamentals

We don't "go online" anymore. We live online.

Online marketing encompasses the promotion of your business online using a variety of ever expanding and evolving channels. These channels include search, social media, video, e-mail, and display ads. Consumers today live across these channels on their computers, tablets and smartphones. Online marketing is focused on being there at the right moment, with the right message, to capture the customer.

The Internet has transformed the way we buy and use products and services. It also has completely changed how we consume content and media whether for information, news or entertainment.

Now, with the Internet on mobile devices, that experience is available and accessed anytime and anywhere. This places the customer in the driver's seat relative to the buying process. Potential customers have immediate access to the resources to conduct research, compare alternatives, share their experience, and ask their friends for advice and recommendations.

All these actions happen continuously and simultaneously. Marketing techniques have radically changed in order to adapt to this new world. What were once standard operating procedures are now marginalized and obsolete as online continues to become dominant.

Print media continues to drop in readership and people are abandoning cable TV for streaming services like Netflix, Amazon, and YouTube.

We have migrated from ownership to access models for movies, games, music and software. We don't have shelves of DVDs, VHS cassettes, or CDs; we stream Pandora or Netflix. And we use SaaS providers (Software as a Service).

Streaming music, audio books, and Podcasts are alternatives to radio. Google Search and Maps have replaced the Yellow Pages. And Yelp allows the consumer can see reviews and even pictures of the business.

Even as we walk our attention is on our screen and we miss advertisements in the shop windows and next to the bus stops. In physical stores shoppers are using their phones to scan barcodes and compare prices. They are chasing deals and deciding whether it's cheaper and more convenient to buy online.

Your business and offerings need to stand out in this noisy environment of online and mobile channels. With so touch-points, and a multitude of channels, online marketing can feel overwhelming. But its actually freeing to be creative and engage customers across so many potential platforms. You just need a contextual framework in which to operate.

Digital Marketing Landscape

Lets take a look at the history of digital advertising and then review the current landscape. The first widespread digital advertising started in the early 1990's. Display banners for Sear's products started appearing on the bottom of the screen for customers of an online service provider of the time, Prodigy. At that time they were much like magazine ads, visual but not interactive.

In 1993 the first clickable ad was created by a law firm in Silicon Valley and from there things took off. In 1994, web banner advertising was mainstreamed and stayed so until 1998 when the first search advertising keywords became available through a company that was eventually acquired by Yahoo.

Google launched AdWords in 2000 and the rest of digital marketing fell into place. From 2000 until now the landscape has evolved to include social medial, video advertisements, interstitial advertising and an entirely new marketing methodology surrounding the idea of promoting content not just ads. We've also seen entirely new platforms catered to improving ads, tracking ads and serving ads, emerge and gain massive market share.

And there was the radical and rapid shift from desktop to mobile. In July 2007 Apple introduced the smartphone and its adoption was dizzyingly rapid. By

2010, Mobile became a dominant platform and Mobile advertising spend has been increasing 90 percent each year.

As the adoption of digital media continues to increase, we're seeing people spend longer periods of time online. Digital channel activity is growing rapidly, and with it, the allure and impact of digital marketing. In 2000 it would have been really difficult to effectively to promote yourself online and now, it's foolish not to.

Adidas announced recently that it is going totally digital in it's advertising in order to capitalize on engagement with its customers. More companies will likely follow suit as traditional media and advertising become less relevant to consumers.

Throughout these years we've witnessed some incredible shifts in how people respond to online marketing, consume content, and make purchasing decisions.

Search is the number one source currently used when making a decision to purchase something. And the top three search engines are: Google, YouTube and Amazon. You probably guessed the first one but the second two are less intuitive but have massive audiences and search activity.

Search as the top decision making tool for purchasing holds true across the spectrum from consumers to sophisticated business decision makers. A website's visibility in search is the most valuable online real estate. Searchers are an ideal target audience because they are expressing intent in your niche.

This is why Search Engine Optimization, SEO, is so critically important. Paid search is also a key piece of digital marketing and advertising. The current leader to buy ads from is Google AdWords. Keywords are bid on in an auction format and the top payers, along with Google's algorithm for ad relevancy, are shown to searchers at the top of the list or in the side bar.

Email was the initial digital marketing format and a quality email list is still extremely valuable. Your email list, along with your website, is the marketing property you own. That independence from platforms like Facebook and Twitter make it very valuable.

Now everything has to be mobile friendly. Almost half of all emails are opened on mobile devices and that landscape is continually evolving.

Along with mobile email, the digital market place demands a mobile compatible website. Most website templates are now dynamic and sense whether the viewer is on a desktop, laptop, tablet, or phone. These are called responsive and adaptive websites. Any website you design needs to be adaptive and responsive and mobile compatible.

There have been dramatic developments in marketing automation. Applications like automated bidding for keywords, automatic remarketing to people who have visited your site, and even populating bespoke advertisements based on what a user was searching for.

Automation is a big component of email campaigns. MailChimp has powerful automation tools available to create email sequences that will send to your list or onboard new subscribers.

Social medial engagement is essential for many brands. Facebook has recently said it is changing its newsfeed to move away from advertising and more towards friends and family. While this makes good sense for consumers of social media, it sent Facebook stock down as it diminishes their monetization strategy. But Facebook's reach is unparalleled worldwide.

Content marketing is effective because of the engagement and trust it develops. Creating relevant content for audiences generates significant ROI for those doing it well. Users report interesting content as being one of the top reasons they follow a brand.

Content marketing is reforming. Consumers now demand more authenticity and genuine value of information in content. They are weary of sensational headlines, click-bait and may be responding less effectively to previously common techniques such as top 10 lists (listcles).

Stay in tune with the online marketing landscape as it evolves. As new tools and trends emerge, test them out and see how they perform for your brand and products.

Let's Break it Down

There are basically three types of media we use in online marketing:

- **Paid,**
- **Owned**
- **Earned.**

Paid media is advertising that you pay for. This includes paid ads on channels like Google Adwords, Facebook, YouTube and Amazon. Google Adwords comes in two basic varieties: text and display marketing.

Owned media encompasses the channels you own like your website, your list of customers that you use to send out e-mails, and your blog and its readership.

Earned media is the realm of organic reach through Social Media platforms like Twitter, Linkedin, Facebook, Instagram, Pinterest, and Snapchat. Shares on your social media accounts, mentions on other blogs, and mentions in articles are ways various channels function within earned media.

These platforms all overlap, as do users as they interact with each. Together, they constitute the foundation of online marketing. To sum it up, online marketing is the process of putting your business front and center along the journey your customer takes on the internet, web and mobile devices.

Digital Strategy

Creating a coherent digital strategy is critical in order to take full advantage of the opportunities to connect with your customers online.

Having a digital presence in these channels just for the sake of it is not effective. The key is to develop and follow a dedicated strategy that results in a measurable return on your investment.

The importance and value of building out your online presence in a strategic manner is obvious but it's easy to be tempted to dive right in.

There is a saying attributed to Abraham Lincoln: "Give me six hours to chop down a tree and I will spend the first four sharpening the axe."

This is why we started with fundamental marketing concepts like AIDA, STP, and the 4 Ps. These concepts provide the framework for strategic marketing thinking.

Three Strategic Areas

Online marketing is a broad topic. In order to get our arms around it in a structured way, we are going to categorize strategy into three strategic areas that share common goals.

These three strategic areas are:

- **Business**
- **Customer**
- **Marketing**

Our goal is to develop a coherent online marketing strategy. In order to do that, we first need to understand the business plan at a high level. Here are some questions to ask:

- How do you intend to be perceived by your market?
- Who constitutes your market? Customer Segments.
- What are the use patterns of you customers relative to digital technology?

A clear and well thought out strategy keeps you focused. It serves as your road map as you explore new marketing channels. The strategy will determine what channels are best to build into in order to reach your customers

It's easy to chase seductive opportunities that take you away from your main purpose.

Every business needs to create it's own strategy. The focus is on creating product/market fit and shared value. Shared value is when the needs of your customer overlap with the goals of your business. The marketing strategy is developed with shared value in mind. Go back and review the Business Model Canvas and the Value Proposition Canvas to help organize your thinking in this area.

Adopt the mindset that you're marketing an experience for your customers: the user experience. As we explore our three strategic areas, focus on the idea of creating a shared value experience.

Business Strategy

The first of our three strategies is Business Strategy. This entails articulating the Mission statement, Objectives, and Value proposition. You need to be able to state your business purpose crisply and succinctly in an Elevator Pitch. These four elements put the business in focus and provide context for the customer and marketing strategies.

First we need to address the basics. These are:

How much of your business is digital?
Do you have the right organizational structure in place?
How will your online marketing efforts fit with your existing process?
Do you have the resources necessary to execute your strategy?

One of the big challenges of online marketing is keeping things current and relevant. This is a commitment of resources and time.

You can only plan an effective strategy if you have a clear understanding of your business. You need an understanding of the big picture. A big picture view is necessary to determine which channels make the most sense to invest your time in. And when you encounter obstacles, you need that big picture view to address the issue and pick a new route that gets you to your destination.

As we go through these strategic thinking and planning steps, we don't want to fall into the trap of paralysis from analysis. This is broad-strokes thinking. We want to have a bias towards action. At this stage, we're just trying to get a dart on the dartboard. Over time, you can refine your strategy iterate towards the bull's-eye.

We're now going to identify the mission statement, objectives, your value proposition, and the elevator pitch.

Mission Statement

We start by defining our mission statement. This is one sentence that summarizes what you are trying to do. It should be able to stand up on its own. Your mission statement will keep everything else in check. Every decision you make relative to your

205

business should be measured against the criteria of the mission statement. If an idea seems great but is not in line with your mission statement, discard it. Focus is about eliminating great ideas that don't fit. Take a lesson from Steve Jobs:

"People think focus means saying yes to the thing you've got to focus on. But that's not what it means at all. It means saying no to the hundred other good ideas that there are. You have to pick carefully. I'm actually as proud of the things we haven't done as the things I have done. Innovation is saying no to 1,000 things."

Objectives

Next, describe at least three organizational objectives. These should be the elements that are required to keep the business running and to maintain your brand identity. It can be anything from selling product to increasing email list signups. These constitute what the business is set up to do.

Value Proposition

Next, identify the value proposition of each objective:

- Why do you stand out?
- What makes you unique?
- Why would someone choose you over your competitor?

Select one or two value propositions that differentiate your brand for each of your objectives.

Elevator Pitch

Finally, develop your elevator pitch. Your pitch helps you think concisely because you can explain it clear and crisp. Online marketing has many channels that limit the amount of information you can communicate. Think Twitter. So this is a great opportunity to practice expressing and messaging in a concise manner. Emphasize the elements that are specific differentiators to your business; what makes you stand out.

Understand Your Business

This process helps you understand your business better. And that helps you understand where you want your online marketing efforts to take you. Next, we'll be looking at how to develop our customer strategy.

Customer Strategy

We need to know who our customers are, what motivates them, and where we find them. With our customer strategy, we're trying to do three things:

- Reach the correct audience. It would be a waste of time and advertising spend to pursue the wrong audience.

- Understand that audience, what motivates them as it relates to our offering and objectives.
- Know where we find that audience, what marketing channels we can leverage to connect them with.

A review of the STP Segmentation, Targeting and Positioning section will help with developing a customer strategy.

Remember that the digital consumer is in control. They are able to follow their interests and whims landscape that is niche and personalized. This means that when you go to identify your audience you have to be very specific with whom you're targeting. Its about micro targeting niche audiences and delivering bespoke messages that address their needs, wants, aspirations, desires, concerns, and interests.

Unlike physical shops and stores, there's no street traffic to market broadly to. Your audience expects a refined niche experience and you are able to seek out this micro targeted customer with a precision unlike any marketing efforts of the past.

We first need to define our target audience: their age range, interests etc. We can get more specific as we gain feedback and data. We just need a solid and sensible starting point, begin and iterate.

We need to think like a customer. Put yourself in the shoes of your target market. Who is your audience? What are their goals and aspirations? What are they looking to accomplish? What are the pain points and frustrations we are eliminating or the delight and entertainment we are providing?

Next we need to think where we are going to find them online. Here, you want to identify what platforms and mediums this audience is using. Is it social? If so, what network? Is it a blog? Are they likely to be searching on Google, or visiting a particular website? Are they watching YouTube videos? Take note of which channels you think resonate the most with your audience.

From here, we need to drill in and understand our goals for each customer segment. For each segment, we need to understand four things. First, what is our business goal for this segment? These goals are basically a more granular version of our overall business objective.

Second, what is the shared value for this segment? If you recall, shared value is when the goals of your customer overlap with the goals of your business: the product/market fit.

Third, we'll look at the key performance indicators KPIs. These will be what you're measuring. It could be how many units you expect to sell, or how many people visit your website.

Fourth, we want to create a target objective. This target will be directly related to our key performance indicator. It may be how many units you want to sell in a given timeframe or how many signups to your email list.

Take the time to think through your core demographics, the goals for each, and what your final targets are. The next step is to take that information and build a marketing strategy around it.

Marketing Strategy

Now that we have taken some time to understand our business and our customer, we are ready to figure out how we are going to execute our online marketing. Each strategy has built on the preceding strategy and each gets more specific.

Our marketing strategy winds up being a bundle of targeted plans, each designed to address one goal for a specific customer segment. This granularity is what makes our marketing strategy actionable by breaking it down into tactics.

A marketing strategy will focus on a goal as it relates to a customer segment. From there we examine the channels we plan to market on and develop a marketing idea for each of the medias available to us: paid, earned, and owned.

We haven't yet discussed all the channels available but we can think of the ones we know like Facebook, Twitter, LinkedIn, our blog, YouTube, Amazon and others.

For our paid media, we'll need to identity what we intend to do under each channel. Not every channel has to participate in each medium. For example, we may not do any paid media on Twitter and rely on earned activity.

Next, we do the same for our earned media. Because this is our organic effort, we're really identifying what we'd like to see happen. We ultimately want to complement and leverage the efforts in paid and owned to influence our earned media and vice versa. Each category should support and enhance the others.

In the earned category, we plan to create viral campaigns. In an effort to help encourage wider distribution we'll be adding share links and questions in our articles and other content to inspire conversation.

Finally, make note of what you can do with your own media as it relates to each channel. This might be as simple as posting on Facebook or it might involve a complex automated email campaign.

Online marketing is an iterative process and you'll work to continuously improve upon these initial ideas. As you build out a new audience, new objectives, and new channels you want to make sure you have addressed adequate coverage with your marketing strategy.

It's important to be flexible and ready to course correct. As you collect more and more data and feedback, you'll be able to get closer and closer to your real targets. You may also learn that your plan was too aggressive or too conservative. There's a lot to think about when you build your marketing strategy.

Spend time doing research to further understand your business, your customers, and the marketing channels available to you. You may choose to implement all of the strategies available to you or you may choose to be more selective. Both are valid options depending on what you're setting out to do. Your marketing strategy is the final piece of this puzzle; it's the implementation plan.

Revisit your assumptions often, measure them against feedback and data, and revise them accordingly and often. Try things, experiment, and course correct.

Surveys and Questionnaires

A great way to do customer discovery and customer development is to use questionnaires and surveys. There are web-based services that allow you to create questionnaires and analyze the results. And you can access potential responders from your email list, social media, or though the service provider. One of the best and easiest to use is SurveyMonkey.

The terms Survey and Questionnaire are relatively synonymous and are used interchangeably but lets differentiate the two because that is what marketers do; they differentiate. This is by no means definitive but it give a sense of how to approach two concepts of querying customers in order to gather information for segmentation and targeting.

A survey is a more general term than questionnaire. A survey is defined by Oxford Dictionaries as: "a general view, examination, or description of someone or something. In order to conduct an examination, a number of techniques may be used, from observation, research, sounding of opinion etc." A survey is the result of open-ended questions. Here you are doing qualitative research.

This is opposed to a questionnaire, which is defined as a set of printed or written questions with a choice of answers, devised for the purposes of analysis or statistical study. This is more quantitative research. The fixed answers can be aggregated up and results expressed as a percentage or other number.

In both cases you can get customer feedback on products and services and solicit suggestions about what else you can provide and what they feel is important or good about what you are doing or propose to do.

A caveat is that customers don't always know what they want or need. Henry Ford remarked that if he asked people what they needed they would have told him a faster horse. In many cases people can't conceive of the benefits of something they have never known.

You can also couch questions in a way to get potential customers excited about your motives by inquiring into their dreams and aspirations. You can use a questionnaire as a marketing tool to promote engagement with customers.

You must also be aware and take care of the biases inherent in the sample group you are questioning. If they are your social media contacts then they are self-screened in a certain way. If they are from your email list then the ones who initially signed up based on your free give away, or lead capture strategy, are predisposed to that; and the ones that have stayed and not unsubscribed are attuned with the content you have been providing.

Find some sample sets that are not previously biased toward your offerings. Don't preach to the choir.

You can get less immediately biased groups from the survey provider. Survey Monkey is a great questionnaire tool and good place to start.

You can spot trends, identify preferences, prioritize feature sets for MVP, refine messaging based on questionnaire results that are tempered by taking into account potential biases and preferences of the group responding.

Digital Marketing Terminology

There is terminology specific to online marketing and apply to touchpoints along the Customer Journey.

One of the most important pieces of online marketing is your **Call to Action**. This is an instruction you provide to your audience as a way to provoke a certain response. Calls to Action typically use a verb, such as *Save Now* or *Buy Today*. You'll find them in banner ads, on website landing pages, and in social media posts.

The traffic that comes to your site has to come from somewhere, whether it was an advertisement or an email. Traffic comes when someone Clicks on your Call to Action. We want to measure the **Click-through Rate**. As marketers, we'll often measure performance by how many clicks an ad receives. Every time an advertisement is shown, it counts as an impression. The Click-through Rate is calculated as how many people clicked on the ad in relation to the amount of impressions.

As you drive traffic to your site, you'll want to measure how long someone stays on your website. The **Bounce Rate** is when a visitor arrives on your website, but leaves after visiting only one page. They're said to have bounced and your Bounce Rate is the percentage of these visitors. A Bounce Rate can apply to an entire website or a single page.

The term **Abandonment** is used when a user does not complete the goal you intended for them. A user is following a particular path say to checkout from an e-commerce store or to complete an online form for more information, and then they leave the process early. In marketing we aim to reduce Abandonment.

There are tools now to identify those visitors who abandon a shopping cart or other activity and then you can re-market to them. These are high percentage leads because they have exhibited an interest in your offer.

As you begin to scale up your marketing efforts you'll encounter paid advertising and the term **Ad Impression**. Each time your advertisement is displayed to a user it counts as an Impression.

Impressions are related to **Frequency**. Frequency is the amount of times an individual will see your ad. If your ad had 10 Impressions, with a Frequency of two, then five individual people would have seen that advertisement.

When a user completes your goal, whether it's buying a product or downloading an application, they're said to have **Converted**. Your **Conversion Rate** is the percentage of visitors who entered into this experience and actually completed the goal. To understand how a user converted or when, we need to use what is called a **Tracking Pixel**. These are minuscule one-by-one pixel images that are embedded in your website. They track conversions, website visits, abandonment, and ad views.

Advertising only makes sense if it brings you a positive return on investment and to analyze ROI, we look at **Cost Per Acquisition** or **CAC**. This is how much it costs you per goal completion. For example, if you ran an advertisement with a goal of getting an application download and that ad cost you $100, then if one person downloaded the app, despite the hundreds of potential customers that clicked on it, the Cost Per Acquisition for that single user would be $100.

The **CAC** is then compared to the **Lifetime Value** or **LTV**. Every customer has a value relative to how many purchases he or she make over the course of time. Some will buy once and never return, others will become repeat buyers. Your lifetime value is a prediction of the average net profit attributed to that relationship. With paid advertising, you want your Cost Per Acquisition to be lower than your Lifetime Value or CPC<LTV. If this is not the case, you are losing money.

There are two basic kinds of paid advertising: text ads that are driven by keywords in Search Engines like the Google Ads platform, and Banner or Display ads.

Banner Advertisements and Display ads refer to visual images, either static or animated, that are used to generate brand awareness or entice a user to click. Banner or Display Advertisements contain a Call to Action.

When you run these advertisements, the Call to Action will drive someone who clicks on it to a **Landing Page**. It's important that the user arrives on a page that is specific to your promotion. If you don't use a targeted webpage, it's unlikely they'll convert. This page they first arrive on from the ad is called the **Landing Page** or **Splash Page**.

Let's compare **Paid** and **Organic** search results. When you conduct a search on Google, you have two types of results: paid results, which are typically the first couple of links and a handful of links on the right sidebar; and Organic listings which are not paid and instead achieve their rank through the search engine algorithm prioritizing them as the most relevant. Attempts to rank high with the search algorithm are called **Search Engine Optimization**.

Attribution is a term that has gained prominence in marketing as a performance metric to gauge the effectiveness of ads and content.

Attribution in digital marketing is giving appropriate credit to the sources, which ultimately bring a prospect to your paywall and have them convert into a paying customer. Each step contributes to the ultimate goal.

Attribution is a measure of the touchpoints along the customer journey and how much weight to give to each in the sales funnel. In this way we can measure the Return on Investment of each step and eliminate or refine underperforming steps and double down on better performing stages.

There are many attribution models to help identify the sources that helped you acquire the new business. Google Analytics is a very popular and effective one.

Designing and Managing Digital Marketing Campaigns

Now that you have a solid grasp of what digital marketing is and the tools, techniques, and platforms that are available. Its time to pick and choose which best suit your needs and begin to implement some campaigns. Here are some summary thoughts as you start creating action plans for digital marketing.

We are in a period of rapid innovation and evolution relative to the tools and techniques of digital marketing. New technologies are continually being created and adopted and new ideas are being explored. The options available as a marketer are potent but can be overwhelming.

It's important to keep in mind that your marketing strategy doesn't need to include every marketing channel available. You may end up using a handful of the ones we discuss, or you may find success in leveraging other avenues that are not part of these core components. With such a wide array of choices, it is important to evaluate which channels make the most sense.

Because we have limited resources of time and budget, we need to prioritize which channels to use. And, if you're exploring a new channel, it's a good idea to explore how it'll impact your day to day operations. In order to gauge the effort versus the return, we can evaluate each based on the effort required to build out the channel, and the value received in doing so. We need to examine the areas of our online marketing strategy like SEO, Search marketing, Social media and Video and decide what channel we're using for these areas.

Here is an example of a mosaic of channels and platforms that we can assemble: For SEO, we will focus on Google. For Search marketing, we'll use Google AdWords, and with Social media, we can start with Facebook. For video, we'll use YouTube. Now we can estimate the effort relative to the value.

SEO takes significant effort but has high value in pushing traffic to your website. Google Adwords is less effort but also costs money but the targeted nature of the channel has high impact and high value. YouTube for many may be a lower value channel and making videos can be higher effort (by the way YouTube is the second biggest search engine platform in the world). Facebook is pretty low effort and the value can be less as well, unless you are using targeted Facebook advertising, which can be higher value but also costs.

We're simply comparing and scoring these in relation to one another to get a feel for the return on investment, ROI, we can expect and where to deploy our resources and focus our efforts.

Parting Thoughts on Marketing

You now have a solid understanding of the principles of marketing. These principles are timeless and have to do with making people aware of your offering, communicating the value of products and services, and developing trust between customers and brands.

Marketing is about delivering the right message about the right product, at the right price, at the right place, at the right time, and to the right person.

You are also familiar with the tools, techniques, and platforms of digital marketing.

Now it is time to put this new knowledge to use. Create some campaigns, measure the results and course correct as you go along. Good luck and the greatest success in all your marketing efforts!

Accounting

Let's dive into the underlying structure of business: the numbers. You need to know the basics of accounting and have a proper accounting system in place in order to run a business. It is the fundamental way that you keep track of *how* your business is doing and *what* you are doing. It is the most telling and intimate record of a business.

Learning accounting and understanding how to read financial statements can seem daunting and complicated. Yet you already have a finely calibrated sense of accounting from your daily life: it's all about money, ain't a dang thing funny...

You have implicitly learned and understand the fundamentals of accounting from your experience of getting and spending. This knowledge is what you can always use as your touchstone. Every day you balance your checkbook, stretch your paycheck, pay your bills, manage your credit cards and car loan and mortgage and rent. You are running a pretty complicated enterprise! Though it may sometimes seem like it, accounting is not an arcane exercise; it is a foundational and practical part of everyday life.

Accounting needs to make sense and be direct and clear. It is the way to record all the transactions of a business and communicate them to others not intimately involved in the particulars of that business. So we need to keep it simple and direct. Keep Occam 's Razor in mind, which is the principle that the simplest solution is always the best and try to eliminate unnecessary elements.

There are two basic parts to accounting knowledge: bookkeeping and financial statements. Bookkeeping is how you enter business transaction information into your accounting system and how you track these entries. Financial statements are the reports that organize the transactional information of bookkeeping in standardized forms so an interested party can quickly grasp the financial position and performance of the enterprise. You will learn how to read **financial statements** and how **bookkeeping** entries are made, revised, and checked.

Prior to the 1980s when personal computers revolutionized accounting with software programs and spreadsheets, accounting and bookkeeping required a relatively high level of expertise, experience, and concentration. Systems had to be essentially created from scratch and each number and account was generated, entered, and written by hand on ledger sheets. You really had to know your **debits** from your **credits** and be the calculator. Now computer systems assist in creating the structure and guide the process of making entries. This makes accounting practice much more accessible and less cumbersome.

The twentieth century saw helpful innovations in accounting before computers. Adding machines and then hand held calculators were huge helps in relieving the burden of adding and subtracting columns of numbers and in reducing errors. You can imagine how tedious and mind-numbing accounting must have been before that. Poor Bob Cratchet.

In the past several decades the practice of accounting has been transformed with spreadsheets and accounting software. You are so lucky to be learning and becoming an accounting user now! You can now add and subtract and manipulate columns of numbers in spreadsheets and save them as a handy record of your work. Accounting software such as QuickBooks is easy to set up and use, and gives you prompts for how to input numbers and helps check for errors. We can also import and export between spreadsheets and accounting software and word processors to generate reports. These innovations have removed some of the biggest barriers to starting a business and running it professionally. Lucky us!

Bifurcating Accounting

Accounting tracks the monetary aspects of a business operation; where the money comes from and where it goes.

To paraphrase the humorist and actor Robert Benchley: "there are two kinds of people: those who divide things into two groups, and those who don't"

To get a grasp of accounting let's break the field into two groups: **Bookkeeping** and **Financial Statements**.

Bookkeeping is the process of recording each and every transaction that takes place within a business: every check that is cut, every invoice received and entered, all the money that comes in as **Revenues** and all the money that goes out as **Expenses**; and all the **assets** and **liabilities**. It is a record of all purchases, sales, receipts and payments. These business transactions occur on a daily basis and must be properly recorded in "**the books**". The books is a slang term referring to the **General Ledger** and the various journals that are kept by a business. The general ledger is a list of all the accounts grouped by the types of transactions.

Financial Statements are the reports generated of the aggregation of the bookkeeping activity. There are three main financial statements: **Balance Sheet, Income Statement,** and **Cash Flow Statement.** The two to focus on initially are the Balance Sheet and Income Statement.

Cash

The lifeblood of business is cash and keeping track of your cash position is an absolute priority. Things come to a grinding halt when the bank accounts are empty. You need cash to pay bills, purchase supplies, pay salaries (people become ornery if they don't get paid), and keep the lights on. Your accounting system keeps track of how much money is coming in (revenues) and how much is going out (expenses); how much cash you have is what is left over.

Budgets

How much cash you have on hand is the measure of how much business activity you can perform in the foreseeable future. Based on your budget, you can estimate how long you can operate with a certain amount of cash in the bank. How much cash you need to spend each month for your proposed operations is called you "**burn rate.**" For operating businesses the burn rate is extremely important, as is the forecasting of when revenues will be received to replenish the coffers. If you are in a pre-revenue start up phase of developing a business, the conservation and disciplined use of cash is paramount. The budget is your plan of cash use.

The amount of cash you have, divided by your burn rate is called your "**runway**". It is a flight metaphor related to how much time you have before you need to "take off," i.e. begin replenishing cash with either revenues or a round of funding. This metric is also called your horizon to revenues.

Revenues from sales increase the cash position and fund future activity. For Start-up enterprises, the amount of cash raised is equivalent to how much development activity you can perform before you will need to achieve revenues and sales or go out and do another round of fund raising. The "**runway**" represents how long the enterprise can operate, based on the budget (and disciplined execution and adherence to that budget), before things come to a grinding halt or more money is raised. Cash is your main resource. You cannot be effective without it. A slang term for thinking of cash in this way is called "dry powder," an old fashioned gun powder analogy.

Each month it is good operating and managerial practice to compare your actual accounting results to your previously prepared budget. When you compare Actuals to Budget you are looking for variances: differences between them. These are the numbers that you need to understand. Why were you over or under budget? Was it a onetime unforeseen event or a recurring expense that you overlooked in the budgeting process? This kind of analysis forces you to have detailed answers to these questions.

If you are over budget it better be for a very good reason like it accelerated timetables or expanded opportunities. Caveat: expanding opportunities can be seductive and not necessarily productive.

What seem to be expanded opportunities can dilute efforts and actually reduce chances of success. You can't successfully chase all the possibilities that present themselves. Part of disciplined execution and management is focusing on the specific goals and eliminating or reducing distractions; even if they seem attractive. Remember the Sirens from the Odyssey…

Keeping Track

Your computer-based accounting system helps keep track of all of these considerations so you can report and operate your business in an organized and planned manner. In comparing actuals to budget you may need to export or import data between your accounting system and a spreadsheet program. The current versions of software have easy functions to accommodate import and export sharing between programs.

Now we will discuss bookkeeping and the basic process of making journal entries, posting them, and creating financial statements from that information.

Bookkeeping

Preparing and maintaining the accounting books is the task of bookkeeping and bookkeepers. Bookkeeping creates of a record of every transaction that a business makes. As you get money in and pay bills and have money going out, every transaction gets recorded in the books. Records are maintained of every transaction: all receipts, invoices, check stubs, purchase orders and packing slips are kept in orderly files related to each time period (months, years), by transaction type, vendor, or account.

Bookkeeping is about recording transactions as journal entries of debits and credits and posting them to the general ledger.

Setting Up the Books

When we talk of the "books" what we refer to is the group of all the accounts of the transactions of an enterprise. This list or group makes up the general ledger.

The general ledger is the collection of all asset, liability, equity, revenue and expense accounts. Transactions are grouped together in some related way as accounts and accounts are grouped and categorized into the General Ledger ("GL").

Transactions are usually related by vendor, customer or type of transaction. For example, all of your office rent payments would be grouped in an account called "Landlord" or "Office Rent" or something similar. Your sales income might be grouped by customer, or simply in a general "sales revenue" account; all of your electric bills and payments would be recorded in an account set up for the utility company.

This list of accounts and vendors is the basic organizing principle of your accounting system. When you initially start an accounting system for a company you create a **chart of accounts** that classifies different groupings of business transactions.

The chart of accounts is a listing of all accounts used in the **general ledger** of an organization. The chart of accounts simply a laundry list of all the accounts. Usually when you begin working for an existing company the chart of accounts already exists and as new vendors occur, a new account is added. The *vendor list* shows information about the people or companies from whom you buy goods and services, including banks and tax agencies.

You need to be familiar with this organizing structure conceptually, but remember; rarely are you called on

229

to set up a **chart of accounts** and **vendor list** from scratch. In most accounting situations you will be introduced to an already set up and functioning system.

If you are in a position of starting a company you will lack internal supporting resources. At some point early on you can hire an experienced accountant as a consultant to help set up your system, including the chart of accounts and vendor list, and coach you and review your initial entries.

If you are involved in a start up or small company, having a pro review your books and processes on a regular basis like once a month or quarter is a good idea. Another set of eyes is always helpful. Be honest about the level of your abilities but don't be intimidated. After reading this book you know enough of what you need to identify, interview and hire an accounting consultant or a staff accountant when the time comes.

The Accounting Cycle

The accounting cycle refers to the sequence of activities that occur in the accounting process from the occurrence of a transaction though the generating financial statements.

- Recognition of the event as a transaction and identify and file the source document: receipt, bill, check, invoice etc.

- Analysis of the transaction to determine which accounts are affected and in which direction (debit or credit)
- **Journal Entries**: the transaction is recorded in the journal as a debit and a credit. (a transaction can have more than one debit or credit, but the debits must equal the credits so that they balance)
- Post to the Ledger: the journal entries are transferred to the appropriate **T-accounts** in the **general ledger**
- **Trial Balance**: an unadjusted trial balance is generated and calculated to verify that the sum of the debits is equal to the sum of the credits. This is a point in the process where some iterative work may have to be done to locate any errors if and when the debits and credits don't initially balance.
- **Adjusting Entries**: are made of accrued and deferred items (the ones from the operations section of the cash flow statement)
- Adjusted Trial Balance: a new trial balance is calculated after making the adjusting entries
- Financial Statements: prepare the financial statement from the adjusted trial balance
- Closing Entries: transfer the temporary accounts such as revenues and expenses to owner's equity.
- After-closing Trial Balance: prepare a post-closing trial balance in order to check all the accounts

The good news is that your accounting software will perform these tasks for you. You only need to enter the transaction. However, you need to be familiar with the process so you can quickly troubleshoot any mistakes if the balances between debits and credits don't match. You will make lots of these mistakes but there is no need to be concerned. Even very experienced accountants make errors. The key is to realize it and quickly locate them and fix them. The accounting cycle process provides the step-by-step methodology and helps us error-prone humans.

The accounting cycle is a methodical set of steps that help ensure the accuracy and conformity of financial statements. You follow these steps like a recipe. Computerized accounting systems have helped to greatly reduce entry and mathematical errors in the accounting process, and the uniform and rigorous process of the accounting cycle also helps reduce mistakes and maintain consistency. Accounting is a detail-oriented activity. The steps in the accounting cycle act as a checklist that helps promote accuracy. The deity is in the details.

Bookkeeping Flow

There is a process flow to how business transactions are entered and recorded into the accounting books. The Accounting Cycle section above details the steps of the flow. The following section provides more details about the steps in the bookkeeping parts of the cycle.

Transactions are initiated through a form of documented request: an invoice, or a bill, or a contract. These are entered as obligations: a payable, or receivable, or as a cash disbursement, or revenues. In other words, either you receive money (**revenue** or **sales**), or pay money (**expenses**), or you are owed money (**account receivable**), or you are obligated to pay money (**account payable**).

Each transaction is entered as a **Journal Entry**. Each journal entry impacts two accounts by essentially reducing one account and increasing another. This is called **double entry** bookkeeping. The two entries offset each other as a **debit** and a **credit**. A transaction can impact more than just two accounts. In this case there will be debits and credits to multiple accounts. But the sum total of the debits must equal the sum total of the credits. An example would be paying for a piece of equipment partially with cash and partly with a loan; this would impact three accounts and the total of the cash and loan would equal the price of the equipment.

All journal entries are posted to the general ledger. In a specific period like a month, or quarter, or year, they aggregate up to form the basis of the financial statements. This journal entry process is the start and the essence of bookkeeping and since financial statements are the summation of all the bookkeeping entries, it is the foundation of the entire accounting process.

Debits and Credits

Debit and **credit** are the two most basic accounting terms to become familiar with. They represent the fundamental concept of bookkeeping. However, the practice of double entry bookkeeping and the application of debits and credits to accounts is not intuitive and will take some time to get used to. With that in mind, let's discuss the concepts more.

In accounting, there are two sides to every transaction and they are called **debit** and **credit**. Each journal entry affects at least two accounts; it can affect a group of debits and a group of credits but they must equal each other. This is a concept that may take a while to get your head around and get used to. But you will. Think of a situation where you lend someone $10. Like Shakespeare said, there are two sides to this IOU type transaction: the borrower and the lender. You record that you expect the money back (**asset**) and the other party records that they expect to pay it back (**liability**).

All transactions are two sided like this example: one account is enhanced and one account is depleted. Or think of a deli counter transaction: you get a sandwich and the deli gets money. But each side records two entries. From the deli side, they get money, which increases their revenue, and they give up a sandwich, which depletes their inventory. From your side, you get a delicious sandwich which is an asset (albeit temporary), and you give up money, which depletes your bank account. Each side records a double entry transaction. Each sides transaction entry is a mirror image of the other: what you gain, they give up, and vice versa. Accounting is a zero sum endeavor.

Debit and Credit can be tricky concepts to initially understand. Here is another attempt at a simple explanation. A Debit increases the resources of the enterprise and a Credit reduces the resources. So with Asset accounts, ones that are resources, a Debit will increase the account. With a Liability account, ones that are obligations of the enterprise, a Debit will decrease that account; because the decrease of a liability, like say a loan, means in essence to increase the resources of the company. Think of this as if you pay off a credit card, you have increased your resources by no longer carrying that debt obligation (and at the same time you save a ton of interest payments!)

Credits are the mirror image opposite. When you pay a bill, you credit cash (an asset account) because you have reduced the amount of cash you have. If you take out a loan, you credit the loan account (a liability account) because you have increased an obligation of the company.
You will probably have to refer back to this concept of debits and credits several times. Just acknowledge that this concept may be challenging and don't become frustrated, it will become clear with use.

History of Double Entry Accounting

The concept of debits and credits may seem mundane; if not obvious, but in fact double entry bookkeeping is one of the great innovations in the history of civilization. Its invention and adoption represents one of the great inflection points in history.

The first recorded description of double entry bookkeeping was in 1458 in a work titled: *Book on the Art of Trade*. The author's name was Benedikt Kotruljević, who was born in Ragusa or what is now known as Dubrovnik in 1416. It is considered a great intellectual breakthrough and he is famous in Dubrovnik. Bookkeeping in this manner enabled merchants, entrepreneurs and their investors to keep track of every penny they received or spent.

The invention of double entry bookkeeping is usually attributed to being invented in Milan by Luca Pacioli. Luca wrote the *Summa de Arithmetica, Geometria, Proportioni et Proportionalita* in 1494 and was living with Leonardo da Vinci as his math teacher at the time.

The Medici's and other banking families of Florence first implemented the idea in a functional way in the late 1400s. This concept was their trade secret that allowed Florence to become a very rich and powerful city-state conducting wide ranging international trade. It gave the city the financial resources to become the center and engine of the Renaissance, change the course of history, and start humanity on the course of becoming modern; of becoming us.

Double entry bookkeeping represents an ingenious work-around for a society that had yet to discover the powerful number zero. It is strange for us to imagine the idea of zero as being a breakthrough innovation.

The concept of Zero came to the West through Persia and the Ottomans via India. The two countervailing numbers that cancel each other out in double entry bookkeeping were a way to show the impact of a transaction on two parties or on assets and liabilities whose net effect is equal to zero.

The history of accounting is tied to the history of trade and thus the history of human progress. Accounting is an extremely important and influential innovation. Keep this legacy in mind as you study and learn it.

Accrual vs. Cash Accounting

Most accounting is done on an **accrual** basis as opposed to a cash basis. Accrual means that transactions are recorded when they occur, not when cash is received or dispersed. Conversely, cash basis accounting calls for the recognition of an expense when the cash goes out the door, regardless of when the expense was actually incurred; and recognition of revenue only when cash is received, not taking into account when the corresponding sale was actually consummated. Although cash basis accounting may seem logical at first glance, it leads to confusions in recording and reporting the operations of the business.

Accrual accounting provides you with a more accurate picture of the business activities. Here is an example of accrual accounting: your business has sold a product and the customer has 60 days to pay; the transaction is booked as a receivable so it is recorded that revenue was generated at that time but cash wasn't collected; when the cash is collected, the receivable is cleared out (credit) and cash is recorded (debit).

On one side of the equation, the customer received the product and a transaction clearly has occurred. On the other side, the cash has not been collected for the sale. The receivable records the obligation. This completes both sides of the transaction with a debit and credit recording.

If you recorded this transaction on a cash basis you would record the cost of the sale two months before you recorded the receipt of the cash, so you would have more expenses one month and more revenues in another. That is not an accurate picture of what has occurred. Take a look at the Khan Academy videos (KhanAcademy.org) on accrual vs. cash accounting. Sal does a great job of explaining it by running through some comparison examples.

Accrual accounting operates on the principal of matching expenses and revenues in the same period for a given transaction. There are basically two kinds of accounts that are created to record accrual type activities:

- **Accounts Receivable** (AR) which deals with money that is owed to you but not yet received
- **Accounts Payable** (AP) which deals with bills that have been received and recorded but not yet paid

Accrual accounting is based on the **matching principle**. The **matching principle** states that expenses should be recorded during the period in which they are incurred, regardless of when the transfer of cash occurs. If cash has not yet been collected related to a sale then the expense should be matched to an **Accounts Receivable**. If a bill is acknowledged as something to be paid but the check has not yet been cut, then the liability should be entered as an Accounts Payable.

A transaction is usually determined to have occurred based on this cause and effect relationship. If no cause-and-effect relationship exists such as a sale or purchase, costs are recognized as expenses in the accounting period they occurred.

Prepaid expenses are not recognized as expenses in the period that you pay them. They represent an asset that will be used over time. Prepaid expenses provide future benefits. Prepaid expenses are booked as assets until they are used and the benefit is received. At this point, that used or spent portion is recognized as an expense. As a prepaid expense is used up, an **adjusting entry** is made to update the reduced value of the asset. In the case of prepaid rent, the cost of rent for the period would be deducted from the Prepaid Rent account.

The matching principle and accrual accounting allow for a more objective and accurate analysis of profitability. By recognizing costs in the period they are incurred, a business can see how much money was spent to generate revenue, reducing "noise" from timing mismatches between when costs are incurred and when revenue is realized.

Payroll

Payroll is an accounting function that administers paying all employees, calculating the appropriate withholdings for taxes, and processes all the checks or direct deposits. Payroll is performed on a regular repeating schedule.

Typical schedules are: weekly, every two weeks, or on the first and fifteenth of the month. The first and 15th is a good schedule as it smoothes out the differences in the amount of days in each month. An employee receives two checks per month and can better plan their monthly budget and expenses. Also it ends on the last day of the year which is important for keeping annual payroll accounting less complicated. Payroll is paid for work completed; employees are paid for the prior period's work.

There are a number of withholding deductions that are made from gross payroll. These withholding deductions include: Federal and state taxes, Social Security, workers comp, and Unemployment. They are calculated on an individual basis per employee.

QuickBooks and other accounting software provide schedules for calculating these. New schedule come out annually and need to be updated as tax rates and other details may change. Accounting software also provides for the printing of checks and including the reporting the withholding amounts and net pay. Special checks are ordered for the printer and usually include, besides the check number, two copies of detail portion: one for the employee and one for your files.

There are also payroll services that outsource the entire payroll process. The number of employees, the size of the payroll, and your in-house resources are determining factors of whether to employ a payroll service or do it in-house. You may decide to outsource at first and bring it in-house as you grow, or vice versa. It is something to routinely consider as your company grows. An added advantage of payroll services consists in the fact of having more controls and procedures in place when cutting large numbers of checks, and also offsets some liabilities if mistakes are made.

Fraud Prevention

Controls and Procedures

There are many points in the accounting cycle that are vulnerable to fraud. Bookkeepers and accountants have big responsibilities. As such we need a solid sense of business ethics. We handle the day-to-day money operations and need to be scrupulously honest and not tempted to steal. A company is prey to fraud and stealing from the personnel who report the transactions, maintain the books, and cut the checks. And the people who are responsible for this work are prey to rationalizing bad behavior. A glance at the business news any day provides many examples of these type bad actors.

From a business operator's perspective we need to be aware of these temptations and institute controls and procedures to protect against them. These concerns are also extremely important if you are lucky enough to be a successful performer or artist. There are a lot of tragic stories of musicians and other artists being ripped off by their accountants and managers or a combination of the two. It is crucial to have knowledge of accounting in order to review your books with your accountant and manager and scrutinize the methods being used.

Separating the duties associated with managing and reporting the money that comes in and goes out of a business is extremely important in order to protect against fraud. This process is codified and formalized in the Controls and Procedures document. It is also important to have mechanisms in place to quickly detect any unusual transactions and track down their origins.

This kind of scrutiny will aid in preventing anyone tempted to defraud you. The perception of easy money and the prospect of getting it can easily lead to a distorted perception of reality.

Documented procedures need to be developed *and followed* relating to who:

- Opens the mail,
- Records the transactions,
- Reviews and authorizes payments
- Prepares the checks to pay bills
- Reviews and signs the checks,
- Reconciles the accounts,
- Reviews the books.

These functions need to be separated and records reviewed on a regular basis in order to help prevent fraud. You may not be able to eliminate the possibility of fraud but you can take steps to create an environment in which it is difficult to perpetrate it.

Good accounting systems prevent fraud

Your accounting system also provides a record of every transaction and, when managed properly, helps insure against fraud, theft, and "leakage". Review of financial statements is an important part of identifying and preventing fraud. We have all heard horror stories of entertainers and other victims who were taken advantage of by unscrupulous managers and accountants.

Learning accounting and how to read and assess accounting records or "books" through financial statement review will help protect you and your assets against such a fate. Just an aside: The incredible longevity and success of the Rolling Stones is due in no small part to their business savvy (and incredible musical and songwriting talent!) Mick Jagger is a graduate of the London School of Economics. Word to the wise…

Computer- Based Accounting Systems

We are now going to discuss accounting software. There is absolutely no reason to do accounting manually these days. Software packages are inexpensive and have major advantages such as speed and accuracy of operation, record storage and, the ability to see the real-time state of the company's financial position.

There are many different software packages to handle business accounting. I recommend QuickBooks as the accounting software to start. QuickBooks is by Intuit who also owns TurboTax. It has become the standard accounting software for small businesses because it has a huge installed base of experienced users.

There are many consultants and small business accountants that can help you set it up and get running. The company provides very good instructional tutorials and support. And there is also tons of instructional information on YouTube and other sites such as Lynda.com. In most cases you can set it up and operate it yourself. You can learn basic QuickBooks in a matter of hours with these online resources and tutorials.

Find an experienced user and ask a few questions if you run into an impasse. There is a cloud based version that is attractive because it is less expensive as an entry option and is convenient from an IT standpoint. You don't have to load and install the program on your computer, just set up an account and you are ready to go. There are many alternative systems to QuickBooks that you can explore online. But taking the easy alternative means one less thing to think about.

Users of Accounting Information

Management needs to know how the overall company is performing or how their division is doing. Managers may need feedback ASAP on how a new marketing campaign or pricing strategy is working. When and how transactions are booked is very important to users of accounting information. Users need timely information about how the business is doing in order to make decisions.

Besides the internal interests of management, there are external users of accounting information such as:

- Bankers who are interested in your credit worthiness and ability to repay loans,
- Vendors who are interested in your ability to pay and your credit worthiness,
- Investors who want to know whether to invest or how their investment is performing,
- Stock Analysts who research companies and opine on whether or not they are good investments for their clients,

- Potential customers, especially of big ticket items or services, who want to know that the company is sound and will be around to offer support and spare parts, and
- Taxing authorities who want to know how much money the business has made or lost.

Reporting the results of business activity on an accrual basis is important to these parties that have a stake in the company's performance and health. Accrual provides a much more accurate picture of the operations to those who are not intimately involved in the day-to-day operations but need to know the operational details.

The way this kind of reporting of the accounting information is prepared, organized, and conveyed is in Financial Statements. We covered financial statements in a previous section. Go back and give it a quick review. You want that understanding solid.

Budgeting

Budgets are financial projections developed for a relatively short and predetermined period of time. Most budgets are prepared for the next year and divided into detailed monthly budgets. Budgets can be expected to be reasonably accurate because they represent estimates of relatively short time periods and because they rely on historical information about the company.

Budgets are created, reviewed, and approved and then used to measure the actual performance of the company each month. Did the company under or over perform relative to the budget? The differences between the actual accounting prepared at the end of the month and the budget amounts is called a Variance.

Variances are reviewed and discussed to see why some line items went over budget and why some may be significantly under budget. Budgets are developed using historical performance data, which means that they are relatively predictive of the levels at which a company should be operating. And the budget will reflect the goals that management hopes to achieve in the coming year.

Budgeting is part of the planning process and reviewing the actual results against the budget on a regular basis is good management practice.

Financial Projections

Financial projections are less accurate than budgets because they are forecasting sales and expenses three to five years into the future. The ability to predict the future with any level of accuracy diminishes, as the timeframe gets more remote and removed from the present.

Financial projections are made for start-ups or new divisions of companies. This is done for long term planning and valuation purposes. Financial projections are used to assess whether a project is financially worth pursuing. They serve as an instrument to analyze whether or not to make an investment or fund a project or venture.

Spreadsheets

Budgets and Financial Projections are prepared in spreadsheets. The rows and columns are perfectly suited for a quick summation of revenues and expenses in columns and rows. The actual accounting figures can be imported into a spreadsheet from the accounting software for variance analysis.

Many of you are probably very familiar with spreadsheets and how they operate. Here is a short summary for those of you becoming familiar with them.

Spreadsheets are computer programs used a lot in accounting as worksheets. Arranged in the manner of a mathematical matrix, they contain a multicolumn, multi-row layout. Using them makes your life simple when adding columns of numbers and it gives you clear a record of those columns and calculations. This can be convenient six months later when you can't remember how the heck you came up with a certain number that is throwing your books out of whack.

Microsoft Excel is the most common spreadsheet program, both powerful and easy to learn. Become familiar with the basic functions and features of Excel. There are great online tutorials from

Microsoft from absolute beginner through sophisticated applications of Excel. There are also many third party tutorials freely available on YouTube.

Managerial and Cost Accounting

What we have been discussing so far is called Financial Accounting: recording transactions and preparing financial statements. This book is about Financial Accounting. Another part of accounting is Cost Accounting. While Financial Accounting information is of interest to users both internal and external to the company, cost accounting is a set of techniques that is strictly applied and used only internally

The goal of cost accounting is to clearly understand the costs associated with the products produced and services provided by a company. Understanding costs in detail is extremely important in order to figure out the best and least expensive ways to make products.

Cost accounting is an important management decision-making tool. Managers use cost accounting to make decisions to maximize profitability.

Differences between Financial and Cost Accounting

Financial accounting aims at recording and presenting the results of an accounting year in the form of an

Income Statement, Balance Sheet, and Cash Flow Statement. Cost Accounting aims at computing the costs of production or services in a rigorous analytic manner that facilitates cost control and cost reduction.

Financial accounting reports the results and position of business to management, government, creditors, investors, and other external parties, while Cost Accounting is an internal reporting system to aid management in their decision making processes.

In financial accounting, cost classification is based on various types of transactions, such as salaries, repairs, insurance, inventory etc. In cost accounting, classification is made on the basis of functions, activities, products, and processes. It is a different approach and way of looking at costs and how they aggregate up. Cost accounting classifications and presentation is directed at internal planning and control and serves the information needs of the organization.

Financial accounting aims at presenting a 'true and fair' view of the transactions, profit and loss for a period, and the Balance Sheet on a given date.. These concepts are not the focus in cost accounting since we are not making reports to share with the general public. Check out our book on Cost Accounting for a detailed look at this discipline.

Tax Accounting

Tax accounting is also its own specialty and profession. The rules differ from state to state in the U.S. and tax laws and rules change on a regular basis. Keeping up with these changes and their implications is a full time job.

Tax accounting in the US is governed by the Internal Revenue Code and overseen by the Internal Revenue Service (IRS) which dictates the specific rules that companies and individuals must follow when preparing their tax returns. Tax accounting principles differ from Generally Accepted Accounting Principles (GAAP).

There are several taxing authorities that you need to be aware of and remain in compliance with: Federal (IRS), and State and local authorities, such as county or city. Hire the services of a CPA that specializes in taxes to help you initially prepare and file quarterly estimates and tax returns.

Never defer paying taxes and contemplate using the tax money to finance the business. You may rationalize that you only need it to cover expenses for a short while and then will pay the taxes later. This is a slippery slope and a recipe for disaster; do not fall into this trap.

Parting Thoughts on Accounting

The Foundational Importance and Impact of Accounting in Modern Life

The history of accounting is several thousand of years old and can be traced back to the great ancient civilizations.

The early development of accounting dates back to ancient Mesopotamia and the Sumerians, and is closely related to the basic developments of writing, counting and money. The Egyptians and Babylonians had developed extensive auditing and accounting systems.

By the time of the Emperor Augustus two thousand years ago, the Roman government had access to detailed financial information relating to their empire.

The invention of double entry bookkeeping is attributed to Luca Pacioli. He was a Franciscan monk and is referred to as the father of accounting. The book in which he describes double entry bookkeeping was a mathematics text called the *Summa de Arithmetica, Geometria, Proportioni et Proportionalita.* He wrote it in 1494. Luca was living with Leonardo da Vinci at the time in Milan and was Leonardo's math tutor.

The first actual recorded description of double entry bookkeeping was in 1458 in a work titled: *Book on the Art of Trade.* The author's name was Benedikt Kotruljević. He was born in Dubrovnik in 1416.

Double entry bookkeeping is one of the great intellectual breakthroughs and turning points in history. It is the basis of modern accounting. This method enables traders, merchants, and entrepreneurs, to accurately keep track of every transaction in detail. It provides investors with an accurate summary of the business activities of an enterprise.

Accounting allows people to organize massive amounts of transactional information and produce summary financial statements. These financial statements distill the information into readable form that communicates the operational performance of a business.

The income statement shows total revenues minus total expenses, leaving either a profit or loss. The balance sheet illustrates the assets, the debts, and the difference between them as owners' equity.

These financial tools have enabled business owners, investors, and governments to allocate resources more effectively. For example, if a business person owned two shops, they could look at each income statement and review the profits or loss. From this information they are able to determine in which one to invest more money, effort and time; or which one to close.

As this type of analysis developed, more decisions began to be made using the information provided by accounting. This led to more efficient and effective use and deployment of capital. Capital grew, and as it did so did the surplus benefits to society.

From analysis of the income statement the idea of the return on investment (ROI) evolved. ROI enabled investors to compare investments objectively with the simple ratio formula. They could then double down on the better performing ones.

Investors, bankers, and the business community started to add calculations and assesments of risk to the analysis. An entrepreneur might ask: if we could make a $1,000 on investment A and a $1,000 on investment B, which one has the least risk thereby making the investment safer? Or which investment has the more important outcome, making bearing the risk more acceptable? This combination of risk and return into business analysis became the basis of **Corporate** **Finance**.

Organizing financial information and the results of operations into the balance sheet has had a great impact as well. The balance sheet shows how assets are financed and grow by reducing accounting into a simple elegant equation: Assets = Liabilities + Owners' Equity. The equation shows that everything owned is financed with a combination of debt and equity.

With these insights owners, investors and entrepreneurs were able to value their assets more accurately and to sell them to others for what they were worth. People began to make better and wiser decisions and became financially literate. This drove markets to develop around the world. Wealth has been created on an unprecedented scale, lifting millions of people out of poverty. Accounting is foundational in the modern capitalist economic miracle.

Next Steps

In this section we have gone over bookkeeping; financial statement preparation, budgeting and financial projections.

Accounting is not a spectator sport. You will really learn accounting by doing it. But first you need to know what to do. Jump-starting through the complexity of that paradox is no small feat.

Your intention to learn is the first step. Purchasing this book was the second step.

Journeys start with initial steps. But they are of no use to you unless you read it, comprehend the ideas and internalize the concepts. As you are reading this: Congratulations! You have digested the material. No one can take that away from you. This is an accomplishment that you can be proud of.

Now that you have read through it once, you may want to return to sections again more thoughtfully until you own this subject.

Now you are part of this tradition. It's now time to put your accounting knowledge to work! Go forth and prosper!

Accounting Concepts, Principals, and Glossary

Accounting Principals

Accountants often need to make judgments. We make decisions relative to recording and presenting transactions in the clearest and most meaningful way. We use consistent principles to guide our decision-making process. Here are some general rules and concepts.

- **Matching principle:** This principle states that a company's revenue should be matched with the expenses that relate to that revenue. The concept of simultaneously recognizing the revenues and expenses that jointly result from the same transactions.

- **Principle of Conservatism:** Conservatism relates to decisions about presentation and reporting. Reporting should err on the side of generating the least attractive financial result. If there's a decision about revenue, the conservative choice is to delay recognizing revenue in the financial statements. Expenses should be posted to the financial statements sooner rather than later. These choices generate financial statements that are less optimistic and less likely to mislead investors and potential investors. The idea is to manage expectations and not mislead investors and other parties that make decisions about the financial viability of the company based on the presentation in the financial statements.

- **Materiality:** refers to the judgment standard of what level of detail is significant to report on financial statements. It is about relevancy and importance. The concept that accounting should disclose separately only those events that are relatively important. Materiality defines the threshold at which financial information becomes relevant to the decision making needs of users. Information is deemed material if its omission or misstatement could influence the economic decisions of users. Accounting information is deemed material if the judgment of a reasonable person relying on the information would have been changed or influenced by the omission or misstatement. Materiality relates to the significance of transactions and is relative to the size and circumstances of individual companies and situations.

- **Fair value accounting** is a financial reporting approach in which companies are permitted to revalue certain assets and liabilities based on estimates of the current prices. Because historical prices can be misleading, companies make estimates of what they currently would receive if they were to sell the assets or would pay if they were to be purchased. An active market or other objective basis of valuation is very important in this regard.

- **True and Fair View of Financial Statements** are auditing and financial reporting concepts. True and fair view in auditing means that the financial statements are free from material misstatements and faithfully represent the financial performance and position of the company. **True** means that the financial statements are factually correct and have been prepared according to GAAP in the US or IFRS for international companies. They do not contain any material misstatements that may mislead users. **Fair** means the financial statements present the information faithfully without any bias and that they substantially reflect the economic transactions being reported.

Common Accounting Terms Glossary

These are important words and phrases, in alphabetical order, you will become familiar with as you study and acquire a working knowledge of accounting:

Account
An account is a device for accumulating additions and subtractions relating to a single asset, liability, or owner's equity item, including revenues and expenses. An account is a record used to classify the transaction activity that is recorded in the General Ledger.

Account balance
An account balance is the sum of debit entries minus the sum of credit entries in an account. If positive, the difference is called a debit balance; if negative, a credit balance.

Accounting

Accounting is a service activity whose function is to provide quantitative information, primarily financial in nature, about economic entities that is intended to be useful in making economic decisions. Accounting is the recording and reporting of financial transactions, including the origination of the transaction, its recognition, processing, and summarization in the financial statements.

Accounts Payable

Accounts Payable is an amount owed *by* the enterprise for delivered goods or completed services. Accounts Payable is a liability representing an amount owed to a creditor. In most companies checks are cut in batches and obligations are first entered through Accounts Payable accounts before they are paid. It is normally a current liability.

Accounts Receivable

Account Receivable is an amount owed *to* the enterprise from a completed sales transaction or for services rendered. Accounts Receivable is an asset related to sales revenue. It is a claim against a debtor arising from sales or services rendered. This is normally a current asset.

Accrual Basis

Accrual basis is a method of accounting that recognizes revenue when earned, rather than when collected and expenses when incurred rather than when paid. It is the method of recognizing revenues as goods are sold (or delivered) and as services are

259

rendered, independent of the time when case is received. Expenses are recognized in the period when the related revenue is recognized independent of the time when cash is paid out. Accrual basis creates an accurate picture of transactions. Enterprises use the accrual basis for their accounting as opposed to a cash basis. Accrual accounting is a consequence of implementing the Matching Principle.

Additional Paid-in Capital (APIC)

The Additional Paid-in Capital (APIC) account is where the amount paid for a share of stock, less the par value, is recorded. Another alternative title for the account is *capital contributed in excess of par value*.

Adjusting Entries

Adjusting entries are journal entries usually made at the end of an accounting period to allocate income and expenditures to the period in which they actually occurred. It is an entry made at the end of an accounting period to record a transaction or other accounting event, which for some reason has not been recorded or has been improperly recorded during the accounting period. It is an entry to update the accounts.

Adjusted Trial Balance

An adjusted trial balance is a listing of all the account titles and balances contained in the general ledger after the adjusting entries for an accounting period have been posted to the accounts. The adjusted trial balance is an internal document. It is not a financial statement but is used to create the financial statements.

Amortization

Amortization is the process of liquidating or extinguishing a debt with a series of payments to creditor. It refers to the calculation and schedule of the paying off of debt with fixed repayments in regular installments over a period of time.

Consumers are most likely to encounter amortization with a mortgage or car loan. Amortization can mean the accounting for the payments themselves. An amortization schedule for a mortgage is a table showing the allocation between interest and principle.

Amortization can also mean the spreading out of capital expenses for intangible assets over a specific period of time (usually over the asset's useful life) for accounting and tax purposes. Amortization is similar to depreciation, which is used for tangible assets, and to depletion, which is used with natural resources. Amortization roughly matches an asset's expense with the revenue it generates.

Asset

An asset is what the enterprise owns. An asset is defined as having probable future economic benefits obtained or controlled by an entity as a result of past transactions. For example: land, factories, office buildings, equipment, vehicles, cash in bank accounts, other investments, accounts receivable, and intellectual property such as patents and trademarks.

Audit
An audit is a systematic inspection of accounting records involving analyses, tests, and confirmations. It is a formal examination and official endorsement of the accuracy of the financial statements of the enterprise conducted by an independent certified public accountant (CPA). In the U.S., an audit is based on GAAP and FASB rules. Most companies are required to have an audit performed each fiscal year.

Balance Sheet
A Balance Sheet is a summary report of a company's financial position on a specific date that shows Total Assets = Total Liabilities + Owner's Equity.

Bookkeeping
Bookkeeping is the process of analyzing and recording of financial transactions in the accounting records. Transactions include purchases, sales, receipts and payments by an individual or organization.

The Books
The "books" is a general term referring to the General Ledger and the various journals that are kept by a business. *Book* can be used as a verb: to record a transaction.

Book Value

Book value is the value of an asset according to its balance sheet account balance. For assets, the value is based on the original cost of the asset less any depreciation, amortization or impairment costs made against the asset. It refers to the net amount.

Budget

A budget is a financial plan that is used to estimate the results of future operations. A budget is an estimate of revenue and expense activity for a fiscal year or period. It is used to help control future operations. A budget can be created for a department or a project. In a corporation, budgets are aggregated up to the corporate level and reviewed and approved by the board of directors. The budget then becomes an operational document for the coming year and actual results are measured against it. In governmental operations, budgets often become the law.

Capitalize

To capitalize is to record an expenditure that will benefit a future period as an asset rather than to treat it as an expense in the period of its occurrence. It is an accounting method used to delay the recognition of a significant expense by recording the expense as a long-term asset. In general, capitalizing expenses more accurately depicts the situation as companies acquiring new assets with a long-term lifespan can spread out the cost over a specified period of time. That period of time is an estimate of the asset's useful life, when it will be contributing to the generation of revenues.

Cash

Cash is currency and coins, negotiable checks, and balances in bank accounts. We all know what cash is but in accounting it refers to the first account in the Assets category of the Balance Sheet. This is aggregated from all company bank accounts and it is derived as the bottom number on the Cash Flow Statement.

Cash Flow Statement

A cash flow statement is a financial statement that shows how changes in balance sheet accounts and income affect cash. The cash flow statement breaks the analysis down into operating, investing and financing activities.

Chart of Accounts

The chart of accounts is a listing of all accounts used in the **general ledger** of an organization. The chart is used by the accounting software to aggregate information into an entity's financial statements. It is a list of the names and numbers, systematically organized, of accounts.

Common Stock

Common Stock is the type of stock that is present in every corporation. Shares of common stock provide evidence of ownership in a corporation. These shares represent the class of owners who have residual claims on the assets and earnings of a corporation after all debt and preferred shareholders' claims have been met. Holders of common stock elect the corporation's directors and share in the distribution of profits of the company via dividends. If the corporation were to liquidate, the secured lenders would be paid first, followed by unsecured lenders, preferred stockholders (if any), and lastly the common stockholders. If a company is acquired, the proceeds go to the shareholders after the debts are paid off.

Cost of Goods Sold

Cost of Goods Sold (COGS) is the direct costs attributable to the production of the goods sold by a company. This amount includes the cost of the materials used in creating the good along with the direct labor costs used to produce the good. It *excludes* indirect expenses such as distribution costs, marketing and sales force costs.

Credit

A credit is an entry on the right side of a double-entry accounting system that represents the reduction of an asset or expense or the addition to a liability or revenue. It is the countervailing entry to a debit.

Current Assets

Current Assets are balance sheet accounts that represent the value of assets that are reasonably expected to be converted into cash within one year in the normal course of business. Current assets include cash, accounts receivable, inventory, marketable securities, prepaid expenses and other liquid assets that can be readily converted to cash.

Debit

A debit is an entry on the left side of a double-entry accounting system that represents the addition to an asset or expense or the reduction to a liability or revenue. It is the countervailing entry to a credit.

Debt

Debt is an amount owed usually for funds borrowed. Debt is the general name for loans, notes, bonds, mortgages, and the like that are evidence of amounts owed and have definite payment dates and schedules. The lender agrees to lend funds to the borrower upon a promise by the borrower to pay interest on the debt, usually with the interest to be paid at regular intervals. Debt is a Liability to the company (an asset to the lender) and is shown on the balance sheet net of how much has been repaid.

Depreciation

Depreciation is a method of allocating the cost of a tangible asset over its useful life. It is the process of allocating the cost of an asset to the periods of benefit. Businesses depreciate long-term assets for both tax and accounting purposes. Different depreciation schedules are used for different fixed assets. Depreciation schedules can vary in length and also in how fast depreciation is incurred. There are accelerated depreciation techniques that apply more depreciation to early years in the schedule. Depreciation can also mean a decrease in an asset's value caused by unfavorable market conditions.

Dividend

A dividend is a payment made by a corporation to its shareholders, usually as a distribution of a portion of profits. When a corporation earns a profit or surplus, it can re-invest it in the business (called retained earnings), and/or pay a fraction of the profit as a dividend to shareholders. A dividend can be paid in cash (cash dividend) or stock (stock dividend).

Double-Entry Accounting

Double entry is the system of recording transactions that maintains the equality of the accounting equation. Each entry results in recording equal amounts of debits and credits. Double-entry accounting is a method of recording financial transactions in which each transaction is entered in two or more accounts and involves two-way, self-balancing posting. Total debits must equal total credits.

Equity

Equity is a claim on assets. Equity is short for owner's equity or shareholder's equity. It consists of the net assets of an enterprise. It is the residual interest in the assets of an entity that remains after deducting its liabilities. Net assets are the difference between the total assets of the entity and all its liabilities. Equity appears on the balance sheet. Remember the balance sheet formula: Assets = Liabilities + Equity.

Expense

An expense is funds paid by the enterprise. For example: paychecks to employees, and payments to vendors for goods or services. It is a decrease in owners' equity caused by the using up of assets in producing revenue or carrying out other activities that are part of the entity's operations.

FASB
FASB stands for Financial Accounting Standards Board and is an independent, private, nongovernmental authority for the establishment of *generally accepted accounting principles* in the United States.

Financial Statements
Financial Statements are a series of reports showing a summary view of the various financial activities of a company. There are three major financial statements: Balance Sheet, Income Statement, and Cash Flow Statement. Each statement tells a different story about the financial activity of an enterprise. Financial statements also include the notes thereto.

Fiscal Year
A fiscal year is a period of 12 consecutive months chosen by a business as its accounting period for annual reports. Most fiscal years are a calendar year (January 1- December 31) but a fiscal year can start and end on any month. For example most government agencies run a fiscal year from October 1 – September 30.

Fixed Asset
A fixed asset is any tangible item with a useful life of more than one year, for example-office buildings, factories, major equipment and vehicles. Computers

used to be thought of as fixed assets but personal computers now cost less than $1,000 and have useful lives of not much more than a year and so are usually expensed instead of capitalized as a fixed asset. A fixed asset is an asset and is listed on the Balance Sheet.

GAAP

GAAP stands for Generally Accepted Accounting Principles which are conventions, rules, and procedures that are required to be followed in preparing financial statements. GAAP defines accepted accounting practice in the U.S. These principles are defined by FASB. They include both broad guidelines and detailed practices and procedures.

General Ledger

The general ledger is the collection of all the financial statement accounts including: asset, liability, equity, revenue and expense accounts. The general ledger is what is used to prepare financial statements.

Income Statement

An Income Statement is a summary report that shows revenues, expenses, gains or losses over a specific period of time, typically a month, quarter or fiscal year. An income statement is structured as: Revenue – Expenses = Net Income. Net Income is also referred to as Profit or Earnings. The *earnings-per-share* amount is usually shown on the income statement.

Intellectual Property

Intellectual Property (IP) is a broad categorical description for the set of intangibles owned and legally protected by a company from outside use or implementation without consent. From an accounting standpoint, Intellectual property can consist of patents, copyrights, and trademarks. IP are assets listed on the balance sheet and valued at the cost of procuring them net of depreciation.

Journal Entry

A journal entry is a group of debit and credit transactions that are posted to the general ledger. All journal entries must net to zero so debits must equal credits. An explanation of the transaction is included, if necessary.

Leverage

Operating leverage refers to the tendency of net income to rise at a faster rate than sales when there are fixed costs. Financial leverage means the use of long-term debt in securing funds for the enterprise. A measure of financial leverage is the debt to equity ratio. It is calculated as the ratio of a company's loan capital (debt) to the value of its common stock (equity). Debt/Equity.

Liability

A liability is an obligation to pay a definite amount at a definite time in return for a past or current benefit. It is what the company owes. For example: loans, taxes, payables, long term debt from a bond issue.

Line of Credit (LOC)

A line of credit is an arrangement between a financial institution, usually a bank, and a customer for short term borrowings on demand. The borrower can draw down on the line of credit at any time, but cannot exceed the maximum set in the agreement.

Liquidity

Liquidity refers to the availability of cash, or near cash resources, for meeting a firm's obligations.

Mark-to-Market

Mark-to-market or fair value accounting refers to accounting for the "fair value" of an asset or liability based on the current market price, or for similar assets and liabilities, or based on another objectively assessed "fair" value. Fair value accounting has been a part of Generally Accepted Accounting Principles (GAAP) in the United States since the early 1990s.

Net Income (loss)

Net Income (loss) is the amount the company made or lost for a specific period of time. It is the excess of all revenues and gains for a period over all expenses and losses of the period. It is the bottom number on the Income Statement. To arrive at net income take total revenues minus total expenses. Net Income is sometimes called Profit or Earnings.

P & L responsibility

P&L stands for profit and loss statement or income statement. P & L responsibility is one of the most important responsibilities of any executive position. It involves monitoring, and being judged on, the net income after expenses for a department or entire organization. The executive's performance is judged on the financial results. The executive has direct influence on how company resources are allocated and how tactics are developed to implement strategy.

Par Value
Par value is the face amount of a security. The Par Value account is a stock equity account shown on the Balance Sheet. It is a way to keep track of the amount of shares outstanding. The par value is a small monetary value attributed to each share. It is an arbitrary number, usually $.01

Preferred Stock
Preferred Stock is a class of corporation stock with claims to income or assets after bondholders but before common shares. Preferred stock provides for preferential treatment of dividends. Preferred stockholders will be paid dividends before the common stockholders receive dividends. These dividends are sometimes paid in stock instead of money.

Principal
Principal refers to the face amount of a loan. It is the original sum invested or lent.

Retained Earnings
The percentage of net income not paid out as dividends, but *retained* by the company to be

reinvested in its core business, or to pay debt. It is recorded under shareholders' equity on the balance sheet and is measured as owners' equity less contributed capital.

Revenue
Revenue is funds collected by the company usually from sales. It is the monetary measure of sales or services rendered.

SEC
Securities and Exchange Commission, the agency authorized by the U.S. Congress to regulate, among other things, the financial reporting practices of public corporations.

Shares Outstanding
A company's stock currently held by all its shareholders, including restricted shares owned by the company's officers and insiders. Outstanding shares are shown on a company's balance sheet under the heading "Capital Stock." The number of outstanding shares is used in calculating key metrics such as a company's market capitalization, as well as its earnings per share (EPS).

Stock
Stock, or shares, is the general term used to describe the ownership certificates of a company. Stocks are the investment instrument or vehicle of equity.

T-accounts

A T-account is an account from shaped like the letter T with the title above the horizontal line. Debits are shown to the left of the vertical line and credits to the right. Accountants and bookkeepers often use T-accounts as a graphical aid for visualizing and understanding the effect of the debit and credit on the two (or more) accounts related to a journal entry.

Trial Balance

A trial balance is a listing of account balances. All accounts with debit balances are totaled separately from accounts with credit balances. The two totals should be equal. Trial balances are taken as a partial check of the arithmetic accuracy of the entries previously made.

A company prepares a *trial balance* periodically, usually at the end of every reporting period, as the initial step in preparing financial statements. This statement of all debits and credits is used to quickly locate any disagreements indicating an error. The trial balance is a trouble-shooting tool.

Vendor List

The *vendor list* shows information about the people or companies from whom an enterprise buys goods and services, including banks and tax agencies.

Management

Effective business leaders and managers apply the toolkit and skill sets we are exploring in this book.

Being effective is about gaining the intuition and the ability to know when to apply what, and how to best apply it.

Effective leaders and managers are able to communicate well and be decisive without being rash. In order to be effective you need to know the terminology and how to use the tools.

Management and Leadership require a synthetic sense of the entire business activity.

What You Do and Who You Are

The study of business management should not be intimidating. These ideas are not foreign to you. Managing your daily life has prepared you to understand all the aspects of management and leadership.

Working on business management skills will help you better manage your daily life. This leads to a virtuous cycle of improvement and success.

Who you are as a businessperson need not be a separate identity from the one you already have developed. Yet we need to commit to a personal development process because we are taking on expanded responsibilities and expanding the scope of those around us who we influence directly and indirectly. Our actions and the consequences of those actions will affect others and in some cases profoundly.

If you want to take on the mantel, assume the responsibility to become the best you possible.

Be Yourself, Only More So

Most problems in a business come from issues related to people management. There is a lot of ambivalent advice about how best to approach and deal with people management. Fortunately there are new and growing ways of automation, which will allow you to eliminate some of those issues. Nonetheless, thinking through them will remain a high priority and daily concern.

To be genuine and authentic in your business dealings, you have to be fully you. This isn't about obtaining a business guise in which to command authority.

Work from your intuitive sense of Management and Leadership. This is your platform. You have been developing interpersonal skills all your life with siblings, parents, friends, teachers, and work colleagues. By now you have probably developed some strategies that are effective in addressing problems. You have some meaningful experience dealing with people and understand how to get them to do what you want.

We all also harbor habits that no longer serve us.

Part of your self- assessment now is to look at your personal interaction skills and to cull out those that are dysfunctional. Commit to abandon them and focus on developing the productive ones.

Remember, you already run a complex enterprise called your life. Granted, it will take some discipline to maintain focus on developing these skills.

Set up a pleasant environment in which to study. If you get into a habit that makes you feel good you will look forward to these breaks away from your daily routine. And in a week you will find you have made some real progress. This in turn will encourage you to continue, and then more progress will allow you to build more confidence and self-esteem and this will ultimately become a virtuous cycle.

Management and Organizational Structure

We will start off with a discussion of how to organize, manage and lead an enterprise.

The most significant resource in just about any enterprise is its people, its human resources. The biggest expense line item in most any company is salaries and other compensation to employees, contract labor, and consultants. These will usually run well over 50% of total expenses. Besides of the monetary impact, directing employees and organizing people in an enterprise so that everybody moves in concert towards common goals and a shared mission takes the most attention from management.

The main question is how to best motivate people to focus on the tasks that contribute to the overall goals of the enterprise. An organization can easily lose momentum and fall into the doldrums. If employees feel underappreciated, not empowered, or if they just don't understand the vision and direction of the enterprise they might will quickly lose interest in their job and perform poorly. This is not surprising since we only can do a great job when we feel valued and appreciated.

As managers we need to learn how to be sensitive to our employee's needs, find ways to make them feel valued, keyed in to the mission of the business, as well as empowered to make solid decisions and move things forward. This means creating an atmosphere of positive momentum, acknowledge and celebrate successes, tolerate yet quickly address mistakes, give employees autonomy to make decisions, seek and encourage their suggestions for improvements, and celebrate people as valued team members who understand and their role in the overall organization. Generating this sense of momentum and engagement is a pivotal task of management and leadership.

Cultivating Employees

Part of making people feel empowered means allowing them the autonomy to figure out how best to do their appointed tasks and fulfill the requirements of their job. As a manager, you need to learn how to delegate effectively. This means creating an organization that is process-oriented so that others can understand and take over tasks. It also means giving people authority to make decisions and take responsibility for fixing problems and addressing issues that arise instead of having those issues always kicked upstairs.

You want to cultivate a work force with a certain amount of autonomy. This means creating an environment that encourages self-confidence and decision-making. It means creating a safe environment where mistakes are acknowledged, addressed and fixed without adverse repercussions.

A business will progress when employees feel comfortable with taking risks or at least are not risk averse. They should never feel that making a mistake might cost them more than making a good decision will benefit them.

One of the major pernicious effects of an ill-conceived management is a work environment that does not invite making decisions. This is often the case when there is no mechanism in place that recognizes and awards a good decision and refrains from punishing decisions with ill effects. For your employees this means that not rocking the boat is always best; until eventually the organization as a whole succumbs to apathy.

David Ogilvy was one of the great creative leaders one of the prime inventors of modern advertising. In fact, his 1960s advertising firm is the model for the TV show "Mad Men". He wrote great memos and papers for his staff on communication, leadership, management and many other topics. Here are some of his thoughts on management.

One of the things he cautions against is the danger of negative internal politics and bickering. A dysfunctional work environment has destroyed companies. We all have experienced how toxic office politics can be. Here are seven ways Ogilvy suggested to curtail dysfunction and promote healthy competition:

- Always be fair and honest in your own dealings: unfairness and dishonesty at the top can demoralize a staff and the company.

- Never hire relatives or friends

- Sack incurable politicians

- Crusade against paper warfare. Encourage you people to air their disagreements face-to-face

- Discourage secrecy

- Discourage poaching

- Compose sibling rivalries

Move Fast and Break Things

Facebook's famous motto "Move fast and break things" encourages the opposite of this behavior. This attitude is extreme and should obviously not to be taken literally, but it nonetheless emphasizes the need to move fast and tolerate some flaws along the way. Too many flaws can slow down your success as you stop to fix them and lead to customer wariness if products end up being too flawed. So tempering perfectionism is an important part of management.

There has been a lot of emphasis lately on encouraging failure as part of the process of learning and moving forward. If you are not making mistakes then you are not moving forward fast enough. The motto is: Fail fast and fail forward. These ideas encourage us to break out of the risk averse mode of operating that is fatal to organizations in the long run. Management is always about creating good organizational structures and incentives, developing and nurturing talent, effectively communicating goals, and properly measuring results. You must be an effective role model and genuinely embody all of these attributes.

Human Resources

Human Resources (HR) refers to the functions in an organization that hires, fires, and creates and administers the rules of employee conduct and the relationship between employer and employee. HR has become very sophisticated in the last several decades as a greater appreciation of the strategic importance of leveraging an organization's talent pools has developed.

Hiring

The first tip of good management is: **<u>hire well</u>**. That is easy to say and really challenging in practice. Besides attempting to assess technical skills and work ethic you are trying to gain concerning psychological and emotional insights of potential employees in order to asses if they will be a good fit and provide synergies to the organization.

A new hire is a big commitment. It is the beginning of a deeply complex and engaging relationship like marriage. As in dating, people tend to present a virtuous façade at first that may hide other personality traits. There is an entire body of new work on how to develop a better initial assessment that might allow you to predict with greater certainty, which will be a good, great, or disastrous fit for a particular job.

Just as in dating, mating and marriage, it is often easier to get into a relationship and very difficult to extricate oneself. In other words, front end assessment work in the hiring process is crucial.

Screening and understanding the psychological makeup of a potential employee before hiring is crucial You want to know if this potential hire will flourish in your organization and help energize others, if they will be a toxic element that poisons and erodes the esprit de corps, or an unremarkable seat warmer somewhere in between.

You are looking to identify a person that is a team player with talent, expertise, and experience to perform the task at hand. You also need to assess if they have the flexibility and capacity to learn and contribute as the environment evolves.

Hiring an employee is one of the most critical decisions you can make. When interviewing, people are on their best behavior and often throw everything they know at you. Some are very smooth interviewees but may turn out to be all talk and toxic to your business.

The basic premise of the book *The No Asshole Rule* (love the title) is that even if someone has stellar talent, if they are an asshole DO NOT HIRE THEM. A catty personality that develops cliques and palace intrigues is toxic to an organization and its ability to function.

I have personally been fooled many times both ways in hiring and assessing people's potential. I have thought someone would fit in and be able to contribute quickly and substantially only to find myself shocked by their lack of performance and ability to disrupt and anger others. But I have also been more than pleasantly surprised by "bland" people who seemed earnest and capable, but grew quickly into stellar performers and inspired others to reach higher.

There have been a lot of recent developments in designing objective criteria for making hiring decisions. Testing and analysis have evolved to help guide the hiring process along quantitative, systematic and predictable criteria. This is especially important in fast growing companies that need to scale up quickly in order to remain competitive.

The author William Poundstone has chronicled the testing and hiring selection process at Microsoft in his book *How Would You Move Mount Fuji* and at Google in *Are You Smart Enough to Work at Google?* Both books detail interviewing tactics used by these companies in their attempt to separate the good prospects from the stellar.

Obviously, better screening processes and tools can help make better hiring decisions, but in most cases it still comes down to trusting your gut and to engage your bullshit detector. An equally, if not more important, question is whether you resonate on a personal level with the person.
When a company is growing rapidly hiring decisions are most critical.

A formal system and process is necessary to acquire top talent quickly and ensure a good fit with the organizations culture and objectives. There is an adage: A people hire A people and B people hire Cs. Inferior hires can quickly devolve into a dysfunctional mess that cannot be remedied.

Do not be timid. Hire people smarter than you and don't be afraid. Steve Jobs considered hiring superior talent to be strategically critical. He said that top talent isn't 10% better than the others; they are 10 times better. These are the people you want. You want super smart creative talent that can make an impact on your company's destiny.

Here is what David Ogilvy has to say on hiring:
The challenge is to recruit people who are able to do the difficult work our clients require form us.

- Make a conscious effort to avoid recruiting dull, pedestrian hacks.
- Create an atmosphere of ferment, innovation, and freedom. This will attract brilliant recruits.
- If you ever find a man who is better than you are – hire him. If necessary, pay him more than you pay yourself.

When hiring look for people who are genuinely humble. Brilliance and intelligence can breed hubris and cloud one's ability to perceive and adjust for shortcomings and faults.

Aside from the brilliant hires you will also need dedicated stable workers; "Steady Eddies" that are superbly capable and can add incremental improvements and efficiencies. These people keep the trains running on time.

Firing

Hiring is critical. Once someone has joined your company it is very difficult to get rid of them. An employee insinuates themselves into all kinds of aspects of the business and it is very disruptive to rip out those roots and replace them. But get rid of sad sacks who spread doom and gloom and who incurably spoil office politics. Do not tolerate phonies, zeros, bozos, or bastards.

There are rules and regulations protecting employees and they are important to ensure against abuses from bad management. But these protections can also become hurdles to making quick decisions about pulling the plug. Cynical or angry bad actors can use these protections as weapons to harm your enterprise if you are not careful.

It is incumbent on you to prevent these situations. But if you find yourself in such a situation fire them, do not to let them fester. Know the rules and regulations and focus your resources on hiring well and developing those new hires to be great individual and group contributors.

The Meta-Hire

Hiring a great HR director is one of the most important hires you can make. This isn't the dusty back office job to which it was once relegated. People will make or break your enterprise and the person who interfaces with them is in a critical position.

Human Resource Development

Training and developing employees is one of the most powerful strategic missions a company has. Developing employee's skills also helps with retention. It is much more cost effective to keep good employees and develop them than it is to search, hire, and train new personnel. Many companies that used to outsource training are now developing in-house training and education programs that are more accurately tailored to their particular business.

Executive education has been viewed as a cherished perk to provide to up and coming talent. But many companies have recently realized that sending a star executive off to an executive MBA program is a double-edged sword. The newly trained executive became more attractive to other companies and would jump ship for other opportunities. To avoid this kind of attrition companies are developing germane in-house programs even at the upper echelon.

Satisfaction

There is nothing more satisfying than helping develop the latent and innate talents and skills of employees. You can actually watch someone blossom and gain confidence as they successfully operate at higher levels. This is one of the greatest satisfactions of running a business and being a manager.

Automated Business Models

On the other hand, employees are the biggest cost line in a business and they can be a headache to manage. Aside from having to pay them, you have to manage their disputes and work around their needs for time off and being sick.

A way around some of these issues is to implement a business model using web-based automation. There are web tools available to automate marketing, sales and payment processing. You can also outsource procurement and order fulfillment and delivery.

In fact, if your product is a digital download, you can automate the entire business. This can remove a lot of potential headaches with employees and free up your time in addition. It also means great operating leverage. Without the expenses of employees, lots more money falls to the bottom line as profit.

Tim Ferriss has written a compelling book on the subject of getting yourself out of the loop of less constructive work by automating your business model and creating cash streams that require minimum amounts of your attention. The book is called *The 4-Hour Work-week* and I highly recommend it. It provides practical steps to incorporating his revolutionary ideas. These are great ideas to entertain and implement in any business in order to leverage your effectiveness and free up time to focus on other important activities.

Another great book that details these kinds of business models is *Bold* by Peter Diamandis and

Steven Kotler. The authors discuss how to employ new methodologies of using web based assets like Amazon's site, Mechanical Turk, and Freelancer.com to hire talent for specific tasks. On Freelancer you can hire engineers, marketers, computer coders and others to develop products and provide services that used to be only available by hiring employees and making long-term commitments. Integrating these online tools is a new way of thinking about and acquiring technical and operational assets to fulfill your business goals.

Contract workers

There is an explosion of new services using web and mobile platforms to match workers with jobs on a contract basis. These business models are called matching engines. One high profile model is Uber which matches people with cars with people needing rides, creating a flexible and efficient on-demand taxi service.

Another example is AirBnB which matches bedrooms and homes with people who need a place to stay. These services compete with taxis and hotels and they rely on the powerful network effects of the Web and ubiquitous smartphones.

Similarly, there are services connecting people with freelancers to solve their problems; companies like: Freelancer.com and Fiver. These new ways of delivering labor and services are challenging our basic assumptions of capitalism and the nature of the firm and the structure of careers.

Using these services and contracting for work with expertise all over the world has become feasible with real time Internet communication systems like Skype and Facetime along with email. Soon real time translation services will make these systems even more useful as we will be able to communicate in multiple languages instantly.

This model has been useful for professionals such as lawyers, doctors, and consulting services. Another idea is using prizes as incentive for creative ideas such as R&D solutions, design concepts such as logos, or the creation of videos. These are ways to match specialization with need and tap underused capacity.

On-demand business models have an attractive set of capabilities and advantages such as reduced need for offices and full-time permanent employees. This can be an asset for people selling their services, as well as for the virtual organizations using them. Computers are used to package a set of particular needs into another groups set of tasks. This is a way to access spare time and spare cognitive capacity, and compensate people for it across the globe.

Amazon's Mechanical Turk is a great example for this operating model. It allows customers to post any "human intelligence task" on line and it allows workers to choose what to do according to the task and price.

In Economic terms, this is part of a revolution that is unleashing latent pools of resources. Ebay has monetized the latent value of our clothes closet, garage and basement; Uber and AirBnB have monetized the under-utilized value residing in out cars and homes; and these talent pool websites are allowing people with skills to moonlight or create careers and access demand for their services around the world. These tools are creating a new generation of supply and demand based markets.

Become familiar with these services and what they offer. You may use them to build your business in a flexible and scalable manner, or you may offer your services through them to others. This is all part of a trend toward self-reliance. The role of the firm in our lives, to order our careers and provide stability, continues to be reduced. Our relationship to parental-type companies is being irrevocably modified.

Race Against the Machines

There are other profound ways in which business and work are becoming automated. Soon they will have to change the name of the department from HR to HRR: Human and Robot Resources.

The rise of Robotics and Artificial Intelligence and other cyborg related workers is changing the fundamental structure of Management, Labor and business. We are moving into a future where many businesses can scale rapidly with non-tangible products and services can be infinitely replicated. Computer programs and algorithms can also perform the interface with customers more efficiently. This trend has profound implications for how we think about work and the nature of value and productivity.

How we relate to automation not only has implications for how we think about business models and operating leverage, but also about how we perceive ourselves and our careers developing over the course of a lifetime. These developments have profound implications for our sense of self worth and how we impute meaning to our lives.

Blue collar jobs in manufacturing have been impacted over the recent decades as robotic systems have replaced workers on factory floors and assembly lines. Repetitive tasks represent relatively straightforward processes and lend themselves to automation. Now entire factories are operated by a handful of workers monitoring computer screens.

As the leadership guru Warren Bennis predicted: "The factory of the future will have only two employees, a man and a dog. The man will be there to feed the dog. The dog will be there to keep the man from touching the equipment."

The replacement of manual labor by dexterous programmable machines was the first wave of worker displacement. Worker Displacement 2.0 is now underway as Artificial Intelligence is becoming more widely implemented in practical systems. The virtual personal assistant Siri is a good example of a system that interacts via voice and incorporates language recognition and response. Siri performs tasks by searching and retrieving information and employs a voice activated user interface.

White-collar jobs are now being replaced in fields previously thought impervious to the encroachment of automation. Accountants, lawyers, and other professional fields; science and engineering jobs; courts and call centers are all affected. What we choose to train for and how we position ourselves and think of our strengths and skill sets will be tested as we are confronted with continually encroaching prescience of automation and computing power.

It will be our task to recognize, predict, and adapt to this inevitable change. We are going to be tasked with forging productive alliances with new smart tools and leverage a newly focused understanding of our human strengths in fruitful ways.

Put differently, our relationship to robots and artificial intelligence, and robots equipped with artificial intelligence will increasingly determine how happy, content, and satisfied we are in the future.

This Brave New World offers opportunities to delegate mundane repetitive tasks and even rule based thinking tasks to machines. Innovative and complementary pairing of machines and humans in hybrid models allows businesses to approach tasks in novel and productive ways.

We already recognize that tasks that are difficult for us humans are often easy for machines, and conversely, tasks that are easy for us are often complicated to implement in software and mechanical systems. But I regard this situation as an opportunity to unleash creative and energies.

Management Gurus and Consulting Firms

There is quite an industry surrounding management. A number of prestigious companies like McKinsey, Boston Consulting Group, and Bain provide management consulting services. High profile academics are involved with creating and presenting novel approaches to navigating the constantly changing business environment.

In general, academics create ideas and consulting firms parse and implement them in practical forms. This section identifies some of the main players in these areas some of the topics in leading edge thinking of the past several decades.

Consulting Practice

Management consulting is the practice of helping organizations to improve their performance. Top managers enlist consulting firms to provide insight and outside perspective.

They are tasked with analyzing organizational problems and developing plans for improvement. The main traditional management-consulting firms are Bain, McKinsey, and Boston Consulting Group. They focus on strategy consulting for their clients. The Republican presidential candidate in 2012 Mitt Romney ran Bain and created Bain Capital, their investment arm. He realized astutely that since Bain had such expertise in running companies they were leaving value on the table when they remained only advisors. If they actually owned the companies they could reap the value they created instead of just consulting fees.

Accounting firms developed lucrative management consulting practices in the latter part of the 20th century. They were well positioned to provide these services based on established relationships with clients to whom they could sell more services and further solidify relationships by getting more deeply involved in their businesses.

This model came under attack as a conflict of interest issue after the once prestigious accounting firm Arthur Andersen was compromised in its relationship with Enron. Arthur Andersen relaxed its auditing standards in order to maintain its lucrative consulting relationship with Enron. In the wake of that and other high profile conflicts of interest cases, new government regulations were instituted that made accounting firms divest of their consulting divisions.

The big accounting firms are returning to the management consulting business. The Big Four accounting firms (Deloitte, EY, KPMG and PwC) and companies like IBM and Accenture focus on operations consulting for their clients.

Management Theory

Management theory developed as an academic practice after WWII. There was an initial group of management theorists led by Peter Drucker. Drucker was a wide ranging intellectual and management consultant, educator, and author. He wrote well over 30 books on management and is considered the founder of modern management.

His writings helped develop the foundational thinking about the modern business corporation. He has influenced subsequent generations of business leaders and academics. He was also instrumental in citing the need for, and developing, management education and the modern MBA curriculum.

Peter Drucker

No management book could be complete without spending a moment discussing the immense influence of Drucker. He had a long career and huge influence due to his books, which were published from the 1940s through the early 2000s. Much of what he predicted came to pass and many of his ideas were widely adopted. Here is a list of some key ideas that run through his writings:

- Drucker favored decentralization and simplification and discounted the command and control model. He believed that companies work best when they are decentralized. He observed that corporations tend to produce too many products, hire employees they don't need (when a better solution would be outsourcing), and expand into economic sectors that they should avoid.

- He introduced the concept of "knowledge worker" in his 1959 book *The Landmarks of Tomorrow*. Since then, knowledge-based work has become increasingly important in businesses worldwide.

- He predicted the death of the "Blue Collar" worker. The changing face of the US Industry is a testimony to this prediction, first through off shoring of jobs and now through the implementation of robots and artificial intelligence.

- He created the concept of what eventually came to be known as 'outsourcing.' He used the example of "front room" and "back room" of each business: A company should be engaged in only the front room activities that are critical to supporting its core business. Back room activities should be handed over to other companies, for whom these tasks are the front room activities.

- He understood the importance of the non-profit sector, which he calls the third sector (private sector and the Government sector being the first two). Non-Government Organizations (NGOs) play crucial roles in the economies of countries around the world.

- He had a profound skepticism of macroeconomic theory. Drucker contended that economists of all schools fail to explain significant aspects of modern economies.

- He contested the long-standing opinion that the main focus of microeconomics is price, citing its lack of showing what products actually do for us. This critique stimulated commercial interest in discovering how to calculate what products actually do for us, how to think of value, value creation, and value proposition as opposed to price.

- He believed in respect for the worker and regarded employees as assets not liabilities. He taught that knowledgeable workers are the essential ingredients of the modern economy. Central to this philosophy is the view that people are an organization's most valuable resource, and that a manager's job is both to prepare people to perform and give them freedom to do so

- He believed in what he called "the sickness of government." Drucker made nonpartisan claims that government is often unable or unwilling to provide new services that people need and/or want, though he believed that this condition is not intrinsic to the form of government. The chapter "The Sickness of Government" in his book *The Age of Discontinuity* formed the basis of New Public Management, a theory of public administration that dominated the discipline in the 1980s and 1990s.

- He stressed the need for "planned abandonment." Businesses and governments have a natural human tendency to cling to "yesterday's successes" rather than seeing when they are no longer useful.
- He believed that taking action without thinking is the cause of every failure.
- He stressed the need for community. Early in his career, Drucker predicted the "end of economic man" and advocated the creation of communities where an individual's social needs could be met. By the 1980s, he suggested that volunteering in the nonprofit sector was a key way to fostering a healthy society where people found a sense of belonging and civic pride.
- He stressed the need to manage business by balancing a variety of needs and goals, rather than subordinating an institution to a single value. This concept of management by objectives and self-control forms the keynote of his 1954 landmark book *The Practice of Management*.
- He firmly believed that a company's primary responsibility is to <u>serve its customers</u>. Profit is not the primary goal, but rather an essential condition for the company's continued existence and sustainability.
- He believed in the notion that great companies could stand among humankind's noblest inventions.

- He developed the_business tagline "Do what you do best and outsource the rest" in the 1990s. The slogan was primarily used to advocate outsourcing as a viable business strategy. Drucker began explaining the concept of outsourcing as early as 1989 in his Wall Street Journal (WSJ) article entitled "Sell the Mailroom".

Drucker's work had a tremendous impact on the management thinking in Japan and its rise to industrial prominence in the 1980s.

Management Pundits

Here are a few other influential management thinkers whose names and work you should be familiar with.

Tom Peters came to prominence in the mid 1980s with *In Search of Excellence.*

Michael Porter came to prominence with his insightful analysis of the structure of industries and the dynamics of competition.

In the past couple of decades, management theory has been driven by two economic shifts of tectonic scale: the digital revolution in computers and the internet and the growth and expansion of developing countries like China and India. The second change has been chronicled by a brilliant group of Indian management theorists led by the work of C. K. Prahalad. Their work focuses on subjects such as

- The expanded buying power of developing country consumers, what Prahalad coined the fortune at the bottom of the pyramid.
- The virtues of frugal products and product development. An example of this is the introduction of the $4 smart phone in India.
- How to navigate the challenges of doing business in places with poor infrastructure and weak institutions.

Prahalad's famous book is *The Fortune at the Bottom of the Pyramid*.

Clayton Christensen documented the dynamics of the digital revolution with his seminal idea of disruptive innovation. This concept states that successful innovators create new markets that render existing business models obsolete and established businesses irrelevant. Think of audio cassettes and the Walkman, VCRs, cameras and film and the long list of products and businesses that have since come and gone. He is currently considered the world's leading management guru.

Christensen's famous book on the subject is *The Innovator's Dilemma*.

There is a new generation of management theorists working on how to respond to and navigate the disruptions related to technology especially robots and artificial intelligence. These new models of management and work have powerful implications for the fields of Organizational Behavior and Organizational Design.

The most profound implications for organizational behavior and design however arise from a model that is not only theoretical but has been implemented in the revolutionary and successful project that has created the largest information repository in the history of humankind: Wikipedia. Jimmy Wales is the brilliant architect of this system that is completely voluntary and non-hierarchical. Check out his TED talk to get a better understanding of how it is structured and operates.

Managing Up

We usually think of management as a project of giving orders and direction to underlings so they can carry out the tasks you have planned in order to meet your objectives. But we all have bosses and stakeholders to whom we must answer and we need to be aware and know how to manage those relationships as well.

Your job satisfaction and career depend on having a healthy and positive relationship with your boss. Consciously trying to reduce potential frictions in this relationship will make your life so much easier. Some bosses are wonderful people and patient understanding mentors. Some bosses are stone-cold assholes. War stories about bad bosses are legendary and I will bet you have a few of your own. No matter what your boss's temperament, it's in your best interest, and your responsibility, to make the relationship function.

There are many reasons why people higher up the ladder that you must deal with are difficult. In many cases, managers are overextended or overwhelmed. As you move up the management hierarchy, workloads tend to expand with responsibilities and managers not used to delegating can find themselves swamped.

A great way to enhance your relationship and make yourself indispensible is to look for opportunities to take on work and take the burden off your boss. No one is indispensable, but you can *make yourself* so valuable to your company that your boss will think that she *can't* possibly *get along without you.*

Some bosses are downright incompetent and they were promoted into a position of incompetency. This situation is called the Peter Principle which states that in an organizational hierarchy, employees will rise or get promoted to their level of incompetence. And that is where they will languish. They will fail to get promoted beyond a certain job because it has become too challenging for them.

The Peter Principle was first observed by Dr. Laurence J. Peter His book *The Peter Principle* was first published in 1968. He sums up the Peter Principle with the saying: "the cream rises until it sours." The Peter Principle can be solved to some degree through continued education and training. But even with proper employee management training this is a major challenge of organizational behavior.

Organizations tend to get clogged with middle management unsuited to the tasks confronting them. Over time, someone who is not competent enough to carry out his or her new duties will fill every position in the hierarchy. Your boss may have, in fact, arrived at that level. The Harvard Business Review ran a special series on managing up, asking experts to provide their best practical advice for navigating this dynamic.

A summary of these pieces provides a good primer on how to maintain an effective, productive working relationship with your own boss. For more information Google "Managing Up" and find links to HBR pieces. The following is adapted and excerpted from their work.

There are different types of manager so consider the type you have. Different types pose different sets of challenges and require an equally unique set of skills to handle. Perhaps you're dealing with:

- A brand new boss, someone you've never met before.
- A manager you don't see face-to-face because she works in another location
- An insecure boss
- An all-knowing or indecisive boss
- A manager who gives you conflicting messages

- A long-winded boss
- A hands-off boss
- A manager who isn't as smart as you
- A boss that's actually a board of directors

No matter what type of manager you have, there are some skills that are universally important. For example, you need to know how to anticipate your boss's needs. The best executive assistants offer a good model. You need to understand what makes your boss tick, and what ticks her off, if you want to get buy-in for your ideas. Problems will inevitably come up, but knowing the right way to bring a problem to your boss can help you navigate sticky situations. There will, of course, be times when you disagree with your boss. Learned to disagree in a respectful, productive way.

Despite your best efforts to build a good relationship, there may come a time when you've lost your boss's trust. It happens. And while it may take some diligent effort on your part, it *is* possible put the relationship back on track, even if you feel like your boss doesn't like you.

If you feel this talk of bad bosses doesn't apply to you and think, "I have a great boss," be careful. Being too friendly with your manager can be equally tricky. Working relationships without enough professional distance can deteriorate quickly. You also don't want your boss to be your only advocate at work. You need to find ways to demonstrate your worth to those above her as well.

The most important skill to master is figuring out how to be a genuine source of help — because managing up doesn't mean sucking up. It means being the most effective employee you can be, creating value for your boss and your company. That's why the best path to a healthy relationship begins and ends with doing your job, and doing it well.

Managing Forward

Managing forward, also known as managing expectations, is the skill of setting and communicating realistic goals, targets, and timetables. This is important so that harboring overly optimistic expectations doesn't disappoint others.

Managing expectations is an underrated skill. We need to be aware of, and develop it as a skill set, so we can avoid a lot of the drama that goes on in every office, and in our personal relationships.

Emotional drama engendered from disappointment impedes our ability to focus on and accomplish important tasks. Things get delayed, derailed, and mired in minutia. Not managing expectations well can be very costly.

The value and importance of managing expectations can be seen in the markets. Value is lost in public company stocks when analyst and investor expectations are not met.

Promise Less, Deliver More

Leaders who are adept at managing expectations are able to more seamlessly navigate the obstacles of their business and personal lives. They know how to communicate, organize, and direct conversations to focus around getting things accomplished. When expectations are not met, or *perceived* not to be met, leaders lose credibility and projects lose momentum.

Here are some strategies to improve your ability to manage expectations.

Don't Make Assumptions

And be aware of the ones you do make. Have you heard the one about Assume? When you assume, you make an ass of u and me. Ass-u-me.

Don't fall into the trap of assuming someone has the same understanding of a situation, project, deadline, or task that you do.

Avoid this snare by having a conversation in which you openly and explicitly discuss what's expected, how it might be accomplished, and how success will be measured. Our vision of the future is cloudy at best and we need to remember to communicate the various contingencies that we are aware of and also explicitly acknowledge the possibility of unexpected issues arising in the future.

We should develop strategies about how we will deal with the knowns and the unknowns. Always discuss alternate plans and develop possible work-arounds. Allow people to contribute and entertain alternatives as a way to get buy in.

Leave plenty of opportunities for questions. This is the time to agree and commit to what will be delivered, and when. *When* something is going to be completed is one of the most common points of miscommunication.

Communicate

Make a point to communicate with everyone involved frequently. Err on the side of over-communicating in the early stages of a new project or as a key milestone or deadline approaches. Low stakes conversations can eliminate surprises and help mitigate and address problems and issues.

It may appear to be time consuming more work, but it's especially important if you have a new team that isn't used to working together or new leadership that may not have developed a level of trust in the team's ability to deliver. If people feel included and aware of what is going on, they are less likely to feel ambushed by delays or budget issues.

By frequently checking in throughout the course of a project, you also have the chance to provide real-time status updates and manage any delays, risks, or contingencies.

When something unforeseen develops and becomes apparent, report it ASAP. Don't try to buy time and hide it and hope to fix it before anyone finds out. Being honest and upfront about a delay is way better than promising to deliver and missing your deadline.

Set Realistic Expectations

Expectations need to be realistic and achievable. If you don't feel the ones that are being set are realistic, you can, and should, push back. This is a negotiation. The key here is refine them in a way that acknowledges the organization's needs and balances those with the team's abilities.

People don't want to know about potential setbacks and there is an implicit incentive to over-commit so as not to rock the boat. Do not give in to this temptation to please. Confront the uncomfortable realities up front. Acknowledging limitations, and being open about what can be delivered and when, instills confidence.

This is important when designing marketing and messaging materials and is especially pertinent to on-line businesses like downloadable digital products and apps. When designing and launching minimum viable products you really need to communicate what the feature set is and manage expectations of what customers are receiving.

Speed to market is crucial and conventional wisdom has it that if you aren't a bit embarrassed by your initial offering then you waited too long to launch. When people are paying you money for something and they don't get what they expect, that's when they reach for the refund button.

Preconceptions

The challenge when managing expectations boils down to managing two variables:

1. Communication

2. Preconceptions

People have different preconceptions based on their experiences and they will use past experiences as a benchmark for what they expect from you.

Communications and Memos

Taking the time to craft explicit written directions can ultimately save a lot of time and wasted effort. Inefficiencies arise when instructions are misinterpreted, not heard, or understood incompletely. Written communications help minimize this pitfall.

Management by Email

Many people disparage email as impersonal and lacking in communication cues like eye contact, tone of voice, and body language. There is certainly truth to these criticisms but the medium's asynchronous nature and its transcendence of space more than make up for the its shortcomings.

Email is a great management tool. There is not a lot of wiggle room for interpretation of directions and tasks when they are written. It is great for disseminating to groups, and the discipline required of writing forces you to be clear in your request. Your directives are or should be explicitly laid out and clearly documented.

Emails preserve fidelity of communication, whether directed to a group or based on from person to person to person as a message is forwarded. We are all familiar with the old game of *telephone* where someone starts with a phrase and it is whispered from person to person until the last person says what they heard and then the initial person says what started and everyone laughs at the difference: Purple Monkey Dishwasher!
Avoid miscommunication. Email communications help avoid this trap.

But a word of caution: Do not become the servant of your email. Use email judiciously and continually root out unimportant sources of email.

Tim Ferris has great advice about how to help you ruthlessly rid yourself of distractions. Low priority tasks dilute focus on big impact activities.

Focus on being efficient and combating procrastination. Tim also has good advice for email habits, including not to look at email too often, use spam filters and the unsubscribe function to weed out extraneous junk mail, use auto-respond for repetitive responses, and delegate to assistants who can handle day-to-day reactive email activity.

Ferris goes so far as to say try looking at email once a day, once a week, or even longer, which might seem extreme but ultimately frees us up for more important tasks at hand.

Organizational Behavior

Organizational behavior is the study of how groups and individuals perform and interact. It applies to the fields of psychology and sociology and seeks to understand how people operate in work environments and how to better align the firm's goals with that of individuals and groups within the firm.

The understanding of individual, group, and organizational behavior can be critical to your success as a leader and manager. All of the variables that impact behavior are beyond the scope of this book. Be aware of major insights into organizational behavior when you are trying to understand individual human behavior in the workplace, and the interaction between people and the organization. Approach this discipline with the intent to understand, manage, and predict human behavior.

Organizational Design

For effective management, form matters. In order to create an organizational form that follows a viable business model and strategic function, we need to have an understanding of the various business structures and how they operate.

How a company is organized dictates how efficiently it can operate. Different organizational structures are better suited to perform in different environments of operations and addressing particular markets. Should a company be organized by functions like marketing, accounting and manufacturing, or should it be organized according to markets and integrated around the profit and loss performance of that market? The organization of departments and lines of reporting have palpable consequences for how a company is managed, how it reacts to change, and how it addresses its markets.

The way management levels are structured and the way lower level management interacts with the overall mission of the enterprise are important design concerns. The U.S. Army, for instance, has a strict hierarchical structure and obedience to orders is paramount. In contrast, the U.S. government is loosely organized and there is latitude and autonomy in carrying out directives.

When Eisenhower won election as president, the outgoing president Harry Truman remarked "Poor Ike; when he was a general, he gave an order and it was carried out. Now, he's going to sit in that office and give an order and not a damn thing is going to happen."

In today's world we can rely on email and Skype and other technologies to bring people together to work effectively without concerns for geography. We don't need to be in the same office any longer. We can contract with people with specific skill sets to create and organize teams to fulfill certain goals on a project-oriented basis.

These developments create flatter, less hierarchical organizations based on flexible networks. To accomplish our work and meet our needs in these environments, we rely on individuals and organizations over which we exercise no direct control. Purposeful management in these situations takes negotiation skill.

The value of a firm derives from its organization. Organizations driven by some form of hierarchy create economies that make doing things cheaper than buying them from a vendor. This brings up the question of when to do things in-house and when to out-source it. The answer to that question needs to be based on constant strategic assessment of the core competencies and goals of the firm.

Not too long ago, maintaining organizational control used to mean creating a hierarchical structure with layers of management aggregating and reporting up information and dictating instructions and communicating goals down the pyramid. Today, computers, other information systems, and communications networks have had led to leaner management structures and have created "flatter" organizations.

Leadership

A true leader can be defined as a person who possesses great social influence and charisma and can enlist the aid and support of others in order to manifest a vision and accomplish a common task. The genesis of all enterprise is an idea.

All projects begin as a vision through imagination. They are carried out with an attitude of great optimism: namely the belief that what is merely an image in one's mind can be made concrete in the external world. Leaders first need to convince themselves and then get people to share their conviction that this vision is worth the effort.

No doubt, the idea or the vision is crucial, but ultimately it is the execution what separates simple dreams from concrete life-enhancing or life-changing products and services. Leadership is based in inspiring the execution. Visions without action are hallucinations. T.S. Elliot said in *The Hollow Men*: "Between the idea and the act lies the shadow." The term Executive means to execute.

Leaders like athletes are tasked with playing the game while observing it as a whole. Leaders need to develop "court sense". Leaders have developed the art of keeping a sound perspective that allows them to be engaged in day-to-day tasks, yet still see the big picture without getting lost in details. This takes focus on, and devotion to the vision and a sense of the future.

Warren Bennis is an American scholar and author who widely regarded as a pioneer of the field of Leadership studies. His research in the 1960s led him to foresee a change in organizational structure toward less hierarchical, more flat and adaptive institutions.

He anticipated this trend in both private and public institutions. He has written many books on the subject of leadership and is the go-to resource for more information on the subject.

Here are some examples of Bennis' wisdom on leadership:
- Create a compelling vision, one that takes people to a new place, and then translate that vision into a reality.
- Becoming a leader is synonymous with becoming yourself. It is precisely that simple, and it is also that difficult.
- People who cannot invent and reinvent themselves must be content with borrowed postures, secondhand ideas, fitting in instead of standing out.

- Leadership is the capacity to translate vision into reality.

An enterprise is formed and organized in order to carry out tasks. Every enterprise needs a leader. The leader, whose vision is simultaneously ambitious, feasible and compelling, sets the direction. The leader must be able to articulate the vision in ways that make people want to participate in making it a reality. She must be able to create a shared sense of purpose that marshals resources in the direction of that vision and its goals.

It all starts with the vision – the idea. Developing and holding a vision takes courage and the ability to think big. Don't hold back. A big, bold, audacious vision can be a competitive and strategic advantage.

If you are living your dream, you can help others live theirs. Take time to dream and think, believe in yourself and your ideas, behave and act positively. Break down your vision into ambitious, but achievable, goals. Find and surround yourself with like-minded believers and treat them with respect.

These skills are innate in some. And some learn them. In the best cases leadership skills develop naturally from the compelling nature of the initial vision. In other words, even the leader is in thrall to the vision and feels compelled to make it happen. A truly great idea is always bigger than any individual while still needing him and her to manifest it.

317

Harvard Business School professor Howard Stevenson stated: "Entrepreneurship is the process by which individuals pursue opportunities without regard to the resources they currently control."

Bismarck defined statesmanship as the art of the possible. Both these ideas get at the heart of leadership. A leader must articulate a vision that is both desirable and feasible. Followers need to share the desire to achieve the goal and feel it is possible to attain.

Timing is a trait a leader must possess and develop. As part of feasibility of vision the development and convergence of enabling technologies, channels and markets need to be understood and clearly conveyed.

Wayne Gretzky said, "Skate where the puck is going, not where it's been." It is critically important to develop a sense of timing. The early bird gets the worm, but the second mouse gets the cheese. That can mean being persistent or waiting until the enablers are distinctly on the horizon.

The art of leadership is in navigating between being too early and not feasible and being too late and losing an opportunity to competition. This means continuously monitoring the changing technological, social, demographic, economic, legislative, political, and competitive demands of your business environment and how those changes impact implementing your vision.

Leadership requires strategic thinking. This means to continuously monitor the external environment and be ready with revising tactics to meet the strategy goals. It requires consistency and discipline to remain true to the plan, as well as the flexibility to change both plan and strategy when circumstances change.

Leaders must have a certain comfort level with change and ambiguity. Leaders need to develop the ability to objectively assess the changing needs of the organization and its stakeholders.

The Chinese have a saying "sometimes the river flows East and sometimes the river flows West". Things change with time and different ways of perception emerge. We must be aware of these changes and go with the flow.

The ability to detect emerging patterns and help them take shape is an important attribute of leadership.

A leader needs a passionate vision, skills to communicate that vision, and strategic thinking and implementation skills to make that vision reality. Focus on keeping things moving forward. Leaders are obligated to provide and maintain the momentum.
You will ultimately learn leadership and how to wield it by being in thrall to a compelling vision of the future that you want to actively participate in. It will act like a natural force like gravity and will guide you like a pole star. If you can articulate your vision to yourself and others convincingly, they will follow you and you will follow it.

The practical skills to manage and master the processes of leading are consensus building and decision-making. In our modern world organizations are formed like mosaics of the skill sets required to meet certain goals by carrying out specific tasks.

A leader needs to build consensus around the vision and generate momentum in a constant series of decision-making. In more lateral, flatter, and less hierarchical organizations the ability to carry out these tasks is done through negotiation.

Management and leadership are closely related and overlap to varying degrees based on the personality and situation. Here are some ways to look at the differences:

- The manager asks how and when; the leader asks what and why.
- The manager accepts the status quo; the leader challenges it.
- The manager has his eye on the bottom line; the leader has his eye on the horizon.

Leaders are always questioning:

- What are we doing now that we should stop doing?
- What are we not doing now, but should start doing?

- What are we doing now that we should continue to do but perhaps in a fundamentally different way?

These probing inquiries are significant and applicable to everything the organization does: its products and services, internal processes, policies and procedures, strategies, dealing with complexity and change, the fit between the enterprise and the environment. This questioning stance is part of a continuous process and mindset.

A word of caution, the following makes it sound like leaders do all the sexy and cool work. They do, but don't be seduced into thinking leadership is everything and management is something prosaic, unintellectual, and not worth much effort.

Superior execution trumps everything else in business. Great management skills are based on understanding and being able to implement in practice key concepts of how to marshal and direct resources in order to accomplish defined goals. You can't be an effective leader if no one is following or if you are not going anywhere.

To be an effective leader you must find a balance between planning and reacting to opportunities. You must decide when to plow forward in the face of obstacles and to persevere. You must know when to change direction in order to out-flank obstacles or, even more radically, to change the game altogether and pivot. You must have the wisdom of when to persevere and when to pivot and you must have trust in your convictions. This concept is as artful as life itself. This is art. Leadership is an art.

Effective leadership is about communicating a powerful vision and to continuously question and examine assumptions. It is also the ability to think and act strategically. You must develop alternative scenarios of the future, and assess and decisively pick the best one to pursue.

You need to remain realistic in your thinking without losing the power of imagination and be comfortable with continuously updating your models of the world. The wider ranging and flexible your curiosity, the more powerful and accurate you will be as a leader.

Being a generalist with broad interests is also a plus since you are aware of technological, social, and demographic changes, as well as critical changes in the legislative and political arenas. These all can affect the status and direction of an enterprise.

Strategic thinking is very much a leadership activity and quite different from what experts do. Strategic thinkers specialize in relationships and context, whereas expert thinkers specialize in well-defined disciplines and functions. A leader thinks in conceptual systems and their interrelationships.

Strategic thinkers act on intuition and instinct when information is incomplete. When data is incomplete, they focus on action, whereas experts pay rigorous attention to knowledge, evidence, and data, they focus on understanding.

A leader needs to employ strategic thinking and embrace an intellectual process that accepts change and ambiguity, analyzes the causes and outcomes of change, and attempts to direct an organization's future to capitalize on the changes.

Leading in a rapidly changing environment means you have to analyze while still being decisive. You have to understand you will never have complete information or perfect understanding of the outcome. You must be opportunistic and act with only partial and imperfect knowledge in imperfect circumstances. Teddy Roosevelt said: "Do what you can, with what you have, where you are."

Rational preplanned strategies do not always work out as planned and must be adaptable. Dealing with rapid, complex, and often discontinuous change requires flexible leadership. This means understanding the nature and implications of external change, the ability to develop effective strategies that account for change, and the will as well as the ability to actively manage the momentum of the organization.

Strategy isn't static and changes in course will emerge; one must be aware and willing to adapt and pivot.

"It is not the strongest of the species that survive, nor the most intelligent, but the one most responsive to change."

Charles Darwin

As leaders we are not simply being responsive to changes, we are charged with creating the future. The best way to predict the future is to create it. Create new visions for success and be prepared to make significant improvements along the way.

Our understanding of the future is hazy at best and impacts our clear idea of direction and purpose. To make an idea reality often means 'groping' your way to your goal.

Groping is a process of trying things and monitoring feedback as to their success. If something works, keep doing it and perhaps allocate more resources in that direction. If something doesn't work, tweak and adjust the process and see if anything positive results; if not, abandon that path.

Testing two variations at once and comparing results is called A/B testing. A/B testing has become popular as online methods to employ it and measure it have become available. Google has been an innovator in developing and providing A/B testing methodologies. Groping is a forward leaning methodology that leaders should apply.

Leadership takes constant active vigilance. If the strategy is not actively managed, it will not happen. In his great book *Leadership is an Art* Max DePree says, "The only legitimate work in an organization is work that contributes to the accomplishment of the strategic plan. It takes the orchestration of management as well as leadership to perpetuate these capabilities into the future."

When it comes to the relationship between strategy and leadership let's make a distinction between planning and plans. Plans are static documents that are by definition out of date and lack relevance. Planning is the process of analyzing future scenarios and contingencies and coming up with effective ways to exploit or avoid them. Winston Churchill put it succinctly: "Plans are useless, but planning is invaluable."

Here is a list of qualities that David Ogilvy looked for in creative leaders:

- High standards of personal ethics
- Big people, without pettiness
- Guts under pressure, resilience in defeat
- Brilliant brains – not safe plodders
- A capacity for hard work and midnight oil
- Charisma – charm and persuasiveness
- A streak of unorthodoxy – creative innovators
- The courage to make tough decisions
- Inspiring enthusiasts – with trust and gusto
- A sense of humor

This is a great list of traits to look for in others and to aspire to in yourself.

Lead Wisely

Practice humility. Intelligence, while beneficial in so many ways, can also be a burden on making good decisions. Having greater intelligence can sometimes make you a more foolish person because intelligence breeds hubris. When a person starts thinking they are smart relative those around them, they develop blind spots to cognitive biases that ultimately compromise their ability to understand the world.

On the other hand, one can over-think a decision, or defer making one while continuing to ruminate. This is known as paralysis by analysis. Good leaders have a bias towards action.

Intelligence can also hamper learning. Intelligence can be a hindrance that prevents you from moving past mistakes r learning from them. Intelligent people find it more difficult to maintain an awareness of their own biases. When we become aware of our ingrained biases, we move from being intelligent to being wise.

Be humble about your own abilities. Greek tragedies are based on the consequences of hubris. Intelligence can actively impair our ability to make good decision because we believe in our own superiority. Relying too much on raw intelligence can come at the cost of listening to others' point of view and considering new ideas. Don't forget: You need as many ideas as you can get.

If you surround yourself with stellar people you will not have to exert leadership in any overt manner. Give them a direction, turn them loose and be open to the various ways of approaching problems and attaining solutions that the come up with.

Listen to others and consider new ideas.
Here is some more sage advice from Warren Bennis: "There are two ways of being creative. One can sing and dance. Or one can create an environment in which singers and dancers flourish." He also said: "I am reminded how hollow the label of leadership sometimes is and how heroic fellowship can be." In other words, it is not always about overtly being out in front leading a charge.

"Because the awakened one puts himself behind, he steps ahead. Because he gives way, he gains. Because he is selfless, he fulfills himself. The still is the lord of the restless."
                    Lao-Tzu

Leadership and Communication

Effective communication consists in the right people getting the right information, at the right time. Our job is to target the message and the timing.
Leaders communicate and drive the organization by articulating a common mission, a common vision, and a common set of organizational values and goals. These elements define the essential vision of the

organization and greatly depend on the leadership's ability to communicate it.

There needs to be a fit between the direction and vision of what the organization wants to do and what the organization *can* do. This takes gathering the resources, competencies, and capabilities in the organization. You need to create the organizational capabilities to achieve the stated strategic goals and match the messaging to that fit. It is an utter waste of time to encourage people to do things they don't have the resources to achieve.

Email is a great tool for disseminating the message and creating clear unambiguous communication. Here are ten tips from a great communicator David Olgilvy:

"Good writing is not a natural gift. You have to learn to write well. Here are 10 hints:

1. Read the Roman-Raphaelson book on writing. Read it three times.
2. Write the way you talk. Naturally.
3. Use short words, short sentences and short paragraphs.
4. Never use jargon words like 'conceptualize,' 'demassification,' 'attitudinally,' 'judgmentally.' They are hallmarks of pretense.
5. Never write more than two pages on any subject.
6. Check your quotations.
7. Never send a letter or a memo on the day you write it. Read it aloud the next morning—and then edit it.

8. If it is something important, get a colleague to improve it.

9. Before you send your letter or your memo, make sure it is crystal-clear what you want the recipient to do.

10. If you want ACTION, don't write. Go and tell the guy what you want."

This is a memo he wrote to his staff. We need to aspire to write well and communicate as effectively.

Here are some more tips on writing clearly for effective communication from the CIA manual (the CIA Style Guide is available at http://fas.org/irp/cia/product/style.pdf):

- Keep the language crisp and pungent; prefer the forthright to the pompous and ornate.

- Do not stray from the subject; omit the extraneous, no matter how brilliant it may seem or even be.

- Favor the active voice and shun streams of polysyllables and prepositional phrases.

- Keep sentences and paragraphs short, and vary the structure of both.

- Be frugal in the use of adjectives and adverbs; let nouns and verbs show their own power.

The CIA understands that their intelligence reporting is only as good as their ability to communicate it. Stay focused and stick to the subject. Be clear about what you want done. Look at every word in a sentence and decide if they are really needed. If not, kill them. Be ruthless.

Pay special attention to the power positions in your writing. These are:

- Title

- First Sentence

- Introduction

- Transition sentences

- Argument sentence

- Theme sentence

- Conclusion

- Final Sentence

Maintain emphasis on what is significant: the Purpose, the Call to Action, the Take-away, the Promise. Think of the reader asking "so what?" while reading your piece and answer that question continuously while writing it. What you are asking the reader to do? Describe and point to future directions that inspire with a challenge or rallying call.

The Recap is especially important since there you state what you want. Link back to the intro but remember the recapitulation is not a repeat of what has come before. State it differently and get your point across. Finish strong. Make it memorable. Make it sticky.

In today's world we can rely on email and Skype and other technologies to bring people together to work effectively without concerns for geography. We don't need to be in the same office any longer. We can contract with people with specific skill sets to create and organize teams to fulfill certain goals on a project-oriented basis. These developments create flatter, less hierarchical organizations based on networks.

To accomplish our work and meet our needs we rely on a mosaic of individuals and organizations over whom we exercise no direct control.

Purposeful management in these situations takes negotiation skill.

Become a Better Negotiator

Introduction

This section is designed and intended to help you start thinking about negotiation as a learnable skill that you can develop and hone to resolve conflicts, build agreements, and get deals done.

Negotiations have been carried out for as long as humans have existed. It could be argued that beating a fellow caveman with a club was simply negotiating by other means. Negotiations have become more nuanced, if not always more civil, over time and have produced treaties and trade agreements and have resolved myriad disputes.

New World; New Rules

In today's business world we can effectively assemble a team of world-class talent around any set of tasks we are confronting and get things done quickly, efficiently, and cost effectively.

We can use online platforms that match us with contract workers either to provide our skill sets for hire or locate and contract skills and expertise we need. We don't need to live near each other or be in the same office in order to productively work together. We can email, Skype, GoToMeeting, and other technologies to bring people together to work effectively without concerns for geography. Open up a Skype channel and the person can be next to you all day collaborating in real time.

We don't need to be co-located in the same office any longer. And the positions no longer need to be permanent. We can assemble the mosaic of talent specific to a particular project or phase of a project. Teams ebb and flow and breathe as the enterprise expands, contracts, and evolves.

We can contract with people best suited to a job and create and organize teams to fulfill our vision and goals. This turbo charged approach to human resources is a boon to productivity. But without the clear lines of authority inherent in a static organization, challenges arise.

To accomplish our work, and meet our deliverables, in this new paradigm we rely on individuals and organizations over whom we exercise no direct control. Purposeful management in these situations takes negotiation skill.

Negotiation, Management and Leadership

In this new world where direct lines of authority have transformed into networks of collaboration, negotiation has become the primary form of decision-making and a key to management and leadership.

To get what we want we are compelled to negotiate.

Pyramids of power are shifting into networks of negotiation. The communications revolution has created the ability to form global "virtual" organizations with cross-cultural transactions. And these organizations morph and mutate as the tasks at hand change.

We are participating in a negotiation revolution as we move towards collaboration and cooperation and away from adversarial competitive models and modes of behavior.

We have come to understand that wise agreement is better for both sides than the alternative. This approach is called Principled Negotiation.

Principled Negotiation

The idea behind Principled Negotiation is to use a methodology that removes emotions and egos from the process by agreeing to work together to address concerns rather than trick, win or beat up each other in order to achieve domination. It incorporates agreed upon objective standards to evaluate options and uses collaborative brainstorming sessions to come up with those options.

This process can work in two sided deal making or in complex multi-sided negotiations.

Principled Negotiation is based on engaging all interested parties in a joint search for mutual gains and applying legitimate standards for assessing various options. It is a brainstorming process of finding opportunities and searching for solutions that are better for all sides.

In order to make a negotiation process predictably functional we must separate the people from the problem, brainstorm possible solutions and alternatives, and use objective criteria to judge the alternatives. We must also know your bottom line and come up with our best alternative in case we can't arrive at a satisfactory negotiated solution.

This process is all about engaging the other side in exploring mutually beneficial solutions and agreements. This methodology not only makes the process work, it also creates agreements that are less likely to fall apart.

Navigating Agreement

The idea of navigating negotiations in order to achieve agreement and conflict resolution made a big advance in the early 1980s with the publication of a book called *Getting to Yes.*
Getting to Yes is the book that revolutionized the process of negotiating. It did so by articulating a methodology that can be applied to any negotiating scenario to help increase the odds of a beneficial outcome for all parties.

Getting to Yes was first published in 1981 by Roger Fisher and William Ury. It has gone through a number of editions and has spawned a slew of books and research going into more depth on various aspects of negotiation. Roger Fisher has since died. William Ury is still the most prominent expert on negotiations in the world. He is the co-founder of the Program on Negotiation at Harvard Law School. Its Negotiation Project offers many training programs and lots of great free information through its website, blog, and emails.

This section relies heavily on the ideas and concepts first detailed in *Getting to Yes* and its follow on book *Getting Past No.* These books are both well worth reading.

General Criteria

The first question to ask in any negotiation is what it should accomplish. A negotiating method should provide a high probability process of accomplishing the specific goals while meeting these three general criteria:

- It should do no harm and feasibly improve the relationships
- It should be orderly and productive
- It should produce an enlightened and sustainable agreement

The Problem

Positional Bargaining

In a typical negotiation the different parties stake out an emotionally charged position, argue for it and vehemently against the other, and ultimately end up making concessions along that narrow spectrum in order to reach a compromise. This is an arbitrary and inefficient process that leads to less than optimal results. What happens is that both sides' egos get entangled with their interests and these congeal into opposing positions. Each side then becomes committed to these hardened positions.

Hard Bargaining

Hard bargaining ensues where one side is bent on "winning" at the expense of the other side. This zero-sum approach is usually coupled with arguments and disparaging remarks aimed at the other side and endangers any ongoing relationship.

In a hard bargaining scenario neither side will budge from its position as that would be regarded as losing or giving in. These ossified positions get confused with principles and no one wants to feel, or be perceived, as abandoning their principles.

This standoff is inefficient and, worse, can end up provoking bitter feelings if one or both sides feel treated unfairly or disrespected. That can arouse behavior looking to sabotage any tentative agreement.

Splitting the Difference

Splitting the difference is a popular strategy. Whatever is being contested just split into two or however many equal pieces as there are parties and divide it up. It seem equitable and fair but gets complicated in multi dimensional negotiations. And various sides in a negotiation rarely weight issues exactly the same. Splitting the difference in bargaining is not effective because it doesn't address the legitimate concerns of the parties.

There is an insightful biblical tale that illustrates how splitting the difference is not optimal and uses it as a ploy to create a wise outcome.

Judgment of Solomon

The Biblical parable of the Judgment of Solomon is recounted in 1 Kings 3:16-28. It tells of two young women who came to King Solomon for wise counsel in settling a dispute. Both women claimed to be the mother of a baby they presented.

After deliberating on the issue, Solomon called for a sword. He declared that there was only one fair solution: the child must be split in two, each woman receiving half of the child. Upon hearing this stunning verdict, the boy's true mother exclaimed, "give the baby to her, just don't kill him!" The sociopathic imposter cried out, "It shall be neither mine nor yours—divide it!"

The king had precipitously discovered the true nature of the impasse and declared the first mother as the true mother. A genuine, loving mother would rather surrender her baby to another than have it in any way hurt. He presented her the baby. King Solomon's judgment is considered an example of profound wisdom.

In this instance splitting the difference would in no way address the legitimate concerns of the parties. This parable is the origin of the phrase "splitting the baby" when making concessions between two hardened positions. In most cases narrowly focused concessions also do not address the legitimate concerns of the parties. We need to think creatively and expansively along multiple dimensions of concerns, interests, and needs in order to craft wise agreements.

Soft Bargaining

Being nice and giving in is not the answer either. The standard tactics in soft negotiating are to eagerly make offers and concessions, overly trust the other side, try to be conciliatory, and to yield as a necessary maneuver to no order avoid confrontations. People who perceive themselves to be in positions of limited power many times employ these soft tactics. They then resent the outcome and do what they can to sabotage the results. While the concept of soft negotiating emphasizes the importance of building and maintaining a relationship, resentment and passive aggressive behavior will threaten to undo any agreement that is reached.

Most people see their choices in negotiating strategies as between these two styles of positional bargaining: soft and hard. Both run the risk of producing a careless, unsystematic, unsustainable, inefficient agreement. Don't bargain over positions.

The Alternative

A sustainable agreement must address all parties' interests so that no one feels short changed and thus apt to disrupt or sabotage the deal. We need a process that produces wise agreements, efficiently and amicably and that is what the principled negotiation process delivers.

The Process: PIANO

A straightforward method of negotiating on the merits of legitimate interests can be defined in five strategic steps. These five elements can be employed in any situation to strike a deal or resolve conflict. Each stage in the method addresses an element of the negotiation process. To help make the stages memorable I have created an acronym **PIANO** where each letter stands for an element in the process:

People: Detach the individuals from the problem.

Interests: Emphasize interests, not postures.

Alternatives: Invent multiple options looking for mutual gains.

Norms: Insist that the result be based on objective standards.

Option: Have a clear idea of your course if you cannot strike an acceptable deal.

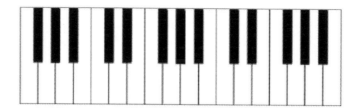

People: Detach the individuals from the problem

The first element addresses the fact that we are emotional beings. Emotions and egos tend to get mixed up with the objective merits of the issue we are attempting to resolve. We risk getting frustrated and angry and expressing volatile feelings aimed at wounding the other side. The other sides are susceptible to the same dynamic and, if not checked, this scenario can escalate quickly. Wounding words are unproductive and cannot be recalled. The process can be derailed before any real issues are even discussed let alone alternative solutions explored.

If we begin by separating the people from the problem, and make this intention clearly stated, then all sides can focus on the issues and problems and not on seeing the other negotiators as the embodiment of those problems.

Ad Hominem

This is not a new or novel idea and was known as a trap to the ancients. Classical logic and rhetoric are concerned with persuasion through constructing and communicating proper and correct arguments. Logical fallacies identify a group of faulty arguments to be aware of so we don't fall into the trap of using them or falling for them.

One of the most famous is the "argumentum ad hominem" or ad hominem for short. Ad hominem is Latin for "to the person". It represents a negotiating pitfall in which an argument is countered by attacking the character, motive, or other attribute of the person making the argument rather than attacking the substance of the argument itself.

Communications

Under the best of circumstances we tend to have difficulty communicating clearly both in stating our needs and in listening and understanding the needs of the other side. It is critically important to have thoughtfully prepared talking points of where our interests lie and be able to explain what is important to us and what feelings the current situation arouses in us. Sticking and returning to our prepared talking points will discipline us not to stray off message and over time clearly communicate our needs and desires relative to the issues and problems we are attempting to address.

Listening is the other side of effective communication. Listen with the intent to understand. If you can understand the other side's concerns you can craft a wise solution. Conflicts can be resolved and deals struck when we perceive that the other side's concerns, needs and issues my not lie along the same axis as ours. In many cases both sides can get what they need if there is a genuine understanding of those needs.

Take the time to actively listen to what the other sides are conveying. A good practice is to repeat back what you believe they are saying. Through this process the other side can agree that you understand them or provide more insight into their perceptions of the situation. When the other side realizes that you are genuinely trying to understand their point of view they will become more liable to listen to your point of view and attempt to understand it.

Critiques and arguments should always be addressed at the problem not at the person. First disentangle any people issues. The participants should commit to working together attacking the problem, not each other. Separate the people from the problem.

Interests: Emphasize interests, not postures

The second element is about unbundling positional posturing from genuine interests. The object of negotiation is to come to an understanding that satisfies and addresses the legitimate interests of the parties.

Adopting a negotiating posture often clouds the underlying interest of what is really important to you and compromising between postured positions is not likely to optimally address what you really are after. Don't limit your options in this way. Focus on interests.

Alternatives: Invent multiple options looking for mutual gains

The third element relates to crafting optimal solutions. The idea is to take this process off-line and brainstorm creative alternatives in a stress free environment. This is the step where free reign creativity comes in. Check out the section on Creativity and Brainstorming later in this book. The goal here is to brainstorm lots of possibilities that promote shared interests and solve common concerns.

This should not be done on the fly or improvised during face-to-face negotiations. Trying to decide or frame options in the presence of an adversary narrows your field of vision of potential alternatives. Pressure and having a lot at stake inhibits creativity.

Before trying to reach an agreement, invent options for mutual gain. Do this during a brainstorming session when you plan and prepare for your negotiation.

Norms: Insist that the result be based on objective standards

Insisting on using objective standards is the fourth element. Agreeing to use a fair standard that is independent of either party is a critical part of overcoming the intransigence of arbitrary positions and posturing. Criteria like market value or appraised value, expert opinion, or law is a way for both sides to defer to a fair solution.

Identifying and agreeing on such criteria allows both parties the opportunity to impartially and objectively search among alternatives for the best outcome. Use objective criteria to assess the pros and cons of various outcomes and judge their value in such terms.

If this is executed well, neither party will feel like they give in to the other. Having agreed upon objective criteria to judge the outcome also allows parties to save face and to communicate the results to their constituencies that may be more suspect of the outcome since they were not involved directly in the negotiations. This helps agreements get ratified and also helps make them more sustainable in the long run.

Agreeing on an objective standard to judge the proposals can be a significant step toward finding a workable solution. Working together and agreeing on criteria fosters a sense of common goals and trust in the outcome.

Options: Have a clear idea of your course if you cannot strike an acceptable deal

You need a credible and feasible Plan B. This process, however rational and methodical, is not a magic formula. Not all deals or negotiations end up with an acceptable solution for a variety of reasons. It could be because of belligerence or intransience, complexity or terms.

Sometimes the parties remain too far apart. We are not trying to achieve a deal or negotiated solution at any cost.

The fifth element is about knowing what your limits are and not going beyond them. A negotiation can become seductive and we must protect ourselves from over-reaching. The heady atmosphere of an auction is an example of a situation where people may lose themselves in the moment and over bid. Auctioneers rely on and cultivate this behavior.

We need to be able to resist this siren's call. The best way to do this is to have prepared our bottom line. Like the disciplined gambler in the Kenny Rodger's song, we need to know when to fold 'em and when to walk away.

We lose all our leverage if we are not ready to abandon a deal if it looks like we are not going to find a suitable solution. This means we have to have a planned alternative to an agreement. We must plan what the alternative plan is and be willing to take it.

Four Stages

The process takes place in four stages: analysis, planning, discussion and closing. In each stage all five elements come into play in different ways.

Analysis

During the analysis stage you are attempting to assess the situation. This means gathering information, organizing it, and thinking about it. You consider all the differing perceptions, hostile emotions, and unclear communications flailing about. In order to be successful, you must really understand your interests and goals, as well as those of the other side.

This is the stage where you parse the problem. Unbundle the various components of the problem so you can consider them and reassemble them into possible solutions. List options already discussed and on the table, as well as any criteria that have been suggested as a potential basis for agreement.

Planning

During the planning stage you generate ideas relative to the five elements in play and decide what actions to take. How are you going to handle the people issues? What are the most important of your issues? How are they ranked?
What are some realistic objectives?

This is the time to generate more alternatives and criteria for deciding among them. It is also the time to detail your bottom line where you will discontinue negotiating and move on to your next best option.

Discussion

During this stage the parties communicate back and forth searching for agreement. Again, the five elements are the best way to structure these communications. Problems concerning people, such as feelings of frustration or anger and differences in point of view need to be addressed.

Difficulties in communications can be acknowledged and talked about. Each side should develop an understanding of the interests of the other side. At that point, both can jointly generate and review options with an eye toward promoting mutual advantages. This is the time to seek agreement on standards for resolving conflicting interests.
This is an iterative stage in the process. This means based on feedback from the discussions and the proposals that are floated, the parties can go back and

reassess and refine their positions moving closer to a solution.

Closing

When agreement is reached, waste no time in drafting any formal documents or contracts and execute them ASAP. Deals can stall and fall apart surprisingly fast if the momentum to close is not urgently pursued.

That outlines the process and the stages of negotiation. Now let's spend some time looking at the process of creativity and how to think creatively to create Alternatives that can then be explored.

Creativity and Brainstorming

Negotiating is a creative act. To navigate conflict and strike a sustainable win-win agreement you need to think creatively. Creative thinking is a skill that can be developed and improved. Creativity is not just for artists and musicians.
Commercial enterprises need to create new products and services that have value for customers. Innovation and invention require novel ideas. Businesses need to solve problems and overcome obstacles. All solutions to problems start as ideas. These are all creative endeavors.

Creativity is usually thought of as an innate talent that people are born with. People are either creative or not, the thinking goes. Creativity is shrouded in mystery and the creative process in mystical mumbo jumbo.

There is the romantic idea of the lone creative genius who has a Eureka moment and something entirely new pops into their head. But creativity is actually synthetic, meaning it is a process that takes known ideas and combines them in a novel way. And this type of creativity can be learned, developed and improved upon.

Creativity is a name for the process of putting concepts and ideas together in new ways. It is a form of systems thinking. It has to do with pattern recognition and pattern forming. It has to do with taking ideas that work in one domain and applying them in another. This is how creativity performs the synthesis of using ideas and concepts as raw material and extruding new ideas.

Sir Isaac Newton who invented calculus and physics, two giant ideas that revolutionized our world, said "If I have seen further than others, it is by standing upon the *shoulders of giants.*"
One of the prerequisites of being creative is to remain curious and devour information from a wide range of subjects.

Creativity is either combining seemingly disparate concepts in a new way or repurposing an idea from one application to another. This is called lateral thinking.

The concept of lateral thinking is related to creativity and problem solving. Lateral thinking is a concept introduced by Edward de Bono. He has written extensively on the subject since the 1960s. Lateral thinking is an approach to creativity and solving problems that is contrasted with step-by-step logic.

In our current world, we have many newly developed platforms and technologies that can be reassembled in novel ways. Thinking about them laterally and figuring out how they can be used to solve problems is a strategy to foster innovation and invention.

Creativity is combining things in novel ways. Arthur Koestler thought of this combinatorial nature of creativity as "bisociation". Routine skills of thinking operate on one plane of thought. A creative act of thinking resides in the collision of two or more thought planes that, out of habit, have not been put together before. And it takes imaginative effort.

Humor works in this way. It is a process of putting two things together in a way you weren't expecting. Creativity works in similar ways in art, science, and business.

Being creative and cultivating creativity is not just for artists. Developing a working knowledge of the creative process is fundamental to being successful. Creativity is critical in all aspects of business. It is a fundamental part of problem solving and conflict resolution. Marketing, Branding, Advertising depend on creative approaches. Brainstorming alternatives in

351

planning negotiations relies on creativity. Product and services and their continuous improvement are creative processes. Deal making is always creative. Leadership is an art; it is creative. Business is a creative act.

Creativity is combinatorial and innovation is collaborative. Getting a diverse group of people to collaborate towards goals that require creative solutions is the essence of managing and leading. You need to get people from different disciplines with different expertise to contribute as peers to an outcome that isn't known in advance. You have to be open to ideas regardless of their origin and create the right environment for them to flourish.

Ideas can come from anywhere. Have humility in the face of creativity. Senior people in companies don't have a monopoly on ideas. Neither does long experience. In fact, experience can hinder creative thinking by limiting possibilities because "it's always been done this way". Encourage ideas from all staff. You need all the ideas you can get.

Cultivate a creative environment. Another quote from Ogilvy is helpful here: "Kill grimness with laughter. Maintain an atmosphere of informality. Encourage exuberance. Get rid of sad dogs who spread gloom."

There is a tension between action and contemplation in management and leadership. Being decisive is a key attribute of a good leader. But it is equally important to think and plan strategically and that takes

352

time and contemplation. We have to be thoughtful and disciplined not to let our tendency to act all the time get in the way of giving ourselves time for deeper uninterrupted thought.

Creativity is not the exclusive domain of some "creative class." It is something we all need to be aware of developing and continuously improving so we can negotiate better and make better decisions based on more compelling visions.

Negotiation Summary

This section outlines a powerful method for negotiating agreement, problem solving, and conflict resolution. This method should be the basis for a joint decision-making process that promotes cooperation and collaboration. Principled negotiation emphasizes a focus on defining basic interests, creating mutually satisfying options, and using fair standards that more often than not have the potential for ending in a wise agreement.

This method is not just applicable to business deals. It is really productive in social settings where maintaining the relationship is paramount but promoting your interests and needs is also important like dealing with family and friends.
In organizational settings it will help you manage those who report to you as well as lateral relationships with colleagues and also bosses.

Operations and Supply Chain Management

How do you make and deliver things in the most cost effective and efficient ways and also maintains the highest quality?

Operations and Supply Chain Management (OSCM) is the heart of a business. It is the skill sets, tools and techniques of creating and delivering products and services. It's all about systems of production and getting stuff to customers.

OSCM is the design, operation and continuous improvement of the systems that create and deliver what an enterprise is selling. OSCM is the series of steps and processes where inputs are transformed into the finished good and that good is delivered into the hands of the customer.

Optimizing the parameters of these systems requires trade-offs between performance measures such as low cost, high quality, and flexibility.

One strategy to outpace the competition and create competitive barriers is to rapidly scale. Rapid increases in scale and scope require the deployment of an effective OSCM strategy.

The Industrial Revolution was predicated on nascent ideas of OSCM. These ideas were put into practice as the divisions of labor, the assembly line, and analyzing productivity and efficiency.

Productivity and efficiency were brutal back in the day; like how many pins could an eight year old make in a typical 12-hour shift. We have tamed a lot of those issues through regulation and oversight, making a kinder, gentler work place. We no longer rely on slave labor or child labor. But it is still a problem in some of the outsourced areas like factories in Bangladesh and enormous labor cities like FoxConn runs.

The goals of OSCM is to manage and reduce costs through increased productivity, cost reductions, sourcing and procuring, and increased efficiencies and effectiveness in the chains of logistics.

It also involves planning and estimating supply and demand, which is used to coordinate and orchestrate the relative quantities and levels of all these activities. There are two key terms to define in relation to key performance indicators and the relevant business goals:

Efficiency: doing something at the lowest possible cost

Effectiveness: doing the right things to create the most value for the company

OCSM can be categorized into these five sequential steps: planning, sourcing, making, delivering, and returning.

OSCM is the set of strategic skills and tools that big retailers like Walmart have used to become successful. Walmart is the largest private employer in the US. For Walmart, leveraging economies of scope and scale is a key strategic element of their success. It is a strategy of ruthlessly optimizing OSCM. McDonald's also has become hugely successful by applying OCSM to create inexpensive fast food of uniform quality.

Hot topics in the field are lean supply chains and sustainability, which increase the efficiency and environmental impact of supply chain processes.

Inventory control and the use of computational methods to optimize systems are another key element of OSCM. Measuring efficiencies such as how long it takes to make a product and measures of quality and defects are important concepts in continually improving OSCM processes. Methodologies like Six Sigma measure and aim to reduce the statistical likelihood of defects to minimal levels.

Computers and information systems are used to gather and codify these metrics. The managerial focus is placed on understanding the implications of the collected information and to how make good informed decisions based on it.

The constant evolution of information technologies has made it feasible and cost effective to capture information directly from the source through systems such as point-of-sale (POS), identification tagging, non-invasive testing for defects, bar code reading and image recognition.

Let's break it down.

Operations refers to the process steps used to transform the resources employed by the company such as raw materials, labor, machines and scheduling, into products that are desired by customers. It can be a physical or electronic product, or a service, or some combination of both.

Supply Chain refers to the processes that move information and material to and from the manufacturing or service and then on to customers. It also includes dealing with follow on support and returns.

Basically you don't want to order too many supplies (or too little), build more than you can sell (or not enough and lose out on customers). You don't want to be carrying too much inventory, which is costly and can become obsolete. You want just as much as you need, when you need it, and you want to turn your products around fast and out the door and into the hands of customers.

Digital products have streamlined things by eliminating some of these concerns. Digital downloads are available anytime and anywhere. You don't need to get them into a physical store and display them for sale. Distribution issues evaporate. The same with inventory concerns. Each digital copy is relatively costless.

Physical products have many more concerns and vectors to optimize when it comes to OSCM.

There is a large body of work and expertise that has developed around OSCM since the 1980s when Toyota started employing these techniques throughout their manufacturing process. Toyota began holding their suppliers to higher standards and treating them like the strategic partners they are.

Networked computers have played an immense role in knitting together and coordinating these activities. There is emphasis now on the importance of being lean and green to ensure competitiveness.

It is obviously critical to successfully manage the entire supply flow: from the sources and supplies, through the value-added processes you do in your business, and on to your customers and delivery. To do this well you need to know what tools and techniques have been developed and are available to you to implement in your own creative and strategic ways.

If you are going to be involved directly in making products or providing services you need to know how best to design, supply and run the processes. OSCM is a mix of managing people and applying technology. The goal is to efficiently create value and wealth by supplying quality goods and services. It's the details that count. The deity, or the devil, is in the details.

Supply Chains and the Global Economy

There are lots of people that have done incredible things that impact our lives in myriad ways, but they are not famous household names.

One such individual is Malcom McLean. Well, he's not totally obscure. In 2000, the International Maritime Hall of Fame named him "Man of the Century". And, if your like me, you follow the proceedings of the International Maritime Hall of Fame with keen interest and enthusiasm.

His insight single handedly transformed our global economy by creating the fundamental component of modern supply chains.

He was an inventor and entrepreneur who developed the modern intermodal shipping container. The intermodal container revolutionized transport and international trade in the second half of the twentieth century.

You've seen those containers stacked on docks in modern ports, on the decks of cargo ships, on railroad cars, and 18-wheelers.

The brilliance of the container is that it standardizes the entire global transportation workflow. The container is an 8x8x40 box. They are even used to make groovy dwellings.

Companies load their goods right into the containers on eight-foot wide pallets using forklifts. Then the box becomes a freight car that is loaded aboard ships with those huge cranes and then offloaded at another port onto a truck bed and driven to its destination's loading platform, and then onto the shelves of your favorite store.

This is the infrastructure of the global supply chain and what makes it possible.
It's standardized. It's universal. It's brilliant.

OSCM and Manufacturing

OSCM was born with the industrial revolution and was really amped up with Henry Ford and his assemble line system for making the Model-T. Then time and motion studies were developed to refine the efficiency and speed of assembly lines and mass production techniques. Frederick Taylor developed these principals of scientific management.

Ford was again an innovator when, after WWII, the company hired en mass a group of super smart operations engineers under the leadership of Robert McNamara. This group had been working on calculating the effectiveness of bombing raids launched from England against Germany. This was in the days before computers. They were based in Washington and used rooms filled with rows of people with mechanical calculating machines like a coordinated human-mechanical computer; real number crunching!

After World War II McNamara realized the value of the team he had assembled and made a deal with the Ford Motor Company to hire the team en masse to optimize their OSCM. They were coined The Whiz Kids and McNamara became the first President of Ford outside the family.

In the 1980s Japan Inc. and especially Toyota developed an array of new and refined techniques to capitalize on manufacturing as a competitive advantage.

Here is a quick recap of how the field has developed over the last thirty years:

Just In Time (JIT) This was a major breakthrough in manufacturing philosophy. Pioneered by the Japanese, JIT is designed to achieve high volume production using minimal inventories of parts that arrive at the workstation in a production line exactly when they are needed. It takes levels of information, integration and coordination that were revolutionary and contributed to the production advantages of the Japanese auto industry starting the 1980s.

Total Quality Control (TQC) relentlessly seeks to eliminate the causes of production-based defects. It is a conceptual part of continuous improvement in manufacturing processes.

Lean Manufacturing JIT coupled with TQC is now the basis of many production and service processes. Lean Manufacturing is the term used to refer to these practices and tools. Lean process ideas have been applied to many business disciplines. One of the interesting ones is in the thinking about Start Ups and entrepreneurial activities. This is the Lean Startup Methodology.

Manufacturing Strategy Paradigm was developed by Harvard Business School faculty to harness manufacturing capability as a strategic competitive advantage. It is based on the focused factory concept that optimizes a set of tasks and limits them for high performance. This type of design and analysis requires trade-offs between performance measures such as low cost, high quality, and flexibility. These techniques have been very influential in the management of factories.

Total Quality Management TQM W Edwards Demming was an early apostle of the quality movement and his legacy is related to TQM. The Baldridge National Quality Award recognizes companies for outstanding quality management systems and their adherence to TQM. ISO 9000 is a certification standard developed to help implement, manage and measure compliance to these concepts. ISO plays a major role in setting quality standards for global manufactures. Many companies require that their vendors meet these standards as a condition for obtaining contracts.

Six-Sigma Quality has to do with refining manufacturing processes to achieve quality by reducing defects to one in less than six standard deviations. A standard deviation is a statistical measure of deviation from a norm. "Six Sigma" is a statistical term that indicates that in a batch of identically manufactured parts, 99.99966% of the items are within the tolerance specified by the customer.

Six Sigma is considered the gold standard of quality and as close as is practically possible these days to attaining the holy grail of zero defects. These tools have been taught to managers as part of "Green Belt" and "Black Belt" programs. Besides manufacturing, Six-sigma has been applied across a wide range of business areas that are repetitive and error-prone. Some examples are: accounts receivables, sales, finance, IT, legal, marketing, HR, R&D and environmental, health and safety services at companies.
Six Sigma is a remarkably versatile set of analytic tools.

Inventory Control

Carrying too much inventory is risky and inefficient. The drawbacks of excessively high inventory levels are the high costs of carrying it and the risk that it won't sell and then you are stuck moving it at a discount or end up eating the costs. There are benefits to carrying inventory that we will now explore.

Inventory acts as a buffer against the vagaries of Demand. You want to design enough capacity to accommodate customers when there is a rush. The optimal capacity can be calculated by measuring flow rate and flow time and applying statistics. Inventory decouples supply from demand as you have a buffer, which can also enhance your ability to accommodate a rush. Inventory protects against the variability of demand and process time (how long it takes to make a product). You can have operations that make to stock or make to order.

Think of a sandwich counter. If you wait until the lunch rush and then make sandwiches to order you will have a significant line and wait time. If however, in the morning you prepare some standard sandwiches that have proven popular, customers can grab a pre-make sandwich and make a transaction quickly. This is more convenient for them and a better business model for you.

Little's Law

Little's Law states that $I - R * T$

I is Inventory

R is Flow Rate

T is Flow Time

This equation codifies the relationship between flow and inventory. Here is an example: if you have 250 emails in you in box and you can answer 50 per day on average, how long will it take you to answer them?

I = 250

R = 50

I/R = T

250/50 = 5 days

By knowing the inventory and the rate you can calculate the time. If you know two of the variables you can solve for the third.

Inventory Turns

As a general rule a company's goal is to sell more in order to generate more profits with less inventory. Inventory turnover is directly related to the efficiency and profitability of a firm. The more inventory turns in a given period the more profitable and efficient the operation. It means that the enterprise is generating its sales while maintaining a relatively low level of average inventory. Two formulas for calculating and thinking about inventory turnover are:

Inventory turns = COGS/Inventory

COGS stands for Cost of Goods Sold.

From Little's Law:

I = R*T

Inventory Turns = 1/T

Inventory is a major component of Working Capital. The higher the level of inventory, the more money tied up to finance it. Items in inventory also risk becoming obsolete, spoiling, or being stolen. Managing inventory levels is a critical function of operations.

Leveraging Information Technology

Companies know that to keep earnings high and sustainable they need to get their products in stores or to customers as quickly as possible. They need to be able to create precise ordering systems so they can make and stock just enough to satisfy the demand they have estimated. Until recently phone and fax was used to place big orders. This was a manual, slow and error-prone process.

Advances in software and technology are enabling coordination and helping provide more stable, sustainable and predictable profitability. Profit margins have improved at many smart retailers due to technology advances.

Efficient logistics have taken on a whole new level of strategic importance. It also helps ease the reliance on price markdowns and sales, which cut into earnings, to move merchandise. You can also order less and order more often, reducing risk and increasing the ability to test a demand and adjust orders if something fails to sell, or conversely, catches on more than was anticipated.

The goal is to have **the right product at the right place at the right time**. These operations goals overlap with similar marketing goals. A company needs to be agile and flexible and have the ability to react to what is selling and what is not. It cannot afford a leaky, mushy system or to carry excess inventory.

Leading companies are using operations and supply chain management techniques to match supply and demand as closely and quickly as possible. This strategy is called minimizing **concept to cash** time: the time between developing a concept and the horizon of receiving revenues from sales of the product.

Computer Simulation

Check out www.responive.net for great operations simulation models that can help you quickly gain some intuition and experience in planning and executing these processes by seeing the implications of manipulating different variables.

This is important for making and delivering physical products, and for services delivered by personnel directly to customers. Strategic new business models have developed surrounding digital downloads and products and services that can scale to demand while not being physical. This eliminates a lot of these concerns. You can sell as many or as few and in any geographical market without concern for stocking or manufacturing or delivery.

This is the basis of the book The Long Tail by Chris Anderson which I highly recommend reading.

Also price has become more fluid of a concept as freemium models have developed where you give something away and charge for upgrades or add-ons after customers have gotten a good understanding of the value you provide. For these concepts Chris Andersen's other book Free is well worth the read. This gets into areas where Operations and Marketing overlap strategically.

Operations and Strategy

The strategy guru Michael Porter came up with a concise and clear framework for thinking about strategic goals as the search for Competitive Advantage. A company can perform effectively by some combination of Differentiation and Cost Leadership.

Differentiation means that you products or services have distinct features that set them apart from other offerings and stand out as being superior in customers' opinions.

Cost Leadership means that a company provides the best value: faster, better, cheaper, to customers.

From a strategic viewpoint managers are always trying to create shareholder value through stimulating growth. Ways of achieving growth can include investment in new technologies, acquisitions, marketing and awareness campaigns.

Relative to these, applications of innovations in operations are relatively reliable and low cost. A firm's long-term viability is vitally related to an understanding of the big picture of all the processes that generate the costs and support the cash flow of the enterprise.

As a businessperson you are positioned to come up with innovative ideas and craft efficient and effective solutions related to operations and supply chains.

Smart management can achieve high levels of value by incorporating these approaches.

Careers in Operations

Career opportunities in operations and supply management are plentiful today as companies strive to increase profitability by improving quality, productivity and reducing costs. Some of the jobs are:

- Manager of a plant, call center, bank
- Hospital administrator
- Supply chain, purchasing, or quality control manager
- Facilities manager
- Project manager

The top of the heap is Chief Operating Officer or COO. No matter what you may end up doing in your career an understanding of OSCM will be a great asset to you and your employer.

Corporate Finance

Finance is a broad topic that can be challenging to initially wrap your mind around. For clarity's sake it can be thought of as organized along economic lines of micro and macro. On the micro side we have individual behavior and personal finance, and the theory of the firm and Corporate Finance. On the macro side we have financial markets, money and banking.

This book will focus on Corporate Finance: how companies make decisions about what projects to pursue, and how the raise money and do valuations.

This book will provide a framework for how financial professionals make decisions. I will present financial markets in so much as how they interact and support corporate finance functions.

Corporate Finance comprises a set of skills that interact with all the aspects of running a business. We will start by exploring the time value of money-- compounding, discounting, and financial valuation. From there, we examine the perspective of a corporate financial manager and think about how, when, and where to spend money.

We'll develop a set of tools for making good financial decisions, like net present value and internal rate of return. Cash creation is key and we will examine financial statements in order to locate and identify it.

We then explore the trade off between risk and return from a Wall Street or capital market's perspective and consider how financial markets define, measure, price, and spread that risk.

You will gain confidence in your knowledge and understanding of finance. The tools of corporate finance will help you as a manager or business owner to evaluate performance and make smart decisions about the value of opportunities. An understanding of Corporate Finance is essential for the professional manager.

The Big Picture

There are common characteristics of successful companies. In particular they are able to consistently accomplish two main goals: they satisfy customers and owners (investors).

Successful ventures identify, create, and deliver products and services that are highly valued by customers. They produce goods that customers want. Customers choose them over competing products and services.

Successful companies price their offerings such that they cover costs and compensate owners and creditors for the use of their money and exposure to risk.

In order to achieve these goals successful companies have skilled people at all levels including leaders, managers, and a capable workforce. They also have strong relationships with groups outside the company including suppliers and vendors. Successful companies excel in customer relationship management.

Successful ventures need skilled people, strong external relationships, and sufficient capital in order to execute their plans.

Great companies manage their cost of capital and raise the least expensive funds in order to execute their plans and support their operations. They need cash to grow their operations and improve their product and service offerings. Companies can reinvest a portion or all of their earnings but they may still need more money to grow and take advantage of opportunities.

Growing companies raise additional funds by a combination of selling stock and/or borrowing. These are the finance objectives related to satisfying customer needs.

The second goal is generating enough cash and value to compensate the investors who provide the necessary capital. To help your company accomplish this goal a finance professional must be able to evaluate any proposal whether it relates to marketing, production, strategy and whether it entails entering or exiting a market, and implement only the projects that add value for investors and owners.

These two competing sets of interests: customers and investors, and the decisions involving them are the realm of corporate finance.

Corporate Finance

Corporations invest in real assets that are intended to be productive in generating income. Some of these assets such as factories, offices, machinery and computers are tangible. Others such as brand names and patents are intangible.

The decision-making tools of corporate finance assess the value of proposed projects and income producing assets based on the time value of money and its relation to risk. The decisions are which projects to pursue and which to pass on. We rank projects based on the present value of their future cash flows. How we do that is called discounted cash flow or DCF valuation and it is the basis of this book.

Corporations finance investments in assets and projects by borrowing, reinvesting profits, and selling stock. These modes of financing assets make up the right hand side of the Balance Sheet under the categories Liabilities (borrowing and debt) and Equity (stock sales and retained earnings).

This raises the two main financial issues that a manager faces:

- What investments should the corporation make?
- How should it pay for those these investments?

The investment decision involves spending money and the financing decision involves raising money.

Corporations can have many owners or shareholders. These owners invest in the company through purchasing stock. Shareholders vary in their wealth, age, investment timing, and tolerance for risk. But they share the same financial objective: they want the management of the company to increase the value of the firm and its stock price.

Successful financial management lies in increasing and maximizing shareholder value. This section will cover the concepts that govern making good supportable financial decisions and how to use the tools of the trade of modern finance. Let's get started by exploring how to analyze financial statements.

Financial Statement Analysis

Accounting and Finance overlap in this area. The launching place for Corporate Finance is the ability to read and understand Financial Statements. The analysis of financial statements and subsequent assumptions and projections based on that analysis is the next step.

Financial statement analysis is the process of analyzing a company's financial statements and comparing the analysis across companies and industries in order to make better operating and investing decisions. This analysis method involves specific techniques for evaluating and quantifying risk, performance, financial health, and the future prospects of an enterprise. We can look at the performance of a particular company over time such as year-to-year results.

This is called **Horizontal Analysis**. And we can look at various performance characteristics within a single time period. This is called **Vertical Analysis**. We can create metrics across an industry segment as an average value to compare our company against.

This is called **Benchmarking**. We can also aggregate up different industry groups and see how they perform relative to each other. This type of analysis can be helpful in gauging where to allocate investment dollars in a portfolio. It can also be used to see how a management team is performing relative to its competition.

Financial Statements are analyzed and scrutinized by a variety of stakeholders including debt and equity investors, government agencies and taxing authorities, and management decision-makers. It is what credit analysts do.

These stakeholders have different interests and apply a variety of different techniques to meet their needs. For example, some equity investors are more interested in the long-term earnings power of the organization and perhaps the sustainability and growth of dividend payments. Some equity investors like hedge funds may be looking for latent risks and pitfalls in order to capitalize on a short position. This means they are looking for companies about to collapse.

Creditors want to ensure that interest and principal on the organization's debt securities are paid on time and when due. Banks and commercial lenders use financial statement analysis as part of their credit analysis to determine whether or not to make loans and lend. Ratings Agencies such as Moody's, Standard and Poors, and Fitch perform financial statement analysis in order to rate the risk and creditworthiness of companies and their debt. Managers use it to see how their company is performing relative to historical performance, their targets, and their industry.

Techniques of financial statement analysis include **fundamental analysis**, the use of **financial ratios** and DuPont analysis. Analysis methods are performed in a horizontal or vertical fashion across a company.

In order to project future performance, historical information is used combined with assumptions about the prospect for the company and the future economic environment. This stream of profits from future years is what is used to calculate the value of a business. This is the foundational concept of **Business Valuation** and **Corporate Finance**.

Before we get into the nitty-gritty of these techniques, let's start with an historical overview of how financial statement analysis developed and has evolved.

History of Financial Statement Analysis

The stock market crash in October 1929 was a catastrophic event that led to the Great Depression and worldwide economic strife. It also led to social unrest and political turmoil. These events called into question the viability of Capitalism and Democracy as unsettling systemic flaws were exposed and many, many people suffered.

A major basis of the problem was that many companies who traded on the stock market did not provide meaningful information about the state of their business. There were no financial statements to review. There was no transparency. In order to clean up the mess and maintain investor confidence in the stock market, the Roosevelt administration created the **Securities and Exchange Commission** (SEC) to regulate and oversee the stock market. Roosevelt needed someone to run the SEC who knew all the dirty tricks of the stock market so they could effectively identify and combat abuse.. The man who rose to the occasion was Joseph P. Kennedy. Joe was future president John F. Kennedy's father and a famous stock manipulator and patriot.

Part of the SEC's new rules were that every traded company had to have financial statements prepared by an outside third party auditing firm under a rigorous set of accounting rules called **GAAP,** Generally Accepted Accounting Principles. These financial statements along with disclosures about the operations had to be filed and made publicly available through the SEC each and every year.

That document is called a **10K**. This kind of disclosure and transparency, allows investors and the public to understand a company's operations and prospects and make determinations about whether or not to invest.

This set of regulations seems obvious and eminently sensible now, but it was bold, and brilliant, and a revelation at the time. **Fundamental analysis,** a system of analyzing this new information, came to prominence almost immediately. To this day, the **10K** is the basic document and fundamental analysis is the tool set for stock market analysis and corporate investment decision making.

Fundamental Analysis

The SEC and financial reporting regulations were instituted in two legislations: the '33 Act and the '34 Act. Benjamin Graham and David Dodd first published their influential book "Security Analysis" in 1934. Warren Buffett is a well-known disciple of Graham and Dodd's philosophy.

The Graham and Dodd approach is referred to as Fundamental Analysis and includes: Economic analysis; Industry analysis; and Company analysis. Company Analysis is the primary realm of financial statement analysis. On the basis of these three analyses the value of the security is determined.

Fundamental analysis is how bankers, analysts, and investors make long-term investment decisions.

Their book has gone through many revisions and editions and is available in a recently revised edition. You may want to check it out; especially if you have any aspirations to be like Warren. Another proponent of Graham and Dodd is Bill Ackman the American hedge fund manager. He is the founder and CEO of Pershing Square Capital Management. Bill is also a billionaire.

Here is the information on the book:

Dodd, David; Graham, Benjamin (1998). Security Analysis. John Wiley & Sons, Inc. ISBN 0-07-013235-6.

Horizontal and Vertical Analysis

Horizontal analysis compares financial information over time, typically from past financial statements such as the income statement. When comparing this past information we look for variations of particular line items such as higher or lower earnings, sales revenues, or particular expenses. Horizontal analysis is used to look for trends that can be extrapolated in order to predict future performance. But remember past performance is not always a good predictor of future performance.

Vertical analysis is a proportional analysis performed on financial statements. It is ratio analysis. Line items of interest on the financial statement are listed as a percentage of another line item. For example, on an income statement each line item will be listed as a percentage of Sales.

Financial Ratios

Financial ratios are powerful tools used to assess company upside, downside, and risk. There are four main categories of ratios: liquidity ratios, profitability ratios, activity ratios and leverage ratios. These are typically analyzed over time and across competitors in an industry. Using ratios "normalizes" the numbers so you can compare companies in apples-to-apples terms.

Liquidity and Solvency

Solvency and liquidity are both refer to a company's financial health and viability. Solvency refers to an enterprise's capacity to meet its long-term financial commitments. Liquidity refers to an enterprise's ability to pay short-term obligations. Liquidity is also a measure of how quickly assets can be sold to raise cash.

A solvent company is one that owns more than it owes. It has a positive net worth and is carrying a manageable debt load. A company with adequate liquidity may have enough cash available to pay its bills, but may still be heading for financial disaster

381

down the road. In this case a company meets liquidity standards by is not solvent. Healthy companies are both solvent and possess adequate liquidity.

Liquidity ratios are used to determine whether a company has enough current asset capacity to pay its bills and meet its obligations in the foreseeable future (current liabilities). **Solvency ratios** are a measure of how quickly a company can turn its assets into cash if it experiences financial difficulties or is threatened with bankruptcy. Both measure different aspects of if, and how long, a company can pay its bills and remain in business.

The current ratio and the quick ratio are two common liquidity ratios. The **current ratio** is current assets/current liabilities and measures how much liquidity (cash) is available to address current liabilities (bills and other obligations). The **quick ratio** is (current assets – inventories) / current liabilities. The quick ratio measures a company's ability to meet its short-term obligations based on its most liquid assets, and therefore excludes inventories from its current assets. It is also known as the "acid-test ratio."

The **solvency ratio** is used to examine the ability of a business to meet its long-term obligations. The ratio is most commonly used by lenders and bankers. The ratio compares cash flows to liabilities. The solvency ratio calculation involves the following steps:

All non-cash expenses are added back to after-tax net income. This approximates the amount of cash flow generated by the business. You can find the numbers to add back in the Operations section of the Cash Flow Statement.

Add together all short-term and long-term obligations. This is the Total Liabilities number on the Balance Sheet. Then divide the estimated cash flow figure by the liabilities total.
The formula for the ratio is:

(Net after-tax income + Non-cash expenses)/(Short-term liabilities + Long-term liabilities)

A higher percentage indicates an increased ability to support the liabilities of a business over the long-term.

Remember that estimations made over a long term are inherently inaccurate. There are many variables that can impact the ability to pay over the long term. Using any ratio to estimate solvency needs to be taken with a grain of salt.

Profitability ratios

Profitability ratios are ratios help discern how profitable a company is. To be profitable, a company has to cover costs. The breakeven point and the gross profit ratio address the dynamics of cost coverage in different ways. The breakeven point calculates how much cash a company must generate to break even with their operating costs. The gross profit ratio is equal to (revenue - the cost of goods sold)/revenue. This ratio provides a quick snapshot of expected revenue that can be applied to the overhead expenses and fixed costs of operations.

Some additional examples of profitability ratios are profit margin, return on assets and return on equity. The higher the value in these ratios, the more profitable a company is. Having a higher value relative to a competitor's ratio or the same ratio from a previous period is indicative that the company is performing relatively well and going in the right direction.

Return on Equity
Return on Equity (ROE) = Net Income / Average Shareholders' Equity

Earnings per Share
Earnings per share (EPS) is the portion of the company's profit which   is   allocated to each outstanding share of common.

Earnings per share is a very good indicator of the profitability of any organization, and it is one of the most widely used measures of profitability.

Activity ratios

Activity ratios are calculated to show how well management is doing managing the company's resources. Activity ratios measure company sales relative to another asset account. The most common asset accounts used are accounts receivable, inventory, and total assets. Since most companies have a lot of resources tied up in accounts receivable, inventory and working capital, these accounts are used in the denominator of the most common activity ratios.

Accounts receivable (AR) is the total amount of money due to a company for products or services sold on a credit account. The length of time until AR is collected is critical because that expected revenue must be financed in some way. The accounts receivable turnover shows how rapidly a company collects what is owed to it and indicates the liquidity of the receivables.

Accounts Receivable Turnover = Total Credit Sales/Average Accounts Receivable

The average collection period in days is equal to 365 days divided by the Accounts Receivable Turnover. This is another ratio that helps gain insight into AR collection:

Average Collection Period = 365 Days/Accounts Receivable Turnover

Analysts frequently use the average collection period to measure the effectiveness of a company's ability to collect payments from its credit customers. The average collection period should be less than the credit terms that the company extends to its customers.

A significant indicator of profitability is the ability to manage inventory. Inventory is money and resources invested that do not earn a return until the product is sold. The longer inventory sits, the less profitable a company can be. A higher inventory turnover ratio indicates more demand for products, better cash management and also the reduced risk of inventory obsolescence. The best measure of inventory utilization is the **inventory turnover ratio**. It is calculated as either the total annual sales, or the cost of goods sold (COGS), divided by the cost of inventory.

Inventory Turnover = Total Annual Sales or Cost of Goods Sold/Average Inventory

Using the cost of goods sold in the numerator can provide a more accurate indicator of inventory turnover because it allows a more direct comparison with other companies. Different companies have different markups to the sale price and this can obscure apples-to-apples comparison.
The average inventory cost is usually used in the denominator to compensate for seasonal differences.

Leverage ratios

Leverage ratios analyze the degree to which a company uses debt to finance its operations and assets. The debt-to-equity ratio is the most common. This ratio is calculated as:

(Long-term debt + Short-term debt + Leases)/ Equity

Companies with high debt ratios need to have steady and predictable revenue streams in order to service that debt. Companies whose revenues fluctuate and are less predictable should rely more on equity in its capital structure. Leverage also has obvious implications for solvency.

Startups rely almost entirely on Equity as they have no revenues or very uncertain revenues that can service debt.

DuPont analysis

DuPont analysis was developed by the DuPont Corporation in the 1920s as a tool to assess their investments across their various companies and operations. As an early conglomerate, they need a tool to assess the relative performance of varied business in order to make decisions of where and how to allocate resources. By now it has been widely adopted as a managerial and investment tool.

What drives ROE?

DuPont Analysis analyzes Return on Equity by deconstructing it into its main drivers.

DuPont Analysis is an expression, which breaks return on equity (ROE) into three parts.
The basic formula is:

ROE = (Profit margin)*(Asset turnover)*(Equity multiplier) =
(Net Income/Sales)*(Sales/Assets)*(Assets/Equity) = (Net Income/Equity)

The three constituent parts are:
- Profitability: measured by profit margin
- Operating efficiency: measured by asset turnover
- Financial leverage: measured by equity multiplier

DuPont analysis enables you to understand the source of superior (or inferior) return by comparison with companies in similar industries or between industries. It also provides a deeper level of understanding by parsing apart the significant variables and drivers of Return on Equity. And ROE is certainly a metric that equity investors (stock investors) find important.

Working Capital

Working Capital is a term used to describe the amount of money and liquid assets available and required to operate a business. It is a financial metric, which represents operating liquidity. Working capital is the difference between current assets and current liabilities. Along with fixed assets such as plant and equipment, working capital is considered a part of operating capital. The management of working capital involves managing inventories, accounts receivable, accounts payable, and cash.

Current assets and current liabilities include three accounts, which are of special importance. These accounts represent the areas of the business where managers have the most direct impact and influence:

- Accounts receivable (current asset)
- Inventory (current assets), and
- Accounts payable (current liability)

Short-term loans and the current portion of long-term debt (payable within 12 months) are also critical, because they represent short-term claims on current assets and are often secured by long-term assets. Bank loans and lines of credit are common types of short-term debt.

An increase in net working capital indicates that the business has either increased current assets or has decreased current liabilities. Financing and managing working capital is a major operating challenge, especially for companies that are rapidly growing.

Managing Working Capital

Receivables and inventory are usually financed with a line of credit (revolving debt like a credit card). Managing receivables aims at making sure that all your customers pay and that they pay in a timely manner; you need that cash in the door! Accounts Receivables turnover is a ratio we discussed earlier that indicates the timeliness of credit sales being paid.

Managing inventories a means not letting inventories build up. You do this by monitoring sales, manufacturing activity, and the Inventory turnover ratio. You want enough inventories so you can accommodate a spike in sales, but you also don't want to risk having too much inventory that you can't unload. This is especially important with products that have a short life cycle and can become obsolete. If not sold in a timely manner this might force you to deeply discount products in order to sell them. This can lead to incurring a loss. Operations Management is the discipline focused on these issues and mitigating potential problems.

You can quickly asses how a company is doing in this regard by looking at their balance sheet and comparing Current Assets to Current Liabilities and seeing if there is a larger amount of Current Assets. Do this comparison for the last few years and you can see if there is a change in Working Capital and if it is due to a build-up of inventories.

The Time Value of Money

"The importance of money flows from it being a link between the present and the future".
— John Maynard Keynes.

Keynes was a brilliant man who deeply understood money and economics. And his insights weren't just intellectual and academic. He made two fortunes: one in the stock market and one in the art market. He understood value and investing and put his money where his mouth was.

The monetary linchpin between the present and the future is interest rates or discount rates. If you have a present value and you want to calculate a future value, we call it an interest rate. If you have future values and you want to estimate their worth today, we use a discount rate. Interest rates and discount rates are two sides of the same coin, to use a money metaphor.

Days of Future Past

There are two sets of data that we use in corporate finance: retrospective and prospective. Retrospective data is compiled in financial statements. These represent the historical performance of an enterprise and can be analyzed, compared, and extrapolated. Ratios are the tools of financial statement analysis and we just discussed them.

Prospective data is compiled in financial projections. These represent management's forecast of how the enterprise will perform in the future. These projections can be analyzed, risk adjusted, and a present value of those future cash flows can be calculated. We will now get into the forward-looking aspects of finance with the concept of the time value of money (TVM).

Time is money, literally. If there is a prospect of receiving a certain sum, then the sooner you receive it, the more it is worth. Interest rates describe this relationship between present value and future value. This is the fundamental concept of finance. We will explore this relationship between present and future value from different angles and I will phrase it in different ways in order to let it sink in.

TVM represents the conceptual basis of finance. This is the underlying principle of how banks function, how stocks and bonds are priced, how assets and companies are valued, how projects are analyzed, and how you should think about the nature and function of money.

A bird in the hand is worth two in the bush.

Receiving money today is worth more than getting the same amount in the future; and the value of the prospect of receiving money diminishes the further into the future the promise to deliver money. The rate at which the value of a dollar in the future decreases relative to a dollar today is inversely proportional to the rate at which a dollar invested today will increase in the future. Take a second to let that point sink in.

The future and the present value are two sides of the same coin (pun intended!) and they are related to each other by the interest rate.

The concept of the time value of money explains why interest is paid or earned. Interest, whether it is on a bank deposit or debt, compensates the depositor or lender for the time value of money. Risk has to do with the uncertainty of being repaid and interest rates reflect the level of this uncertainty or risk. One of the reasons credit cards have such high interest rates is that the risk of other people defaulting on their balance is baked into the rate.

TVM also underlies investment. Investing is about managing risk versus return. An investor is willing to forego spending their money now if they expect a favorable return on their investment in the future. The return required is related to the perceived risk of getting one's money back in the future; the higher the perceived risk, the higher the required rate of return. An investor is willing to part with their precious capital when greed overcomes fear; where the expected return exceeds the perceived risk.

Discounting Cash Flows

The core of corporate finance is calculating the present value of future cash flows. This concept is based on the time value of money. A company is essentially an entity that generates cash flows each year into the future. The trick is estimating those future cash flows and how much they might grow or shrink and what the risks are to realizing them.

This is where you have to polish your crystal ball and do some deep analysis of the business and its markets and competitors. All this information is compiled in a spreadsheet of financial projections and the bottom line represents the future cash flows in each year.

These are discounted back to the present value at a discount rate that takes into account what similar investments, which are just streams of expected cash flows, are priced at in the market and any and all risks specific to the particular enterprise or asset we are contemplating buying or selling.

This is the basic concept of Valuation. Valuation is an estimate of something's worth. Something's worth can be set at auction where people bid and the highest bidder wins. But how do bidders know how much to bid and how much is too much?

The stock market is essentially an auction where investors place bids: how much they are willing to pay for a stock, and asks: how much an investor is willing to sell for. Companies and assets and even startups that don't have any revenues yet are valued using this principle.

This technique of calculating the present value of a stream of cash flows becomes essential when trying to value start-ups that have no revenue history or assets, or companies that are predicted to grow rapidly. In these cases you can't rely on past performance and history in order to come up with a value based on P/E or existing assets.

This is the technique favored by investment bankers, venture capitalists, private equity, hedge funds, and savvy investors, banks and credit analysts, and CFOs. It's not difficult to understand and you will be amazed how useful and powerful it can be.

Present Value and Future Value

$100 invested for one year, earning 5% interest, will be worth $105 after one year; therefore, $100 paid now and $105 paid exactly one year later both have the same value to a recipient who expects 5% return. That is, $100 invested for one year at 5% interest has a future value of $105. This assumes that inflation is zero percent.

The equation in this case would look like this:

$105 = $100 * (1+.05)
The general formula for solving for future value is
$FV - PV * (1 | r)$
Where
FV is future value
PV is present value, and
r is the interest rate
The reciprocal formula to solve for present value juggles the terms using basic algebra and restates the relationship as:

$PV = FV/(1+r)$

It simply puts the (1+r) term on the other side of the equation to solve for PV by dividing both sides by (1+r). If this is confusing just replace (1+r) by the term X for the moment.
$FV = PV * X$
If you divide both sides by X you get:
$FV/X = PV * X/X$

Since the term X/X is equal to one, the term goes away on that side of the equation. So we are left with
$FV/X = PV$
Now replace the X with (1+r) and you see the derivation of our equation.

Take a moment to make sure you really understand this because it is the basis of project finance and asset valuation. This is the formula we use to calculate future cash flows as a present value.

This concept is used to calculate the value today of a projected stream of income in the future. In this case, annual cash flows are discounted and then added together and the sum is the present value of the entire income stream.

Here is a link to the beginning of a series in Khan Academy on the time value of money and present value calculations http://bit.ly/1Ul43VT Sal Khan is great at explaining concepts and these videos will be very helpful in solidifying your understanding of this concept.

Net Present Value

The financial tool that captures the concept of the relationship between the present and future value of money is NPV: Net Present Value. By the end of this post you will know how it works and how to use it. The next five minutes could change your life.

Net Present Value (NPV) is the gold standard analytic technique used in financial analysis and investment decision-making. And spreadsheets like Excel make it super easy to use. Lets talk about what NPV is, how its derived, and how to employ it.

NPV is the concept that ties it all together in understanding corporate finance. NPV is the capstone of financial literacy.

In business we invest in projects that make money in the future. We pay now and intend to reap the rewards in the future. Usually a project or asset will make money as a stream of revenues and profits over years. It could also be a project whose main benefit is savings.

We need the ability to calculate whether that stream of future cash flows is worth more than the money we need to invest to buy it or build it. NPV is the tool we use to make that analysis.

The way we look at decisions about whether to fund a project or calculate the value of an asset is to turn that stream of future dollars into today's dollars.

Then we compare that sum of present values to the cost; if the cost is more than the total present value, we don't do the deal; if it is less, it is considered a good deal.

This is the way projects are analyzed and assessed as go or no go, and how income producing assets and acquisitions are valued for sale, purchase, merger or acquisition.

In those previous blog posts we analyzed and calculated the value of future cash flows and brought them back to present value. **Net Present Value** (NPV) takes this idea a step further and accounts for the transactional aspect.

We must "purchase" the future cash flows either by:

- Buying a bond or stock, or

- Acquiring a company, or

- Purchasing an income-producing asset, or

- Undertaking a project and incurring the costs of developing or building the income-producing asset.

Net present value "nets out" the cost of acquiring the future cash flows. NPV compares the cost in today's dollars to the present value of projected income or benefits also in today's dollars. The deal is only worth doing if the price is less than our assessment of the future benefits.

NPV is the main tool used to value assets and make decisions about projects, purchases, mergers, or acquisitions. The spreadsheets can get pretty complicated when they are populated with all the costs, revenue and expense projections, and assumptions about timing and risk, but the basic idea is always to compare the costs to the future benefits and compare them apples to apples by taking into account the time value of money.

NPV answers a simple question: does the present value of all the money coming in over the life of the project outweigh how much money we have to spend in order to receive it? Net present value is just that, it's the net between the present value of these two streams: the money going out and the money coming in.

We need to determine whether NPV is greater than 0. If it's greater than 0, then the costs are less than the benefits and we should do the project or make the investment.

The decision rule is whether NPV is bigger than 0 or less than 0. We can construct the formula for NPV by following along very closely with what we did in the prior blog post discounting cash flows. NPV is the gold standard but using it along with IRR makes for even better analysis and decision making. I will talk about IRR (internal rate of return) in a future blog post.

NPV is equal to the present value of what's coming in off the project as cash flows minus the initial cost.

This formula is set up as the initial cost, which has a minus sign in front of it, plus Cash flow in period 1, discounted one period back, plus the cash flow in period two, discounted two periods back, plus the cash flow in period 3, discounted back three periods, you get the idea, plus all the other cash flows coming in discounted by their period.

$$NPV = -C_0 + \frac{C_1}{1+r} + \frac{C_2}{(1+r)^2} + \dots + \frac{C_T}{(1+r)^T}$$

$-C_0 = Initial\ Investment$
$C = Cash\ Flow$
$r = Discount\ Rate$
$T = Time$

What we are doing is taking the initial cost and weighing it against the present value of all the cash coming in. We "net" the two numbers. There's a minus sign on the costs, and plus signs on all of the present value cash flows.

We are essentially looking at how all the money going out weighs against all the money coming in.

Think of it like a balance. If we know the initial investment and the stream of money coming in from the project in the future, we can measure the NPV as the difference between the two; its the net between those two streams.

As the initial investment becomes larger, the NPV become smaller. You can see that the NPV, whether it's bigger than 0 or less than 0, depends on that balance between the money going out and the money coming in. Let's work a problem and compute an NPV in practice.

Analyze the stream of cash flows and compute the NPV if the discount rate is 15%

EXAMPLE PROJECT

Today

Year:	0	1	2	Sum (NPV)
	-$3,000	$1,500	$1800	$300

Let's think about whether it's worth it to do this project. In period 0, today, we need to spend $3,000 in order to receive the future cash flows. Is it worth it to spend that $3,000? What do we expect to get in return?

What are the cash flows coming in off the project? We have a cash flow of $1,500 coming in at the end of year one. And we've got a cash flow of $1,800 coming in at the end of year two. If we just sum up the cash flows, a minus 3000 (it is minus because it is a cost) plus 1500 plus 1800, we get an answer of $300. This project is generating cash. It's profitable in this sense. The money coming in is bigger than the money going out.

That's the sum of all the cash flows, but that's without any discounting. We haven't accounted for the fact that we have to wait a year to get the $1,500, and then wait another year after that to get the $1,800. Remember: to use money you have to pay; there is a cost of capital. So what do we have to pay? In this case, we have to pay that 15% discount rate. That is the cost of capital in this example.

Today

Year:	0	1	2	Sum (NPV)
	-$3,000	$1,500	$1800	$300

Present Value: $1500/(1.15)^1$ $1800/(1.15)^2$

NPV @15%

$-\$3,000 + \$1,304.35 + \$1,361.06 = $ **-$334.59**

We need to adjust the cash flows for the time value of money by discounting them to the present value. We take that $1,500 and discount it one period at 15% and we get $1,304.35. Then we take the $1,800 and discount it two periods at 15% and we get $1,361.06. Now when we sum the present value of all those cash flows, we get *minus* $334.59, which tells us that the project destroys value. It's not worth doing.

403

It's a profitable project, but we don't want to do it. Why would we ever not want to do a project that's profitable? It all comes down to the 15% discount rate. That 15% indicates what the hurdle rate is for the profitability of the project. This project might be profitable, but it is not profitable enough to justify the required 15% return. If we, our bosses, or our investors require a 15% return to take the risk of that project, we're not going to be able to deliver it to them with a project like this.

Let's examine what some of the main drivers are in that net present value calculation. First is cash flow. Obviously, more cash is better than less. The second is the timing. The further the cash flow is out in the future, the deeper it gets discounted.

And the third driver is the discount rate. The higher the discount rate, the deeper the cash flows get discounted and the lower the NPV. The lower the discount rate, the less discounting, the better the project. Lower discount rates, higher NPV. Higher discount rates, lower NPV

Net present value is the benchmark metric. It is our best capital budgeting tool. It incorporates the timing of the cash flows and it takes into account the opportunity cost, because the discount rate quantifies, in essence, what else could we do with the money.

The fact that we're discounting implicitly incorporates the opportunity cost. And it incorporates **risk**. If we think the project is a lot riskier, what can we do? We can increase the discount rate to reflect that risk.

NPV is **objective** in the sense that, if we have good forecasting and good discount rates, we can lay this out and calculate it in a way that is presentable and explainable to anybody. It's an arm's length metric. NPV is transparent, we could sit down together with a spreadsheet and go over it and explain all of the assumptions to each other.

Net present value weighs the costs and benefits of cash coming in versus cash going out, and gives us an objective, arm's length, and transparent metric for capital budgeting.

To sum it all up:

Here is the formula laid out in general terms:

$$NPV = -C_0 + C_1/(1+i) + C_2/(1+i)^2 + \ldots + C_T/(1+i)^T$$

$-C_0$ = Initial Investment

C = Cash Flow

i = Discount rate

T = Time

Remember the main drivers of NPV are:

- **Cash Flow**. Obviously, more cash is better than less.

- **Timing**. The further the cash flow is out in the future, the deeper it gets discounted.

- **Discount Rate**. The higher the discount rate, the deeper the cash flows get discounted and the lower the NPV. The lower the discount rate, the less discounting, the better the project. Lower discount rates, higher NPV. Higher discount rates, lower NPV.

Internal Rate of Return

For our last financial decision making tool, we are going to explore using the internal rate of return for deciding how to spend money within the firm. Internal rate of return (IRR) is the discount rate used in capital budgeting that makes the net present value of all cash flows from a particular project equal to zero.

The higher the internal rate of return of a proposed project, the more desirable it is to undertake the project.

The internal rate of return is derivative of NPV. NPV basically tells us whether or not the present value of the cash coming in exceeds the cash going out. NPV calculates the net of the present value of the cash flows. With the internal rate of return we come at the issue from a different angle.

First we compute an NPV and then we're going to ask what discount rate sets the NPV equal to 0; the discount rate that makes the cash outflow equal to the present value of the cash inflows.

IRR Decision Rule

Our decision rule is we're going to invest if that rate is bigger than our hurdle rate.

Internal rate of return is basically asking how hard do we need to discount the cash flows in order to drive the value out of the project? It's a measure of resiliency of the cash flows.

The harder we discount, the more that drives down the NPV. How hard do we have to discount it and still stay bigger than 0? That's what IRR is designed to tell us. This decision rule is very similar to our net present value decision, as we'll see graphically.

What we do with internal rate of return is take the net present value, which is a numerical value, and restate it as a percentage, which makes it more intuitively appealing.

IRR and NPV

It's difficult for us to grasp the meaning of a number. It has little context. If I say the NPV is $2,437,000 it means little by itself. If I tell you the internal rate of return on the project is 25%, it's easy to intuitively grasp. You might think, oh 25% is a good return. It takes the net present value and changes it into a percentage that's easier to quickly grasp and understand.

It gives us a more intuitive and appealing take on the NPV of the project. IRR doesn't tell the whole story though and we will go over some of the things to be careful of in relying on it as a metric. As with the others we have discussed, its best to use it in conjunction with NPV.

Let's think about the IRR in formulaic terms. When we had our net present value formula, the NPV was equal to the initial cost weighed against all of the cash flows coming in off the project in future years.

$NPV = $ - Initial Costs $+ CF_1/(1+r) + CF_2/(1+r)^2 + CF_3/(1+r)^3 \ldots.$

That was our formula for the NPV. What do for IRR is we're going to take that exact same formula, the initial cost, and instead of using r the discount rate, I'm going to replace that with IRR. And I'm going to set that equal to 0. And now I'm simply going to say, what rate sets this series of numbers equal to 0? And all we have to do is solve for the IRR.

$$0 = - \text{Initial Costs} + CF_1/(1+IRR) + CF_2/(1+IRR)^2 + CF_3/(1+IRR)^3 \ldots$$

A spreadsheet is going to help us do that. It's really hard to calculate IRR with pen and paper. But it's easy to do it in Excel or on a financial calculator. They have IRR functions built in.

I prefer Excel or a spreadsheet program on a computer because you can build out the model and save the results. This is important if later your boss asks how you came up with that number. Always save your work for later reference.

Now we're going to solve this polynomial equation for the IRR. And that's going to tell us what discount rate drives all the value out of the project.

Let's look at the relationship between NPV and IRR graphically. Here

409

we have a project that has a positive NPV and we graph the value of the net present value in dollars.

As we discount the cash flows with progressively higher and higher discount rates, the NPV is going to decline until, at some point, it crosses 0.
The point at which that crosses 0, the discount rate that sets the NPV equal to 0, is the IRR.

Any time the discount rate is below the IRR, it's a positive NPV project. So if our hurdle rate is 7% and the IRR is 12% it's a good project. IRR is similar to NPV, except that we have discounted the cash flows to a percentage rate where the discounting just crosses to negative, at 0.

Now we can say, for example, the return on this project, the IRR, is 12%. And that is easier to understand than saying the net present value is $1,613,672, which is just a big number with no context. we don't really know what it means. But if the return is 12%, we can compare: 1% relative to a 7% cost on capital. That's a good project. That's what IRR does for us.

IRR Example

Time	Cash Flow	Trial 1 (10%)	Trial 2 (20%)	Trial 3 (16%)
0	(9,364)	(9,364)	(9,364)	(9,364)
1	10,000	9,091	8,333	8,621
2	1,000	826	694	743
NPV	1,636	553	-336	**0**

Let's think this through in terms of an example. Let's say I were spending $9,364 in order to generate cash of $10,000 in year one, and $1,000 in year two. If I didn't do any discounting at all and just added up the cash flows that would be 1,636. 36

If I discounted the cash flows at 10%, I would discount the $10,000 back one period at 10%, discount the $1,000 back two periods at 10%, give me a net present value of 553. If I instead of discounting at 10%, discounted at 20% instead of 10%, that would give me a net present value of minus 336.

So what must have happened somewhere in between? Somewhere that net present value crossed from positive to negative. If we solve it, that actually happens at exactly 16%. That's the point where we are discounting it enough to draw all the value out of it.

411

In the above example we have to keep guessing and solving for different discount rates until we converge on an answer.

IRR is a really easy thing to do in Excel. Built into Excel is an IRR function. There many tutorials online that will show you quickly how to use that function. It solves that polynomial equation, finds the root, sets it to 0, and gives us the solution.

Calculating IRR

There is no fancy formula for IRR where you can just plug in the numbers and calculate the solution. It can only be done by trial and error iterations. Excel does it for us by crunching through thousands of iterations in a split second. Before spreadsheets became ubiquitous you could estimate IRR with cross-reference tables. Now with just a few clicks, we can get an accurate IRR solution.

IRR Summary

Internal rate of return is very similar to NPV. But it scales that NPV into a percent. It's a more intuitive measure, because it gives us a sense of what kind of rate of return the project is yielding. And it accounts for the timing, the opportunity cost, and the risk of the project in a very similar way to what NPV does. IRR is one of our good capital budgeting tools. We should always compute it alongside of our NPV.

Shortfalls of IRR

There are a couple of things that we need to be careful about with the internal rate of return. By reducing the solution to a percentage IRR is easy to grasp, but there are issues surrounding the information that gets eliminated.

NPV is our gold standard capital budgeting tool. IRR is similar to NPV and we have looked at the benefits of using IRR. But there are a couple of complications in practice that we will now walk through.

The first is loan types of cash flows. When the cash flows get reversed or when they come in and go out, come in and go out, IRR can get confused for some math reasons that we will look at.

Another is the scale issue. We can make poor capital budgeting decisions based only on IRR because doesn't take into account the scale of the project how big it is. When analyzing and choosing between projects, one may have a slightly better IRR but be an order of magnitude smaller and so the amounts of money generated are proportionately smaller.

We would rather have more money than less, but IRR has eliminated how much money we're making overall. IRR puts the solution in percentage terms and we need to be careful about the information that gets lost.

There is also an issue related to the lack of information about the timing cash flows. And finally there are some mathematical complications with IRR that we need to be aware of.

Loan Flows

IRR can sometimes give me a misleading picture about whether or not the project is adding value to the firm when cash flows are reversed during a project.

In a situation where money comes in and then money goes out, the sign, negative and positive, flips. Any time the sign flips in a stream of cash flows, we need to use IRR with caution.

For example, if we spend money on a machine, then the machine generates revenue, and then we have to retool the machine in year three, and we spend more cash, and then generates more revenue, that's two sign changes: money out, money in, money out, money in. Any time the cash flow direction flips a couple of times; you have to hesitate in using IRR.

Loan Flow IRR Example

Project	CF$_0$	CF$_1$	IRR	NPV @ 10%
A	(400)	500	25%	54.54
B	400	(500)	25%	(54.54)

Consider these two projects, A and B. In the first, we are going to spend $400 in order to generate $500 a year from now.

In this case the NPV comes out to 54.54 and the IRR comes out to 25%. In the second project we've got $400 coming in, and then I spend $500 a year from now. This stream looks like a loan. We are getting money in, paying it back later. In the case of project B, the net present value is *minus* 54.54. The whole thing flipped. We aren't making $54; we are losing $54. When we compute the IRR, it's the same 25%.

What happened, did something get screwed up? No, the math is clean. The solution to what rate sets that NPV equal to 0 is 25%. It's just that the NPV flipped sign. We have to be careful any time there's a flip in the sign of the cash flows.

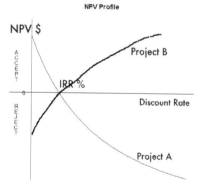

Let's look at it from the graph perspective that we talked about when we talked about IRR. For project A the

NPV is downward sloping and above zero until the IRR. But in project B the NPV is negative and upward sloping until it crosses zero at the IRR.

They have the same IRR, but for a low discount rate, project B is going to give us a negative NPV, whereas project A is going to give us a positive NPV.

We need to be careful when it comes to loan type flows and IRR. What's the solution? Just put it next to an NPV. If you compute an IRR, compare it with the net present value. NPV always serves as a check on whether you're getting the right capital budgeting decision.

Scale and IRR

Another issue is comparing the scale of different projects or investments using IRR. If we have mutually exclusive projects that we want to compare and decide between, it's hard to meaningfully compare them with IRR. Mutually exclusive means we can't pursue both projects because of limited resources. We must choose one or the other. In choosing one, we must forgo the other. As financial officers we want to make sure we decide to pursue the best opportunities that generate the most money.

It's not clear whether a higher IRR indicates a higher NPV. Let's go through an example of how we would compare mutually exclusive projects with the IRR.

Project	CF_0	CF_1	IRR	NPV @ 10%
1	(1)	2	100%	0.82
2	(100)	120	20%	9.1

In project 1 we are just going to spend $1. This would represent an incremental project such as an oil rig and all we are going to do is leave the rig where it is to keep pumping the end of an oil well. That's going to generate $2 in period 1.

That looks like a great project from an IRR standpoint. We are spending $1 in order to make $2. That's a 100% IRR.

Here's the issue: we could move that same rig to a new location. That would cost $100, and would generate $120. That is only a 20% IRR. It looks like project 1 is better than project 2 in terms of adding value, because it's got such a bigger IRR.

But if we compute the net present value, project 1 generates $0.82 per dollar. Project 2 generates $9.10. Project 2 has a much bigger NPV. We should move the rig.

Project 2 is much better from a net present value standpoint because it's generating a lot more value in total dollars for the firm. It's just that project 1 is generating a relatively higher number. IRR doesn't take the scale of the project into account.

The best way to avoid being misled is to put IRR next to NPV. That checks whether or not the IRR is large enough and whether the scale is giving us the right decision with IRR.

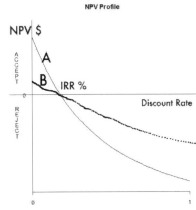

NPV Profile

We can analyze this graphically by looking at two projects. Projects A and B have the same IRR, but Project A has a much higher net present value. Project A is preferable to Project B, because for all discount rates less than the IRR, it's going to generate more NPV.

Always put that IRR next to a net present value in order to check for scale issues.

Multiple or No Solution to IRR

Situations exist where there is no solution to the IRR polynomial.

If you put the cash flows into Excel in the IRR formula and it won't give you an answer, it could be that there's multiple IRR's or no IRR's.

Project	CF_0	CF_1	CF_2	IRR
A	(100)	235	136	[5%,

				30%]
B	(100)	120	(50)	- -

Consider the example above. We are analyzing two projects. In both projects we spend 100. In Project A we plan to make 235 and 136. Project B is forecast to make 120 and negative 50.

In Project A there are actually two IRR's, not one. In Project B there is no IRR.

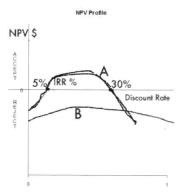

Remember, IRR is the solution to a math equation and there are scenarios where there is no solution to the math problem. Graphically, Project A and B look like this: for Project A the NPV gets bigger for a while, then starts to go down. This project has two IRR's. NPV crosses zero twice as the discount rate increases. It could be that a project is such a total loser that it never gets up to a positive NPV. That is the case with Project B. It has no IRR because it never crosses zero.

Again, how do we address this issue? Make sure to compare an IRR calculation to a net present value. This way you can always check whether or not the

IRR is giving you the right capital budgeting decision.

Shortfalls of IRR Summary

IRR is a good capital budgeting tool. But we need to be careful. Because of the nature of mutually exclusive projects, the scale problem, cash flow timing issues, or whether or not there's an answer or solution, always check next to a net present value.

As long as you aware of these caveats and put that IRR next to the NPV, IRR is a perfectly legitimate analysis tool. IRR provides insight as way to get an idea of what the return on the project is relative to the discount rate.

Bringing it All Together

Lets take stock of all the capital budgeting tools that we've talked about:
- Net present value
- IRR
- Payback
- Accounting ratios

Most CFOs rely on multiple metrics when making capital budgeting decisions. There are pros and cons to payback, IRR, net present value and accounting ratios. What is important to understand is that each one of those data points represents an interesting piece of information.

Using a portfolio of different capital budgeting tools helps make for better financial decisions.

John Graham and Cam Harvey at Duke University ran a survey where they asked CFOs what capital budgeting metrics they rely on. The predominant answers where IRR and NPV. That survey of the practice squares with what we have been saying here. Although in their survey IRR and NPV came out around the same: 75% for both. We have made a pretty good case here that NPV is the gold standard.

We talked about payback period. 57% of CFOs said that they use payback period in helping them make capital budgeting decisions. Payback period falls short in that it doesn't reflect the timing or the risk of the project being analyzed. Payback period analyzes how soon we get paid back on a project and more money sooner is better but we need to be cautious about using payback. Always use it in conjunction with NPV and IRR.

We can also use earnings multiples and other accounting ratios that we talked about. They can provide interesting information but should not be solely relied upon in making capital budgeting decisions. Always include NPV and IRR. Include IRR and NPV next to that return on invested capital or that payback period so that we can make maybe a better decision.

It's your job now to go out into the field and help managers and financial decision makers, especially at smaller companies that might have historically only used payback, to make better financial decisions by using some of the capital budgeting tools that have a better theoretical and empirical foundation.

Summary

NPV should always be your first approach. IRR helps put NPV in perspective by distilling the cash flows into a percentage return. NPV and IRR should always be used in the capital budgeting process.

Payback can be useful, especially if two NPVs are close. One may have a significantly better payback. There's nothing wrong with using payback to help round out that capital budgeting decision.

Accounting ratios can be informative, especially for internal mechanisms of control, but be cautious of using the accounting ratios that don't necessarily reflect timing, risk, and cash creation.

NPV and IRR are the go-to capital budgeting tools. Use payback and accounting ratios such as P/E multiples, return on invested capital to round out the analysis and capital allocation decisions.

Business Law

There are a lot of aspect of law and the legal system as they pertain to business. There is contract law, securities law, intellectual property law, and criminal and civil law and the court system.

The two basic professionals you need to rely on in business are an accountant and a lawyer. I am not a lawyer and this book is not legal advice. This is informational only.

In this book we are going to focus on Corporate law and business entity structure. How you form a company to protect the owners from liabilities is probably the most important legal issue to be familiar with.

Business Entity Structure

Picking what kind of legal entity to operate under is obviously an important consideration. It is also important to know how to navigate and operate in different structures because they have different lines of authority and implications for decision-making.

As companies grow, and demands on the organization change, the business form also should change to better handle the growing complexities of dealing with a larger scale business operation.

Simplicity and low cost are appropriate considerations for small enterprises, and flexibility, formal systems, and liability protection become important as the size of the company increases. From simplest to most flexible there is: sole proprietorship, LLC and S Corp, and C corporations.

A sole proprietorship is the simplest form of business. The main drawback here is a lack of protections for owners against liabilities incurred by the business. In this case, the business and you are pretty much identical. You probably want to protect your house and car and savings from business problems.

Even if you have just one other employee, or vendors and suppliers, things get out of your direct control and oversight pretty quickly and you are held financially and legally responsible for their actions. This is not a good scenario.

The middle ground structure is the LLC or Limited Liability Company. An LLC is a good compromise for a small venture or start-up because, as its name implies, it provides liability protection for the owners and operators and limits liabilities to the assets of the LLC.

The LLC is a good choice if there are few partners and owners. But this form of business gets complicated when there are more than a handful of owners. The accounting and tax reporting on form K1 also gets convoluted and cumbersome with changing ownership and bringing in investors. This choice works best when the ownership is tightly held.

If you are spreading ownership to partners and employees and raising capital to expand and bring in investors, then it is time to consider becoming a C corporation.

There are five main things to consider when analyzing the best business structure:

Ownership: The issues here relate to flexibility of ownership: how easy is it to manage multiple owners and transfer ownership.

Management: What is the relationship of ownership to day-to-day management and how easy is it to transition from one top manager to another. What are the mechanisms for owners to be kept updated on operations and results and how do they voice their concerns and opinions relative to the operations and strategy.

Capital Raising: What alternatives are available for financing the business and how easy is it to slice up the ownership into affordable pieces and coordinate the various owners? This issue is related to ownership and the ways ownership interests in the company can be sold to investors who remain distant to the actual day-to-day running of the business. This is called absentee ownership. These types of owners purchase stock or equity in the company, in other words, a fractional ownership in the company. The other main category of finance capital is debt. Debt or a Loan differs from Equity in that it has a fixed repayment period and interest rate. Debt also has a priority claim on the assets of the company.

Liability protection: This concept represents one of the most significant advances in economics and has fueled Capitalism, business development, technical progress, and economic prosperity over the past 150 years. Different business structures provide different levels of protection from the liabilities and risks of the company such as lawsuits, creditors, and business failure. For example: if a mistake is made, or you employ a bad actor, you don't want your house and savings to be exposed to being taken away to compensate for damages. Liability protection is a big reason why LLCs and corporations are so attractive.

Taxes: How is the business entity taxed? Do the tax consequences of profits and losses pass through to the owners directly or is the entity essentially double taxed at the entity level and then at the personal level for any profits received. Taxation of the individual owners is another important concern. You don't want an inordinate amount of expense incurred employing tax accountants.

To address these issues, there are three basic kinds of business structures:

Sole Proprietorships: is the simplest business structure. This type business organization can be sufficient for an individual or for up to a few partners.

It works well for a straightforward business structure and is good for an independent owner. The big problem with this type of business is the lack of liability protection for the owner against the risks of the business. If the business runs into problems, or is involved in a lawsuit the owner is personally liable for the consequences. However, insurance can help manage some of these risks. The tax consequences flow directly through to the individual owner, a convenient and attractive tax set up. Note that this business structure only works if the owner is comfortable with overseeing every aspect of the business. Otherwise, an organizational structure that affords liability protection is seriously worth considering.

Limited Liability Companies and Partnerships (LLC and LLP)

These structures address the liability exposure concerns of a sole proprietorship and the expense and more complicated set up of a corporation in the form of a compromise. LLCs became popular in the 1980s. LLCs and LLPs work well for businesses with few outside investor groups and stable company ownership.

Professional service groups like Accounting and Law Firms are usually set up as partnerships under LLPs. In this case, taxes pass through to the owners in the form of a K1 statement. You need a good tax accountant to figure these structures out and they get complicated quickly with ownership changes and company growth. You have basically outgrown an LLC when you are past the development stage of a start-up and decide to take on outside investors.

Partnership can be dicey and difficult to maintain. Here is David Ogilvy's advice on maintaining a partnership:

It is as difficult to sustain happy partnerships as to sustain happy marriages. These challenges can be met if those concerned practice these restraints:

- Have clear-cut division of responsibility
- Don't poach on the other fellow's preserves
- Live and let live; nobody is perfect
- "Why beholdest thou the mote that is in thy brother's eye but considers not the beam that is in thine own eye?"

Corporations

The corporation form of business structure has proven itself to be one of the most revolutionary and productive forces of capitalism to date. We rarely think of an organizational and legal structure as being a game changing innovation, but in this case it is difficult to overstate its impact.
Corporations are an ingenious innovation in how humans organize their efforts and protect the owners. This legal concept has been at the center of economic development and an engine of prosperity for more than a century. In the grand scheme of things, that

isn't such a long time. It is a surprisingly recent invention.

The corporate structure allows an enterprise to exist essentially in perpetuity by having mechanisms of governance and capital formation that allow for relatively simple, stable and predictable transfer of authority, power and ownership. It is the most flexible and productive enterprise vehicle ever created. Its importance and influence can be felt in most every aspect of modern life.

I am not exaggerating the importance of the concept of the corporation and want to take a moment to understand how it evolved.

History of the Corporation

Adolph Berle was a famous lawyer and economist who detailed the evolution of the modern corporation in a landmark book *The Modern Corporation and Private Property* published in 1932.

The main concern of this book was to describe the division of ownership and control: those who have ownership over corporations, the shareholders, are separate from the control of the corporation, which is handled by the Board of Directors and the executive management headed by the Chief Executive Officer (CEO) or President. It is governance by plurality and means that more than one person sets and votes on the strategic direction and plan to achieve it. The running of a corporation is guided by a formal set of

429

instructions: the **Articles of Incorporation** and the **Bylaws**.

Separation of ownership and control, along with liability protection and being an actively traded on the stock market are the innovations that allow people to invest relatively modest amounts in giant enterprises. They reap the rewards of their investments in form of their share of the profits and the growth of the value of the enterprise. These incentives and protections are what have allowed capital formation and investment in massive scale enterprises.

The industrial revolution made scale an advantage. These innovations in capital formation allowed enormous enterprises to develop and take advantage of that scale. Not many people can afford to invest the money to start a big operation like an automobile or airplane or computer company. That's why capital formation through stock markets and corporations are an ideal match and present the first form of crowd sourcing. When ownership is diffused to many, capital can be raised from lots of people interested in the prospects and profit potential of a corporation and used to invest in plant and equipment, supplies and employees.

The modern corporation is an ideal match for innovations brought about with the stock market. They create a powerful symbiosis: money can be aggregated in the stock market and allocated and traded to the most promising ventures in the form of corporations. Investors can make their investment decisions based on the performance of the corporations.

Business performance is reported quarterly in the form of profits and other accounting measures. Investor ownership interest is separate from the operating issues of management. They reap the benefits of ownership as the company they invested in generates profits.

Corporate Profits, Shareholders and Stakeholders

The profits of a corporation are divided into two categories: those that are retained for future use and investment within the enterprise, and those that are distributed to the shareholders in the form of dividends. There can be tensions and problematic effects to how profits are allocated and how corporations are run.

Recently there has been vocal demand from shareholders for companies to dividend out more of the earnings and put the money in the shareholder's hands (and pockets). Since the 1980s in the US, maximizing shareholder value and using profits to buy back shares and increase dividends has been the general mantra of US capitalism.

This practice has been popular but is now coming under increased scrutiny and criticism as short-term thinking. It is a practice that can erode the long term viability and sustainability of the enterprise by not bringing adequate amounts of the profits back into the corporation in the form of upgrading equipment,

431

investment in new equipment and training, as well as other things that increase the future prospects of the venture.

Shareholder maximization of this sort focuses on enriching current shareholders, who are the ostensible owners but also have the least long term interest in the company since they can sell their shares quickly in the stock market.

Put starkly, they can advocate for draining the lifeblood of a corporation and exit by selling their shares when the prospects for the future start to look grim or compromised. This can leave other stakeholders like the community, employees and suppliers, in the lurch as they can't switch so easily and have more vested in the long-term viability of the enterprise.

There are advocates for no longer just running a corporation to maximize profits solely for the benefit of shareholders. It has become prominent practice to broaden the awareness of stakeholders and widening the goals of the operation to include other stakeholders.

This more enlightened form of capitalism is practiced in other parts of the world, such as Europe and Asia, where governments, employees and other long term stakeholders have seats on boards and help guide the direction of the enterprise.

The separation of ownership and control is convenient since it gives investors the best bang for their bucks. Executives and employees of the company are essentially working for them and hopefully increase the value of their investment.

Yet this creates a conflict of interest because though executives and workers are motivated differently than the shareholders. Ostensibly all the workers are trying to successfully increase the value of the company and as such increase shareholder value and increasing shareholder value is the stated task of the executives who are planning and running the company.
Often people are more interested in their personal gain, security and well-being than in the firm's future, and this can put their goals and motivations in conflict with those of the owners (shareholders). This conflict of interest is the main reason communism has not been able to operate successful and sustainable businesses: People in power tend to squander all resources for their personal gain.

Those who are focused on the day-to-day affairs and operation of the corporation, the management and the directors, also have the ability to manage the resources of the company to their own advantage. They can do this because there is no effective oversight or scrutiny by the shareholders. How to align these conflicting interest groups and how to properly motivate the workers to achieve the goals of the owners is a key issue of Management, Strategy, and Corporate Governance.

Corporate Oversight

Ways in which these tensions between owners and executives of corporations are managed and mediated are:

- **Voting rights of shareholders**: if shareholders are not satisfied with how the company is being run, they can vote out directors and vote in ones that more align with their ideas of how the company should be run. The annual voting documents are called Proxy Statements and the voting is done at the annual meeting. In most cases, a majority of shares is needed to ratify a vote.

- **Transparency in reporting**: for publicly traded companies, there are regulations that require corporate executives, directors, and their auditors to provide clear and understandable reporting, in documents like 10Ks, as well as accuracy in accounting. There are also mechanisms and documents designed to hold executives accountable for their actions and to address reducing fraud. The Securities and Exchange Commission (SEC) oversees this corporate reporting. The SEC is tasked with overseeing regulations designed to maintain public trust in the basic fairness of the financial markets.

Moral Hazard is a term used to describes lack of accountability, when someone is not held responsible for their actions and the risks that arise from those actions. Reducing and eliminating moral hazard is a key principal of financial and securities regulation. Although eliminating it is not a practical possibility, the goal is to reduce moral hazard to the level of unusual occurrence. This helps significantly to promote trust in the markets and, in turn, encourages investment money to continue to flow into the stock market and supports funding of promising enterprises.

Board of Directors

The Board of Directors charts the course of the company through developing and approving the strategy and the budget. The Board usually consists of an odd number of participants so voting is never tied, and usually consists of outside directors with expertise in various aspects of the business like law, marketing, management, finance and accounting; and directors that are also top executives like the CEO and CFO.

This concept of multiple people with different points of view, experience and expertise, is called governance by plurality.

The Chairperson leads the Board of Directors. The Chair sets the agenda and runs the meetings. Board meetings are set up to discuss the issues at hand and to vote on them, thus in effect setting the course of the company.

The content of the meetings are documented in the board minutes, which are prepared and archived by the Corporate Secretary. The minutes are archived in the board book along with the Articles of Incorporation and the Bylaws.

Executives

The Executives execute the strategy and budget approved by the Directors. The top executive is the CEO Chief Executive Officer; sometimes this role is called the President. Other "C" level executives include:

- CFO Chief Financial Officer, who oversees the accounting, financing, budgeting and reporting.

- COO Chief Operating Officer, who oversees the operations, supply chains, factories, equipment and personnel.

As the digital age has progressed and evolved, two more C level roles have become crucial:

- CTO Chief Technology Officer
- CIO Chief Information Officer

There has been a proliferation of "C" level executive titles in recent years as part of the evolving organizational design and structure of complex enterprises.

Corporate Governance

Corporate governance is documented in the charter documents of the corporation: the Articles of Incorporation and the Bylaws. These documents detail how decisions are to be made that affect the enterprise such as:

- Election and term of Directors (usually 3 years and staggered),
- Voting rights of Shareholders (the owners),
- The scope of power of the CEO,
- How to inform shareholders of news that materially effects the corporation, and
- Scheduling and notification of the **Annual Meeting**.

At the Annual Meeting executives and the board inform the shareholders of the year's progress and performance, as well as the future plans. The **Proxy Statement**, documents the items that were voted on and the vote tally.

Delaware as Corporate Headquarters

In US corporate law C corporations are the most flexible and common form of corporate structure. The state where most companies are incorporated is Delaware. Delaware has become the de facto standard location for corporate residency in the US. Over the decades, this state has developed a legal system especially honed to deal with corporate law and disputes.

From a capital formation or capital raise standpoint, it is a good idea to incorporate in Delaware because venture capitalists and investors are familiar with the laws and structure. This can eliminate a stumbling block in due diligence proceedings related to raising capital and investing.

Nevada has mirrored Delaware's laws and offers more reasonable pricing to incorporate in an effort to lure corporate business and headquarters.

The Role of Corporate Structure

The benefits of corporate structure began to become apparent as the Industrial Revolution evolved, expanded and created the need and the opportunity for large enterprises to undertake large-scale business activities.

Corporations provided the organizational structure to grow and manage large-scale operations in a perpetual manner that transcended a single powerful charismatic entrepreneurial personality like a Carnegie, Rockefeller or Edison.

Corporations also evolved into the perfect vehicle and match for stock and bond markets for capital formation, raising and investment. They developed simultaneously to meet the needs of each other. Corporate structure allowed capitalism and the capital markets to infinitely scale, and capital markets provided the vehicle to aggregate money and invest it in promising projects represented by corporations.

This symbiosis drove the economic development of capitalist countries, especially in the United States.

The concept of Limited Liability and the corporate veil were major contributing catalysts that helped it all fall into place. Regulations to capital markets, like the stock market reporting requirements, allowed investors to review the results and allocate and re-allocate funds based on corporate performance.

The heroic entrepreneurs of early capitalism eventually were replaced by a new group of bureaucratic professional managers as companies grew in scale and matured over time. The MBA curriculum was originally created in the early twentieth century to train competent managers for this new and developing professional field.

Evolving Role

The business world has changed dramatically in the past thirty years with the astonishingly rapid development of technologies, including computers, communications networks, and mobile devices. Companies have been able to develop and grow rapidly without the need for large start up capital. Put differently, in today's economy ideas can be developed, tested, and refined on tiny budgets. The barriers to starting and scaling an enterprise have been dramatically reduced.

A product or service can be developed on a laptop and launched via an App or website and downloaded as many times as there is customer appetite without concerns for manufacturing or inventory.

No longer is big capital an initial requirement to roll out a world changing idea. Marketing and awareness campaigns can be run on-line via targeted pay-per-click PPC advertisements. Ideas, products and services can go viral creating vast awareness on social media.

The interest generated can be converted to sales through credit card or PayPal account charging. This type of model requires little infrastructure other than what is publicly and freely available and supply can scale rapidly to meet any level of demand.

A consequence of this structural shift is a resurgence of high profile entrepreneurs that are leading new enterprises with vision and charisma. Launching companies by converting ideas into products and services relies more on heroic leadership than operational efficiency. There is less initial reliance on the stewardship of professional managers, sometimes referred to as "adult supervision".

However, at some point in the life of every growing company the skills of managers are needed. Many cutting-edge entrepreneurs are adept at continuing to lead their enterprises past the initial ideation stage and have proven to be excellent managers. Others have thought more like owners than employees and stepped aside at the appropriate transition time to let capable others work to increase the value of their equity stakes.

Through this recent transformation of the role and idea of management corporations continue to be the most viable form of legal and organizational structure. The major benefits of corporations is limited liability to protect founders and investors against failure and risk aversion; and a flexible stock structure that provides equity and stock options to investors, key employees and founders.

The early stage barriers with respect to capital for starting a company have been radically reduced. But after a product/market fit and a sustainable business model are established, money is still obviously strategically important in order to scale up production and support marketing and sales. The corporate structure is the vehicle for seeking and attaining venture capital investment and other funding sources.

Human Resource Management

Introduction

Human Resource Management (HRM) refers to the functions in an organization that designs the jobs, recruits, hires, creates and administers the rules of employee conduct and the relationship between employer and employee, and manages termination through firing, severance, or retirement.

HRM has become more sophisticated in the last several decades as a greater appreciation of the strategic importance of leveraging an organization's talent pools has developed.

Designing jobs

What amount of tasks and responsibilities constitute a full time position? Like Goldilocks, the scope and requirements of a job need to be not too much and not too little work. In designing jobs and the requirements of a position, the challenge is to hit the sweet spot between full engagement and overload.
Designing jobs starts with an analysis of workflow and how products and services get made and are delivered, and the nature of the support services that are required. The tasks associated with a particular position are then delineated and a job description is developed. Skill sets are identified to fulfill the tasks and this information is then used to seek out qualified candidates and then to assess their performance once hired.

Recruitment

"Here's to the crazy ones, the misfits, the rebels, the troublemakers, the round pegs in the square holes... the ones who see things differently — they're not fond of rules... You can quote them, disagree with them, glorify or vilify them, but the only thing you can't do is ignore them because they change things...

442

they push the human race forward, and while some may see them as the crazy ones, we see genius, because the ones who are crazy enough to think that they can change the world, are the ones who do."

Steve Jobs, Think Different (1997)

These were the kinds of people Steve Jobs was looking to hire; renegade talent that could think and act creatively and move things forward rapidly. He wasn't afraid to hire smart people; smarter than him. Their challenging, probing questions, aptitude and attitude didn't intimidate him. He knew that hiring mediocre talent would lead to a downward spiral.

When a company is small, it's determined to hire only A players. But as the company grows, fear and politics set in. Some leaders fear that a new employee will be better at something than they are. They may even show them up or take their job.

This fear leads to what Guy Kawasaki (who worked for Apple) refers to as the 'Bozo Explosion'. The moment you hire a B player is the moment the 'Bozo Explosion' starts; the B player hires a C player, the C player hires D players, until one day you wake...and you are surrounded by bozos.

Hire the best. Hire people who are better than you.

LinkedIn

The human resources field is being dramatically reshaped as a consequence of the digital economy. The rise of LinkedIn as a nexus point for job seekers, recruiters, employers, and networking, is an indication and consequence of this transformation.

The social networking site has transformed how employers and prospective employees engage with one another, becoming an indispensable tool for employers seeking the right person to fill a specific position.

Employers use the site both to connect with active job seekers and also to identify desirable candidates to contact, court and hire.

LinkedIn is a great social media tool for business and professional networking. It is also the premier human resources forum for getting exposure to recruiters and employers and upping your chance of landing your dream job.

LinkedIn was launched in late 2002 and has grown to more than 500 million members in more than 200 countries. Professionals are signing up to join LinkedIn at a rate of more than two new members per second. It is your one-stop shop for career networking.

If you are in the job market, get on LinkedIn and polish up your profile ASAP.

Hiring

The first tip of good management is: **hire well**. That is easy to say and really challenging in practice. Besides attempting to assess technical skills and work ethic you are trying to gain psychological and emotional insights of potential employees in order to asses if they will be a good fit and provide synergies to the organization.

The Meta-Hire

Hiring a great HR director is one of the most important hires you can make. This isn't the dusty back office job to which it was once relegated. People will make or break your enterprise and the person who interfaces with them is in a critical position.

Commitment

A new hire is a big commitment. It is the beginning of a deeply complex and engaging relationship like marriage. As in dating, people tend to present a virtuous façade at first that may hide other, less attractive, personality traits.

There is an entire body of new work on how to develop a better initial assessment that might allow you to predict with greater certainty, which will be a good, great, or disastrous fit for a particular job.

Just as in dating, mating and marriage, it is often easy to get into a relationship and very difficult to extricate oneself. In other words, front end assessment work in the hiring process to screen and select appropriate candidates is crucial.

Screening and understanding the psychological makeup of a potential employee before hiring is cannot be overstated. You want to know if this potential hire will flourish in your organization and help energize others, if they will be a toxic element that poisons and erodes the esprit de corps, or an unremarkable seat warmer somewhere in between.

You are looking to identify a person that is a team player with talent, expertise, and experience to perform the tasks at hand. You also need to assess if they have the flexibility and capacity to learn and contribute as the environment evolves.

Hiring an employee is one of the most critical decisions you can make as a manager or entrepreneur. When interviewing, people are on their best behavior and often throw everything they know at you. Some are very smooth interviewees but may turn out to be all talk and poison to your business.

The premise of the book *The No Asshole Rule* (love the title) is that even if someone has stellar talent, if they are an asshole: DO NOT HIRE THEM. A catty personality that develops cliques and participates in palace intrigues is toxic to an organization and its ability to function. They must not be allowed to enter.

I have personally been fooled many times both ways when hiring and assessing people's potential. I have thought someone would fit in and be able to contribute quickly and substantially only to find myself shocked by their lack of performance and ability to disrupt and anger others. But I have also been more than pleasantly surprised by "bland" people who seemed earnest and capable, but grew quickly into stellar performers and inspired others to reach higher.

There have been a lot of recent developments in designing objective criteria for making hiring decisions. Testing and analysis has evolved to help guide the hiring process along quantitative, systematic and predictable criteria. This is especially important in fast growing companies that need to scale up quickly in order to remain competitive.

The author William Poundstone has chronicled the testing and hiring selection process at Microsoft in his book *How Would You Move Mount Fuji* and at Google in *Are You Smart Enough to Work at Google?* These two books detail interviewing tactics used by these companies in their attempt to separate the good prospects from the stellar.

Obviously, better screening processes and tools can help make better hiring decisions, but in most cases it still comes down to trusting your gut and to engaging your bullshit detector. And equally, if not more important, ask yourself whether you resonate on a personal level with the candidate.

When a company is growing rapidly hiring decisions are most critical. A formal system and process is necessary to acquire top talent quickly and ensure a good fit with the organizations culture and objectives. There is an adage: A people hire A people and B people hire Cs. Inferior hires can quickly devolve into a dysfunctional mess that cannot quickly be remedied.

Do not be timid. Hire people smarter than you and don't be afraid. Steve Jobs considered hiring superior talent to be strategically critical. He said that top talent isn't 10% better than the others; they are 10 times better. These are the people you want.

You want super smart creative talent that can make an impact on your company's destiny.
Here is what the legendary advertising executive David Ogilvy had to say on hiring:

"The challenge is to recruit people who are able to do the difficult work our clients require from us.
   • Make a conscious effort to avoid recruiting dull, pedestrian hacks.
   • Create an atmosphere of ferment, innovation, and freedom. This will attract brilliant recruits.
   • If you ever find a man who is better than you are – hire him. If necessary, pay him more than you pay yourself. "

When hiring look for people who are genuinely humble. Brilliance and intelligence can breed hubris and cloud one's ability to perceive and adjust for shortcomings and faults.

Aside from the brilliant hires you will also need dedicated stable workers; "Steady Eddies" that are superbly capable and can add incremental improvements and efficiencies. These people keep the trains running on time.

Talent Wars

This dynamic between top talent and companies goes both ways. Top talent can work at any number of companies and add huge strategic value to the operation. Companies must create a work environment that attracts and intrigues talent.

Recruitment is only part of the equation; retention is also a major concern.
Google encourages employees to spend 20% of their time, one day a week, working on personal projects. It is creative programs like this that attract and retain talent.

Employer and Employee Relationship

Onboarding

Once a new employee is hired the onboarding process begins. Onboarding is also known as organizational socialization. It refers to the process through which new employees acquire the necessary knowledge, skills, and behaviors to become effective members of the organization.

Performance Management

Performance management is the systematic process by which an organization involves its employees and managers in improving organizational effectiveness in the accomplishment of its mission and goals.

Performance Review

A performance review is a method by which the job performance of an employee is documented and evaluated. Performance review is a part of career development and consists of regular reviews of employee performance within organizations.

Employee Handbook

The Employee Handbook details the rules and relationship between employer and employee. This text should be reviewed in detail during orientation and an Acknowledgement should be signed by the employee and kept in their file. Here is an example of the contents of an Employee Handbook.

Sample Employee Handbook Table of Contents

Welcome

452

Training and Development

Human resource management regards training and development as a function concerned with organizational activity aimed at bettering the job performance of individuals and groups in organizational settings.

Human Resource Development

Training and developing employees is one of the most powerful strategic missions a company has. Developing employee's skills also helps with retention. It is much more cost effective to keep good employees and develop them than it is to search, hire, and train new personnel. Many companies that used to outsource training are now developing in-house training and education programs that are more accurately tailored to their particular business.

Executive education has been viewed as a cherished perk to provide to up and coming talent. But many companies have recently realized that sending a star executive off to an executive MBA program is a double-cdgcd sword.

The newly trained executive became more attractive to other companies and would jump ship for other opportunities. To avoid this kind of attrition companies are developing germane in-house programs even at the upper echelon.

Satisfaction

There is nothing more satisfying than helping develop the latent and innate talents and skills of employees. You can actually watch someone blossom and gain confidence as they successfully operate at higher levels. This is one of the greatest satisfactions of running a business and being a manager.

Termination

There are several ways that the employer/employee relationship ends:

- The employee chooses to leave for a better job, or quits because the job sucks. There is a saying: people join organizations but the quit bosses.
- They are fired
- There is a downsizing initiative and employees are offered a severance package to leave
- A long time employee retires

Firing

Hiring is so very important because once someone has joined your company, it is very difficult to get rid of them. An employee insinuates themselves into all kinds of aspects of the business and it is very disruptive to rip out those roots and replace them. But get rid of sad sacks who spread doom and gloom and who incurably spoil office politics. Do not tolerate phonies, zeros, bozos, or bastards.

There are rules and regulations protecting employees and they are important to ensure against abuses from bad management. But these protections can also become hurdles to making quick decisions about pulling the plug. Cynical or angry bad actors can use these protections as weapons to harm your enterprise if you are not careful.

It is incumbent on you to prevent these situations. But if you find yourself in such a situation fire them, do not to let them fester. Know the rules and regulations and focus your resources on hiring well and developing those new hires to be great individual and group contributors.

Automated Business Models

On the other hand, there are good arguments for reducing employees. Employees are the biggest cost line in a business and they can be a headache to manage. Aside from having to pay them, you have to manage their disputes and work around their needs for time off and being sick.

A way around some of these issues is to implement a business model using web-based automation systems. There are web tools available to automate marketing, sales and payment processing. You can also outsource procurement and order fulfillment and delivery.

In fact, if your product is a digital download, you can automate the entire business. This can remove a lot of potential headaches with employees and free up your time in addition. It also means great operating leverage. Without the expenses of employees, lots more money falls to the bottom line as profit.

Tim Ferriss has written a compelling book on the subject of getting yourself out of the loop of less constructive work by automating your business model and creating cash streams that require minimum amounts of your attention. The book is called *The 4-Hour Work-week* and I highly recommend it. It provides practical steps to incorporating his revolutionary ideas.

These are great ideas to entertain and implement in any business in order to leverage your effectiveness and free up time to focus on other important activities.

Another great book that details these kinds of business models is *Bold* by Peter Diamandis and Steven Kotler. The authors discuss how to employ new methodologies of using web based assets like Amazon's site, Mechanical Turk, and Freelancer.com to hire talent for specific tasks.

On Freelancer you can hire engineers, marketers, computer coders and others to develop products and provide services that used to be only available by hiring employees and making long-term commitments. Integrating these online tools is a new way of thinking about and acquiring technical and operational assets to fulfill your business goals.

The Gig Economy

The Gig Economy is the term for workers who construct a career out of working for multiple employers as contractors and also have side hustles that may be business that evolved out of hobbies or other interests.

There is an explosion of new services using web and mobile platforms to match workers with jobs on a contract basis. One high profile model is Uber which matches people with cars with people needing rides, creating a flexible and efficient on-demand taxi service.

Another example is AirBnB which matches bedrooms and homes with people who need a place to stay. These services compete with taxis and hotels and they rely on the powerful network effects of the Web and ubiquitous smartphones.

Similarly, there are services connecting people with freelancers to solve their problems; companies like: Freelancer.com, Fiver, and Upwork. These new ways of delivering labor and services are challenging our basic assumptions of capitalism and the nature of the firm and the structure of careers.

Contract workers

Using these services and contracting for work with expertise all over the world has become feasible with real time internet communication systems like Skype and Facetime along with email. Soon real time translation services will make these systems even more useful as we will be able to communicate in multiple languages instantly.

This model has been useful for professionals such as lawyers, doctors, and consulting services. Another idea is using prizes as incentive for creative ideas such as R&D solutions, design concepts such as logos, or the creation of videos. These are ways to match specialization with need and tap underused capacity.

On-demand business models have an attractive set of capabilities and advantages such as reduced need for offices and full-time permanent employees. This can be an asset for people selling their services, as well as for the virtual organizations using them.

Computers are used to package a set of particular needs into another group's set of tasks. This is a way to access spare time and spare cognitive capacity, and compensate people for it across the globe.

Amazon's Mechanical Turk is a great example for this operating model. It allows customers to post any "human intelligence task" on line and it allows workers to choose what to do according to the task and price.

In Economic terms, this is part of a revolution that is unleashing latent pools of resources. Ebay has monetized the latent value of our clothes closet, garage and basement; Uber and AirBnB have monetized the under-utilized value residing in out cars and homes; and these talent pool websites are allowing people with skills to moonlight or create careers and access demand for their services around the world. These tools are creating a new generation of supply and demand based markets.

Become familiar with these services and what they offer. You may use them to build your business in a flexible and scalable manner, or you may offer your services through them to others.

This is all part of a trend toward self-reliance. The role of the firm in our lives, to order our careers and provide stability, continues to be reduced. Our relationship to parental-type companies is being irrevocably modified.

Race Against the Machines

There are other profound ways in which business and work are becoming automated. Soon they will have to change the name of the department from HR to HRR: Human and Robot Resources.

The rise of Robotics and Artificial Intelligence and other cyborg related workers is changing the fundamental structure of Management, Labor and business.

We are moving into a future where many businesses can scale rapidly with non-tangible products and services can be infinitely replicated. Computer programs and algorithms can also perform the interface with customers more efficiently. This trend has profound implications for how we think about work and the nature of value and productivity.

How we relate to automation not only has implications for how we think about business models and operating leverage, but also about how we perceive ourselves and our careers developing over the course of a lifetime. These developments have profound implications for our sense of self worth and how we impute meaning to our lives.

Blue-collar jobs in manufacturing have been impacted over the recent decades as robotic systems have replaced workers on factory floors and assembly lines. Repetitive tasks represent relatively straightforward processes and lend themselves to automation.

Now entire factories are operated by a handful of workers monitoring computer screens. The leadership guru Warren Bennis predicted: "The factory of the future will have only two employees, a man and a dog. The man will be there to feed the dog. The dog

461

will be there to keep the man from touching the equipment."

The replacement of manual labor by dexterous programmable machines was the first wave of worker displacement. Worker Displacement 2.0 is now underway as Artificial Intelligence is becoming more widely implemented in practical systems.

The virtual personal assistant is a good example of a system that interacts via voice and incorporates language recognition and response. Siri and Alexa perform tasks by searching and retrieving information and employ a voice activated user interface.

White-collar jobs are now being replaced in fields previously thought impervious to the encroachment of automation. Accountants, lawyers, and other professional fields; science and engineering jobs; courts and call centers are all affected. What we choose to train for and how we position ourselves and think of our strengths and skill sets will be tested as we are confronted with continually encroaching prescience of automation and computing power.

It will be our task to recognize, predict, and adapt to this inevitable change. We are going to be tasked with forging productive alliances with new tools and leverage a newly focused understanding of our strengths in fruitful ways.

Put differently, our relationship to robots and artificial intelligence, and robots equipped with artificial intelligence will increasingly determine how happy, content, and satisfied we are in the future.

This Brave New World offers opportunities to delegate mundane repetitive tasks and even rule based thinking tasks to machines. Innovative and complementary pairing of machines and humans in hybrid models allows businesses to approach tasks in novel and productive ways.

We already recognize that tasks that are difficult for us humans are often easy for machines, and conversely, tasks that are easy for us are often complicated to implement in software and mechanical systems. But I regard this situation as an opportunity to unleash creative and energies.

Intellectual Property and Patents

Disclaimer

Information within this book does not constitute legal, financial or similar professional advice. The purchaser of this publication assumes full responsibility for the use of these materials and information. The Publisher and Author assume no liability whatsoever on behalf of any reader of this material. Please consult applicable laws and regulations and competent counsel to ensure your use of this material conforms with all applicable laws and regulations.

This is not legal advice and I do not promise that your patent will be awarded. That will rely on the strength of your invention and ability to adequately describe it and work with the patent office examiner. This section of the book is a brief guide to that process.

Different Kinds of Intellectual Property

There are four types of Intellectual Property protection of which patents are a subset. The four are:

- Patents
- Trademarks
- Servicemarks
- Copyrights

The rights that are protected under patents, copyrights, trademarks and servicemarks sometimes get confused and conflated. These are different kinds of intellectual property protection and they each serve different functions and purposes.

Trademarks and Servicemarks are similar but differ in that a trademark protects attributes of a product and a servicemark protects attributes of a service.

Copyright is a method of protection provided to the authors of "original works of authorship" including literary, dramatic, musical, and artistic.

I will go into more detail below on all four types of intellectual property protection starting with patents.

Patents

A patent is an exclusive property right for an invention and is granted to the inventor. The United States Patent and Trademark Office issue patents. The term length of a new patent is 20 years from the date on which the application for the patent was filed in the United States.

This property right is subject to the payment of application, grant, and maintenance fees. U.S. patent grants are effective only within the United States, U.S. territories, and U.S. possessions.
The right conferred by the patent grant is: "the right to exclude others from making, using, offering for sale, or selling" the invention in the United States or "importing" the invention into the United States.

What is granted is not the right to make, use, offer for sale, sell or import, but the right to *exclude others* from making, using, offering for sale, selling or importing the invention. Once a patent is issued, the holder of the patent must enforce the patent through the courts if there is infringement.

Your patent gives you rights to enforce the patent against infringers but it requires having serious money in the bank to pursue enforcement through litigation. It is not automatic. If a cease and desist letter doesn't stop the infringement, a lawsuit can easily run into the millions of dollars. Check with your attorney if you discover potential infringement on your patent.

International patent rights can be applied for and granted based on an underlying U.S. patent application.

Monopoly

Economists use two terms to describe the nature of competition in markets: perfect competition and monopoly. Perfect competition is where you have lots of alternative products to choose from and they can only really compete on price. In this case profits have been squeezed to zero. This is not a good place to be in business. Monopoly on the other hand is where there is no competition and the seller can command a premium profit for the product.

This is where you want to be positioned. You want to own the market and set your price. Competition is for losers.

This is what makes patents so valuable. A patent essentially gives you a legal monopoly to make, use and sell your invention. You get this legally protected monopoly status for twenty years from the application date. After that time, the invention goes into the public domain. An example of this process is when the patent on a pharmaceutical expires and then generic versions of the drug appear on the market.

There are Three Types of Patents:

Utility

Utility patents are what we will be focusing on in this book. Utility Patents cover the embodiment of an invention. The embodiment appears in the description of patent applications and is the term used to introduce a particular implementation or method of carrying out the invention.
Utility patents are granted to anyone who invents or discovers anything new and useful. A utility patent usually relates to a process, or a machine, but it can also be an article of manufacture, a composition of matter (like a new chemical compound), or any new and useful improvement to something previously existing in these categories.

Utility patents are the most commonly applied for.

Design

A "utility patent" protects the way an article is used and works, while a "design patent" protects the way an article looks. The ornamental appearance for an article includes its shape/configuration or surface ornamentation applied to the article, or both.

Patents may be granted to anyone who invents a new, original, and ornamental design for an article of manufacture. If you are a graphic or industrial designer or an architect, this category may be for you. This category is important to businesses in order to cover the design of their products, things like the tread design on tires or the shape of a bottle.

Design patents are for the cosmetic look only, not for its use. This can be a common confusion. If you intend to protect how something works, it's a utility patent you want to file. The design of a coke bottle is an example of a successful design patent.

Plant

Patents may be granted to anyone who invents or discovers and asexually reproduces any distinct and new variety of plant. There are many patents in seeds that produce more agricultural yield.

Provisional Patent Application

There is a type of preliminary Utility patent application called a **Provisional** application.
Provisional patent only applies to an application process. There is no such thing as a provisional patent. A provisional patent application requires follow-up with a full-fledged utility patent application. This must occur within one year. It is

only possible to file a Provisional Patent Application for utility patents.

Why file the provisional if you need to file a regular utility patent application anyway? Good question. A provisional patent application is quick and less expensive to prepare.
It can speed up the first to file advantage by providing an early effective filing date. The primary benefit is the time prioritizing of one's claim relative to the claims of others.

But you run the risk of not filing the utility follow-up on time. And after one year your invention goes into the public domain and you have lost out. Also the clock starts ticking on your potential patent term. The term of a patent is **20 years** from the earliest filing date of the application. If you chew up a year on the front end with a provisional, which reduces your useable patent term.

Provisional applications are not examined. In contrast to the regular application, the provisional format has less formal requirements. A provisional application doens't required formal patent claims, an oath or declaration. Provisional applications also should not include any prior art disclosure.

It does allow you to use the term "Patent Pending" on the invention.
After filing a provisional, you must file a non-provisional within 1 year.

The non-provisional application is more detailed. But the discipline of the process ensures your invention meets the approval criteria.

Think hard about filing a provisional application. It rarely makes sense. It is my opinion that provisionals are not worth filing. It creates more work and extra costs.

Don't bother getting caught up in the extra step and expense of filing a provisional; go for the gusto!

Trademark and Servicemark

Trademarks and Servicemarks are similar. The difference between the two is that a trademark protects attributes of a product and a servicemark protects attributes of a service. Trademarks and service marks that are used in interstate or foreign commerce should be registered with the USPTO. This registration is used to protect the branding of products and services like brand names and logos.

A trademark is a word, name, symbol, or device that is used in trade with goods to indicate the source of the goods and to distinguish them from the goods of others. A servicemark is the same as a trademark except that it identifies and distinguishes the source of a service rather than a product. The terms "trademark" and "mark" are commonly used to refer to both trademarks and servicemarks.

Trademark rights may be used to prevent others from using a confusingly similar mark, but not to prevent others from making the same goods or from selling the same goods or services under a clearly different mark.

The registration procedure for trademarks and general information concerning trademarks can be found on the USPTO website under the section entitled "Basic Facts about Trademarks." Here is a link to that webpage. (http://www.uspto.gov/trademarks/basics/Basic_Facts_Trademarks.jsp).

Here is an example of a famous trademark dispute.

Apple Corps vs. Apple Inc.

The right to trademark the word "apple" has been contentious. The Beatles music company Apple Corps was first. Eight years later Steve Jobs created Apple Inc. Over the years, the two corporations have battled it out in lengthy litigation.

In the first round, Apple Inc. agreed to pay Apple Corps a cash settlement and stay out of the music business. But with the advent of iTunes, the legal wrangling again heated up.
They reached a settlement after Apple Inc. agreed to buy Apple Corps' trademark rights and then license them back to the music company.
That's a lot of legal fees over a piece of fruit.

Copyright

Copyright is a method of protection provided to the authors of "original works of authorship" including literary, dramatic, musical, artistic, and certain other intellectual works, both published and unpublished.

The copyright protects the form of expression rather than the subject matter of the writing.
The Copyright Act of 1976 gives the owner of copyright the exclusive right to reproduce the copyrighted work, to distribute copies or recordings of the copyrighted work, to perform the copyrighted work publicly, or to display the copyrighted work publicly.

The Copyright Office of the Library of Congress registers copyrights.

Copyrights are big business in the music industry. Publishing income comes from ownership of the copyrights in the songs, not the sound recordings. Songwriters typically own the copyrights in the music and lyrics to the songs they write. They earn money from license fees and royalties from the commercial use of their songs.

There are also publishing companies that purchase the copyrights of songs. Michael Jackson bought the Beatles song catalog. ATV acquired Northern Songs, publisher of the Lennon–McCartney song catalogue, in 1969. Michael Jackson purchased ATV Music in

1985 for $47.5 million. Every time you hear a Beatles song on the radio, Michael's estate gets paid.

Signing away their publishing rights for small compensation in contracts with producers and record companies has ripped off many music artists in the past.

Owners of music copyrights guard their rights and are always on the lookout for hit songs that copy their melody. They sue if they hear something they think is too close to their song. There is a saying in the music business: "If you have a hit, you will get a writ."

Patents and their Statutory Basis

One of the basic rules of law in the United States is the legal protection of private property.

Inventions are considered intellectual property and ownership of that property is protected under patents and patent law.

Trade Secrets

There are two ways to protect an innovation. You can choose to patent it or keep it secret. We have been discussing at length the benefits of patents. Some perceived advantages of trade secrets are:

- Trade secrets can protect "abstract ideas" and patents cannot.
- The protection under trade secret remains for an unlimited period of time.
- There are no filing fees for trade secret protection.
- A trade secret creates cache and an aura of mystery.

Trade secrets are proprietary information that is not publicly disclosed. Trade secrets require agreement between parties not to disclose and are covered under Confidentiality and Non-disclosure agreements between the parties.

An example of a trade secret is the formula for making Coca Cola.

One of the most famous American trade secrets is the recipe for Coca-Cola. The mystique surrounding the formula has lasted more than 100 years. It has been the source of publicity and marketing campaigns. It has also been an enduring intellectual property protection strategy.

In 1886, Dr. John Pemberton created the Coca-Cola formula. Caffeine and sugar are ingredients. Other ingredients have been the source of speculation. One ingredient is the legendary "merchandise 7X". What the "X" factor is in the original formula has never been revealed. It may contain essential citrus oils of orange, lemon, and lime. Lavender may be another ingredient.

Only a small group of executives know the entire formula. No contractor has the complete recipe and each only makes a part of the famous blend.

The formula would have long since entered the public domain had the company patented it. They would have had only twenty years of exclusive rights to their classic blend.
The trade secret approach locks it up forever, as long as the secret is well kept.

There is risk of disclosure. It is not illegal to reverse engineer and copy a trade secret. Patent protection lasts 20 years and is more secure. In a patent lawsuit, independent invention is not a defense.

It depends on the nature of the innovation. You may want to discuss it with potential partners and investors. It may be easy to reverse engineer. In these cases file a patent before disclosing it. If it is a secret recipe like Dr. Pepper or Colonel Sander's KFC spices, then a trade secret works well.

Patents

'I don't care that they stole my idea. I care that they don't have any of their own.'
    Nikola Tesla

In the past decade the patent research, drafting, and filing process has evolved and the tools are now in place that makes it feasible for you to perform all the steps and file your own patent.

The process hasn't gotten easier but the tools of word processing and the database on the United States Patent and Trademark Office website create an environment that empowers all of us to protect and commercialize our ideas and creativity.

This section looks at the patent application process from the standpoint of U.S. patent and filing procedures.

You can file your patent for under $500 and the average value of an issued patent is $1 million. This is lucrative work and well worth your time to learn.

Outline of the Patent Application Process

Drafting a patent application is a surprisingly straightforward process. The hard part is having the idea of an invention. If you have ideas of things you think could be patented you owe it to yourself to read this book and draft an application.

Even if you decide not to file it, this knowledge may come in handy for the next big idea you have. Then you will be ready to draft the application and won't be intimidated because you have done it already.

You only need two things:

- Access to a computer with a word processor. I use Microsoft Word. Apple also has a great word processor called Pages. And Google Docs is also a super (and free!) option.
- Access to the Internet so you can go to the U.S. Patent and Trademark Office (USPTO) website www.uspto.gov where you will perform your prior art search and research patented ideas similar to your invention. This is also where you electronically file your patent application.

Application Process Steps

Pro se is the legal term for representing yourself. You will be representing yourself to the USPTO and the patent examiner in the applications process. Here is an outline of the process so you can get an idea of the steps:

- Come up with a title for your invention
- Write a short description of your invention.
- Use key words from you title and description as search terms in the database on the USPTO website. Copy the Abstract and patent number of patents and patent applications that are similar to yours.
- Write a description of why your patent is different from the similar ones already patented and published applications. This will become the Prior Art section of your application.

477

- Write a Summary of the Invention.
- Write a Brief Description of the Drawings. Every patent application needs to have at least one drawing that shows the parts of the invention.
- Write a Detailed Description of the Invention. This is where you discuss how to make and use the invention in as much detail as you can.
- Write the Claims. This is where you draft the different aspects of the invention each as a separate claim.
- Write the Abstract. This is a separate summary of the invention about one paragraph in length.
- Create the Drawings. You can do this in Word. It must be black and white and they are attached after the Abstract.

That's it! Those are the major sections of the application. When you have completed those parts to your satisfaction, you file it on the USPTO website along with a few short forms and your payment.

Then you wait six to twelve months to hear from your patent examiner who has reviewed your application. He or she will have questions regarding the prior art and your claims and you begin a process of responding to their questions. When they are answered satisfactorily, your patent will be ready to be awarded.

Why Patents Are Valuable

In most cases it only makes sense to patent ideas and inventions that you plan on commercializing. Patents are valuable because they represent a monopoly. You essentially get a 20-year monopoly on the business opportunity detailed by the invention. The patent represents competitive barriers to entry in the markets served.

Patents represent a strategic competitive advantage. In business, a competitive advantage is an attribute that allows an organization to outperform its competitors. A competitive advantage is what creates lasting value for a company.

Patents are a key piece of New Venture Strategy. Patents are strategically important, whether you are an entrepreneur with a start up idea, or working in an established company and have an idea that could expand a product or service line.
Once you have filed your patent, you have secured "patent pending" status.
"Patent pending" is a legal designation that can be used in relation to a product or process once a patent application for the product or process has been filed, but prior to the patent being issued or the application abandoned.

You can then feel free to talk about your invention with potential partners and investors because no one can steal your idea.
Patent pending represents an Asset that you can fund around. Investors like to fund assets. Filing a patent is

a great strategy, and probably the least expensive way, to jump-start a venture.

An astute and experienced business mentor once advised me: "When in doubt, create assets." A patent application costs less than $500 to file and an issued patent is worth $1 million on average. That is tremendous value leverage. This can be the basis of creating significant personal wealth.

Once you learn and become familiar with this process, you can create a patent portfolio that could add significantly to your net worth. It is also tremendously satisfying to see your ideas transformed into valuable intellectual property.
Big companies are big players in intellectual property. Along with branding and Trademarks, patents are considered primary strategic assets. Over 200,000 patents are awarded annually in the U.S. The company that was awarded the most U.S. patents last year was Samsung with over 9,000!

Companies look to create monopolies through their patent portfolio. One patent does not a monopoly make. Astute entrepreneurs and corporate leaders pursue a strategy of developing multiple patents that surround a commercial venture's core ideas. This is called a Picket Fence Strategy.

Patents are the most liquid form of intellectual property, meaning they can be valued and sold. IBM sold a portfolio of more than 500 patents to Facebook and a portfolio of more than 900 patents to Twitter. Twitter paid $36 million for their portfolio.

The Patent Application Process is Also Valuable

The front-end process of drafting a patent application is valuable in and of itself because it will quickly flesh out if your idea is truly novel and what the competitive landscape surrounding it looks like. The patent application process is a disciplined methodology that rationalizes your idea or concept.

If you have an idea for a novel product or service, a patent application can be a great process to initially test that idea against what may already exist. The application process will answer several important initial questions.

First it helps to concretize your concept or idea. You have to think about the different attributes and write them down.

Second it forces you, in a disciplined manner, to articulate and define your value proposition and what is truly unique about it. The process of drafting the application clarifies one's ideas and value proposition. This is a critical aspect of commercialization and will allow you to price your product or service at a premium.

Third the Prior Art search, conducted via key words in the search field of the USPTO database, forces you to examine similar patents and see what aspects of your concept or ideas represent something novel and unique. Searching, evaluating, and responding to prior art is a super methodology for competitive analysis. Your patent will act as a barrier to competitive entry into your market. This mitigates market risk and will make your enterprise more attractive to investors.

Fourth in a matter of hours you can assess whether you are really onto something or whether it has been thought of before. This is valuable to keep from wasting time.

Fifth drafting the application and filing it and receiving "patent pending" status lends credibility to you as a serious entrepreneur and businessperson. It creates a pre-money valuation for investment and licensing opportunities.

The application is a due diligence document that you can share, under a confidentiality agreement, with potential investors. It provides something concrete to analyze and their feedback and critiques can be very valuable. And they may fund your venture!

Sixth you can search and read all the patents in your field and get a sense of the competition.

You can search for Assignees and see what companies control what patents. The assignment of a patent is independent from the inventor. Patents are property. The assignee, usually a company, is the entity that has the property right to the patent. The inventor and the assignee may be the same, but an employee will assign a patent to the company they work for.

You can search on the Class and Subclass of your patent application to also uncover competitors. This is how patents are organized at the patent office. There are over 400 classes in the U.S. Patent Classification System. Each has a title descriptive of its subject matter is identified by a class number. Each class is subdivided into a number of subclasses with its own descriptive title and subclass number.

During the patent search process if you find relevant patents through your keyword search you can copy the classification number and search on that.

All of the information gathered from this process can be placed in your business plan and will make it a much more thorough and convincing document. This work creates clarity, reduces risk, and eliminates vagueness.

Patents create value, but only if they represent a commercially viable product or service. So don't think of a patent as a standalone entity but as an element in a strategic business context that you can execute on or license to someone else to bring to market.

Thomas Edison Patent Master

In the beginning of Edison's career he wrote all his own patents. In one year 1883 he drafted 106 patent applications that turned into patents. Thomas Edison was awarded 1093 patents issued in his name. That is the record!

Word to the Wise: Don't Overspend

There may be many things you can think of that can be patented. But be wise and frugal and only patent inventions that cover products you actually plan on selling.

If it doesn't have realistic markets and meet some customer need, then there is no commercial value and it may not be worth the cost and effort of patenting.

Where to File a Patent Application

The United States Patent and Trademark Office (USPTO) is responsible for granting and issuing patents and registering trademarks.

When you have completed application, you file it electronically with the United States Patent and Trademark Office (USPTO). You file through their website www.uspto.gov. This is the same website that houses the database you will search as part of drafting the prior art section of your application. The United States Patent and Trademark Office is responsible for administering the law relating to the granting of patents.

When to File

U.S. patent law is now "first to file". File as soon as you have your conception and can write a description of how to make and use it. You must disclose the best mode, the best embodiment of the invention and you must have claims drafted. You can be a big winner if you file ASAP!

What Can Be Patented

There are four general categories of criteria that must be met in order to be granted a patent:
- Eligibility: the invention must fall into one or more of four fields of subject matter
- Utility: it must be specifically and substantially useful
- Novelty: it must be distinguished from prior patents and public information
- Non obviousness: it must not be an obvious combination of prior patents and public information

Patent it Yourself!

For more information on how to research, draft and file a patent application check out my book **Patent it Yourself!** It's a handbook on how to get started protecting you ideas and creating a valuable intellectual property portfolio.

Strategy

Strategy in business is the big picture. It is about picking goals for the enterprise and then figuring out what resources are going to be assembled to achieve those goals.

Elements of Strategy

There are three elements of a strategy:

- Objectives
- Scope
- Competitive Advantage

Objectives

Objectives are the goals that define success. For each objective, the strategy must also establish the **metrics** that will measure and define meeting the goals. The goals need to be measurable and achievable. Perfection is the ideal but is not a practical goal.

"You can't ever reach perfection, but you can believe in an asymptote toward which you are ceaselessly striving."

Paul Kalanithi

Scope

Scope defines the boundaries of the organizations potential activities. Scope represents the strategic guardrails or riverbanks. It is the articulation of what the enterprise will and will not do.

Competitive Advantage

Competitive Advantage details why customers buy your products rather than those of competitors. It is essentially the feature set that is superior in the mind of customers to the features of your competitors.

Competitive advantage relates to the tightness of the coupling of Product/Market Fit. Your product or service must satisfy a customer need, address a customer pain point, or provide delight. Your unique value proposition provides the criteria to align the firm's activities and places parameters on future experiments.

Etymology of Strategy

Etymology is the study of the origins of words and how their meaning has evolved over time.

The English word Strategy comes from the Greek στρατηγία which is pronounced stratēgia. In ancient Greek it means the "art of troop leader; office of general, command, generalship" which in turn comes from roots meaning "army" and "lead". It was originally a military term and the concept of strategy has always been tied up with leadership activities.

The Greek verb form means "to plan the destruction of one's enemies through effective use of resources." Many terms related to strategy like: objectives, mission, strengths, and weaknesses, were also developed through military usage.

Business is similar to military operations in many ways. In business we are looking to achieve goals through the effective use of resources, and we are looking to outperform competitors.

Strategy has to do with the view from the top of the organization and how it functions in its external environment. The external environment is made up of customers, competitors, and regulations.

Strategy is what leaders partake in developing, implementing, and monitoring. In a corporation it is the process that the C level executives plan and present to the Board of Directors for their approval. Then the CEO, COO, CFO and others get to work executing on that approved strategic plan.

The Board, and the shareholders or owners, then judge the executives on their ability to perform relative to the plan. That's why they are called executives. Their job is to execute the plan.

There is an old saying: plan the work, and work the plan. This is strategy.

Strategy is the practice of developing and executing a well thought out and detailed plan to achieve the goals of the enterprise. Strategy takes into account that the planning process is done under conditions of uncertainty and limited resources. You plan based on how your best guess of how the future will unfold and then you course correct as you encounter unanticipated events, circumstances, and obstacles.

Strategy is comprehensive. It takes the marshaling of all the resources at one's disposal and directing them toward a defined goal while navigating through a landscape fraught with obstacles.

Strategy is used in many realms besides business. It is an important skill set anywhere that long range thinking and planning can be valuable. Remember: if you don't know where you are going, you may not get there.

Some important areas that rely on strategy are:

- War and military operations
- Politics
- Diplomacy
- Negotiations
- Sports

- Career

Taking the time and effort to formulate strategy is important because the resources available to achieve the goals we set are always limited. It is our responsibility to allocate and use those resources in the most productive manner possible.

Strategy involves setting goals, determining actions to achieve the goals, and mobilizing resources to execute the actions. It also takes into account whether the organization has the appropriate skills and abilities to achieve the proposed objectives.

A strategy describes how the ends, the goals, will be achieved by the means, the resources available.

Strategic planning begins as intentional. It is planned. But we are working with imperfect knowledge when planning and must acknowledge that strategy will emerge and change as the organization confronts its competition and adapts to its environment. These are the two different types of strategy:

- **Intentional**: which is the plan that then becomes implemented
- **Emergent**: the changes and course corrections and adaptations that are developed in response to encounters with the world.

Strategy is a general term for a set of activities. It involves activities such as strategic thinking, strategic planning, strategic implementation, the measurement of results, and course corrections. These steps are interconnected and repeat in a continuous cycle as the organization acts and evolves. This process is called Strategic Management.

Management of the strategic process also entails communicating the strategy throughout the organization and analyzing and implementing feedback. Strategy drives tactics, and tactics inform strategy.

The terms tactics and strategy are often used interchangeably but are two distinct phases of the process of leading an organization. Tactics are the actual means used to achieve a goal. Strategy is the overall plan of which tactics and resources to deploy.

A business strategy is based on a set of guiding principles for the organization usually outlined in the mission statement. These principles are communicated and form the criteria for organizational decision-making in the tactical stage.

Strategy forms the criteria for the alignment of all the day-to-day decisions that are made within an organization.

Strategy informs people throughout an organization on making decisions and allocating resources in order to accomplish key objectives. Strategy is the roadmap. It sets guardrails for the actions people in the business should take, and the things they should prioritize to achieve desired goals.

Strategy also defines what the business is **not**. This helps people in the organization know what **not** to do and what **not** to prioritize.

There is a rich literature on strategy and strategic thinking and there are lots of fascinating books on the subject. Some classics are:

- Art of War by Sun Tzu
- On War by Von Clausewitz
- The Prince by Niccolo Machiavelli

And some recent business strategy classics are:
- Blue Ocean Strategy by W. Chan Kim and Renee Mauborgne
- Competitive Strategy by Michael Porter
- Mind of the Strategist by Kenichi Ohmae

SWOT Analysis

SWOT is an acronym for Strengths, Weaknesses, Opportunities and Threats. It is a popular and quick study undertaken to identify internal strengths and weaknesses, as well as its external opportunities and threats. They are laid out in a 2x2 matrix.
Also internal resources and capabilities need to be taken into account when doing a SWOT analysis.

Check out my MBA ASAP podcast episode with Brenner Adams and his "So What" template. Brenner had the great idea of rearranging the boxes in the 2x2 SWOT matrix to make the analysis better linked to implementation.

Strategic Thinking

Business leaders are like athletes in that they play the game while simultaneously observing it as a whole. It is challenging to maintain perspective and see the big picture while not getting lost in the action.

It is the challenge of keeping emotional distance while being totally engaged. We want to avoid the trap of winning the battle but losing the war.

Leaders develop the ability to think strategically. This takes long-range vision and a sense of the multiplicity of potential futures. Leaders are always scanning the horizon for new developments, threats, and opportunities and thinking about how to either exploit them or defend against them.

Leaders create the vision and managers implement the vision. Both roles take strategic thinking.

Creating the Vision

All enterprises and projects, large or modest, begin in the mind as a vision of the imagination. They emerge from the creative imagination and are nurtured with the conviction that what is merely a dream can be made real and tangible.

To get from vision to reality takes a practical plan. Strategic thinking is part of this translational process.

Strategic thinking requires a certain mindset. It takes a way of thinking that
- Embraces change,
- Examines the causal links and outcomes of change, and
- Attempts to steer an organization towards capitalizing on change.

The operative word here is change. Strategic thinking attempts to understand change and exploit it.

Carpe Diem

Strategic thinking is about seizing opportunities and leveraging available resources in the most productive manner for the long-term viability and success of the enterprise. You have to be opportunistic and make use of the resources at your disposal.

"Do what you can, with what you have, where you are."

Theodore Roosevelt

It's entrepreneurial in its imperative to action and the pursuit of opportunity.

Strategic Thinking Process

Strategic thinking operates on some general premises. Foremost is acknowledging the reality and inevitability of change. We live in a world of ever accelerating rates of change. To use a hockey metaphor, skate to where the puck is going, not where it has been.

Strategic thinkers question current assumptions and activities. They envision possible futures. These possible futures help generate new ideas. Bismarck defined statesmanship as the art of the possible. The art of the possible pertains to strategic thinking as well.

Strategic thinkers imagine and examine the adjacent possible. They guide the enterprise towards those potential futures with the greatest opportunity. They think about future outcomes as a set of probabilities and not binary branches.

Strategic thinking is conceptual thinking. It focuses on systems and how things interrelate and function together. A change in one part has implications for other parts of the system. It is systems thinking.

Strategic thinking takes into account the practical limits on what is achievable. The organization's core competencies and the external environment place restrictions on possibilities.

Strategic thinking translates abstract concepts and generalizations into practical actions.

Timing and Luck

Strategic thinking takes into account timing. Don't fall into the trap of anticipating changes that are a bridge too far. Don't be right too soon. Being ahead of your time doesn't work well in business. The early bird gets the worm, but the second mouse gets the cheese!

Venture Capitalists understand that timing is more important than entrepreneurial talent. It is better to be lucky than smart and luck depends on timing.

Napoleon Bonaparte won battles. Critics said it was because of luck. He responded, "I'd rather have lucky generals than good ones."

Luck depends on timing and on hard work. Believe in the value of luck and you will find the harder you work, the more of it you will have.

Change

The one constant in this world is change. Prepare for it. Embrace it. Strategic thinking assesses the evolving needs of stakeholders. It considers the technological, social, economic, political, and competitive demands of the environment.

A Questioning Mindset

Strategic thinkers are always questioning assumptions and the status quo:

• "What are we doing now that we should stop doing?"

• "What are we not doing now, but should start doing?"

• "What are we doing now that we should continue to do but in a different way?"

• "What can we do better?"

These questions are applicable to everything an enterprise does. This includes products and services, operational processes, policies and procedures, and its strategy.

Focus

Strategic thinking supports the continuous management of the strategy. The periodic process of

497

strategic planning documents course corrections. Feedback and measurement are critical to gauge the relevance and impact of strategy. This in turn influences the thinking.

Strategic thinking focuses on the impactful and the important. Without strategy we are prone to being reactive. We tend to focus on the immediate urgent tasks that spring up. The urgent is not always what is important.

Strategy helps us stay focused on what is important. It gives us criteria by which to discipline our actions and make better decisions.

We conflate urgency and importance. We end up doing minor tasks that seem urgent but are of little long-range importance. And we allow the important life changing projects to languish. This is a form of procrastination.

There is nothing so useless as spending time doing tasks that shouldn't be done.

Strategy is about long range thinking and employing penetrating vision. You are trying to see through walls and around corners. Question and scrutinize assumptions. Understand systems and their interrelationships. Develop alternative scenarios of the future and examine their implications. Challenge the status quo.

Strategy is about scanning the horizon to forecast changes. Identify convergences, in technology, competition, and customer needs and tastes. Include external technological, social and demographic changes. Be aware of legislative and political changes that can impact your business.

Think different.

Strategic Planning

Strategic Planning is the application of strategic thinking to create actionable steps toward meeting goals. It's a process of codifying the steps an organization needs to take to progress towards accomplishing its mission. Strategic planning creates organizational focus by providing criteria for consistent decision-making that is aligned with the organization's goals.

It's about setting goals and developing a roadmap to get from here to there. Strategic planning is assembling the pieces of the puzzle in the most effective way to achieve those goals.

Strategic planning is done as a periodic process of sessions involving strategic thinking and brainstorming. It might be an annual retreat for a day or weekend. The participants convene with the initial goal of reaching consensus on the desired future of the organization. Once the goals are identified, the strategic thinkers develop a set of guidelines and decision rules for pursuing that future.

Strategic planning focuses on core competencies and what is required to create the desired fit between the organization and the external environment. Strategy is seeking to set the conditions for optimal performance.

Strategic planning is a negotiated process that incorporates consensus and judgment. It requires evaluating and analyzing performance metrics to double down on successes and address problems.

There are programmatic ways to conduct strategic planning sessions to stay on track and complete the plan in the fixed amount of time set for the sessions. These sessions aren't just free-for-alls, they need to be kept orderly and led. The strategic planning process provides a sequential series of steps for creating a strategy document.

The end product is a document: the strategic plan. This document reflects the thinking of the moment, but it should not be taken as set in stone. The planning process is dynamic and ongoing. The plan is a static representation of the process at a given time.

The plan is open to modification as we encounter new information. It is not the plan per se, but the planning process that is most useful.

"Plans are useless, but planning is invaluable."

Winston Churchill

Strategic planning provides guidelines and guard rails for decision-making and operations.

Strategic planning takes analyzing and understanding the current situation and the competitive landscape. It takes the analysis of the internal and external environment and develops the optimal fit between an organization's core competencies, competitive forces, and customer needs and desires.

The process is to develop and refine the organization's direction. Success is measured by an organization's effectiveness in its environment.

A common mission, vision, goals, and set of organizational values drive strategy. This is the directional strategy or "what the organization wants to do".

Strategic goals are not just a question of what management wants to do, but what the organization is capable of.

The organization's operations, resources, competencies, and capabilities influence strategy. This internal assessment represents "what the organization can do."

Strategic Plan Template

The 7 Ps is a British Army adage for Proper Planning and Preparation Prevents Piss Poor Performance. Cheeky Brits. But the meaning is crucial. Planning is a key part of launching and growing a successful business.

Strategic planning uncovers critical issues driving a business. These issues can be problems, opportunities, market changes, resource adjustments and anything else that requires a solution or decision.

As part of the strategic planning process, question everything. Challenge all the assumptions upon which the past strategic initiatives have been based. And question the strategic implementation:

- What needs to be addressed?
- What are we doing now that we shouldn't be doing?
- What should we do differently?
- Is there a better way to do something?

These are some of the types of questions that strategic leaders ask to jump-start the process.

A strategic plan is a roadmap to launch and grow your business. It's your map of how to do more with less. Remember a map is not the territory and your plan is not a static document but subject to continuous revision as you confront events and the world.

All plans and maps by their nature, reduce and abstract and by doing so, eliminate information that can prove important. The most accurate plan would include everything.

"The best material model of a cat is another, or preferably the same, cat."

- Norbert Wiener

This partial information coupled with uncertainty about future events means a plan is not a perfect document to act upon and must be open to revision as new information becomes available.

As the great Prussian military genius Field Marshall Von Moltke said:

"No battle plan survives contact with the enemy."

Plans are Useless, Planning is Invaluable

In preparing for battle I have always found that plans are useless, but planning is indispensable.
- Dwight D. Eisenhower

The reason for the military references is that strategic thinking and planning come out of a military background and was appropriated by business.

When it comes to strategic planning, process is more important than the product. It's not the plan document, but the planning process that is valuable and also your ability to course correct in the face of new information. It is important to remain flexible and adaptive and have contingency plans in place to address various possible futures.

Think of strategic planning as having four main interlocking and iterative stages:

- Analysis and Assessment
- Strategy Development
- Strategy Execution
- Evaluation and Refinement

This provides a context for thinking about the strategic plan, not as a fixed static document, but as part of an ongoing organic process.

The strategic planning process and plan address what we trying to fix, accomplish or avoid. Communicating your strategy aligns stakeholders around your priorities. It engages, motivates, and retains both internal and external audiences.

The goal is to answer the question: how will we succeed? Strategies are the methods you intend to implement to achieve your vision. Strategy determines what you want to achieve and why and most important, it answers the question "how". The strategic plan aligns your mission, programs, and capacity.

Elements to Include in the Strategic Plan

The information below outlines the key elements to cover in your plan.

Here is an outline. Your table of contents should look something like below. Feel free to change the order so the flow fits your thinking.

Executive Summary

Elevator Pitch

Mission, Vision, and Values
  Mission Statement
  Vision Statement

Priorities
  Objectives
  Goals
  Action Items

Measurement
  Objectives and Key Results (OKRs)
  Key Performance Indicators (KPIs)

Marketing Plan
  Target Customers

Environmental Analysis
  PEST
  SWOT

Industry Analysis
   Competitive Analysis & Advantage

Human Resources

Operations Plan

Financial Projections

Here is a detailed look at each element.

Executive Summary

The Executive Summary should be first in the document but completed last. Like the name says, it summarizes the other sections of your plan so you need to spend the time crafting the other parts first.

The Executive Summary is critical. Keep it to one page. It should succinctly convey the future direction, priorities and their impact.

The discipline of creating a concise crisp distillation of your strategy is well worth the effort. Many of your key constituents will only read the summary and you want them to understand where you intend to go and to be engaged in the execution.

When Harry Truman suddenly became president after the death of FDR, General Leslie Groves met with him to brief him on the Manhattan Project. Groves brought volumes of material to leave with the new president. Truman ordered Groves to come back with a one-page summary. Groves said he couldn't possibly reduce such a complicated program to a single page. Truman told him that he didn't really understand the program until he could put it on one page. Groves then went and did it. This is great advice to all of us. Keep it in mind as you write your summary.

Elevator Pitch

An elevator pitch is a brief description of your business. It got its name as the challenge of having a description your business prepared that you can deliver in the course of an elevator ride. Included it early in your strategic plan because it is a distillation of what is important and unique about your business.

The clarity of your elevator pitch is key to your business' success. Customers and investors need to understand it. It's the essence of your recruitment. Everyone in the organization needs to be able to clearly and concisely articulate the business.

Mission, Vision, and Values

Here is where you state your purpose and why what your are doing represents meaningful work.

Mission Statement
The Mission Statement Answers the following:

What is our purpose?

Why do we exist?

What do we do?

Your mission statement explains what your business is trying to achieve. It provides the criteria that guide managers and employees to make decisions that are aligned with the company's goals.

Your mission statement is what defines the guardrails of what your business is and isn't. It defines why what the company is doing represents meaningful work. Contributing to meaningful work is what motivates employees.

It is also the main message delivered to external stakeholders, such as investors, partners, potential employees, and customers. It should inspire them to take the actions you want.

Vision Statement

Every project starts as a vision in the imagination. A Vision Statement defines that desired future state and provides direction for an organization.

The vision statement addresses the question: where are we going? And as Yogi Berra said,

"If you don't know where you are going, you might wind up someplace else."

It is critical to articulate a vision that all the stakeholders agree to and are inspired by. It is fruitless to expect people to enthusiastically act upon strategies and tactics if they don't believe in the ultimate goals and vision.

The bulk of the strategic plan is devoted to addressing how we will get there.

Priorities

This general heading includes objectives, goals and action items, and how you are going to measure them. This section attempts to balance the aspirational and forward looking with the specific and tangible.

Objectives

This is where we set priorities. What are the major things we must focus on to reach our vision? What are the "big rocks" that we need to put in place first and foremost?

Address key objectives for all areas of your organization including financial, customer, marketing, operations, and human resources.

Goals

Goals express a result. Goals allow us to focus on the most important actions to reach our strategic objectives. Goals can be formatted using the SMART template: Specific, Measurable, Attainable, Realistic and Time bound.

Strategic planning is all about setting and achieving goals. The ability to execute is the hallmark of successful companies.

Identify your long-term goals. Then, identify interim milestone goals that you must achieve in order to maintain the pace and path to achieving your long-term goals.

Work backwards to create more granular goals for the next months and quarter. Boeing is legendary for the granularity of their plan. They break five-year plans into day-by-day goals and milestones. There are no long-term results without short-term results. When it comes to implementation, take care of the short-term and the long-term will take care of itself.

Revisit you plan regularly, update your progress and revise as necessary. Strategy is an iterative process.

Action Items

This is how you make strategy work. These are essentially assigned and accountable tactics. Who will do what by when?

These are functional items that are aligned with, and support, the accomplishment of the objectives and goals.

Measurement

"What gets measured, gets managed."

Peter Drucker

How will we measure success? **OKRs** and **KPIs** are ways to organize measuring performance.

Objectives and Key Results (OKRs)

Objectives and key results is a framework for defining and tracking objectives and their outcomes. Major Silicon Valley companies including Google, LinkedIn, Twitter, and Uber use the framework. The legendary venture capitalist John Doerr has written and excellent book on OKRs called Measure What Matters. He names Andy Grove, of Intel fame, the "Father of OKRs".

Key Performance Indicators (KPIs)

KPIs are the metrics that will have the most impact in moving your organization forward. Measuring the KPIs, and acting upon the feedback, are how you course correct. Guide your organization with measures that matter.

Tracking your KPIs. Businesses leaders intimately understand and are obsessive in measuring their metrics and KPIs. This is how you know how your business is performing so you can adjust as needed.

A basic KPI such as Total Sales is critical for understanding if the company is performing well. Understanding and measuring the drivers of sales is also critical so you can anticipate and address issues quickly. KPIs help a company be responsive to changes in the environment in which they operate.

List the KPIs you will track in your business.

Marketing Plan

How do your strategic initiatives impact and enhance your brand?

Your marketing plan describes who your customer segments are and how you will move them through your sales funnel. It talks about customer acquisition costs (CAC) and maximizing lifetime value (LTV). Remember CAC<LTV.

Include a detailed summary of your marketing plan in your strategic plan. Emphasize and prioritize the critical elements.

Target Customers

This section of your strategic plan is for identifying your target customer clusters. Use marketing templates like **STP: Segmentation, Targeting and Positioning** to help organize this planning.

It's important to focus your marketing efforts to be effective and efficient in reaching and addressing potential customers. Hone your messaging and ensure it speaks to your target customer wants and needs.

Environmental Analysis

This is where you analyze your organization's position in the larger context of outside influences and competitors. You can use PEST and SWOT formats for clearly organizing this information.

PEST

PEST stands for political, economic, social, technological factors that affect your organization's mission and approach.

SWOT

SWOT is a template that stands for Strengths, Weaknesses, Opportunities and Threats. A SWOT analysis is an exercise for examining your organization's internal strengths and weaknesses in relation to the external opportunities and threats. It is a quick way to assess and describe your competitive position.

Its importance in the Strategic Plan is to rank and determine the best opportunities to pursue relative to achieving your goals.

Use it to identify which strengths and core competencies to allocate resources toward in order to improve your company.

SOWT Analysis

My friend Brenner Adams, a brilliant marketer and strategist, didn't think SWOT was stacked right. So he came up with So What: SWOT.

SOWT is more than an arbitrary list of strengths, weakness, threats and opportunities; it's a formula for action. To complete a SOWT analysis, strengths are aligned with opportunities, and weaknesses are aligned with threats horizontally. Matching strengths to a market or consumer opportunity, for example, leads to insights, which drive quicker and more effective decision-making.

Weaknesses and threats are evaluated the same way: a company will list out the weaknesses they determine internally based on the market, the product or the team. Then, they can compare that list to one of the threats faced, whether from competing products or market risks, and leverage the resulting insight to prioritize the challenges in order to draw actionable conclusions and build plans to mitigate those external factors.

Once you align your strengths and your opportunities, you can get insights. Weakness and strengths determine what actions you need to take to prevent getting surprised and ambushed. You're not going to have every answer, but you become aware what some of the blind spots could be.

SOWT drives initial strategic prioritization and thinking.

Industry Analysis

You want to understand your industry and ensure your addressable market size is expanding. If it is not, consider diversification. Analyzing the structure and dynamics of your industry will help uncover new opportunities for growth.

Competitive Analysis & Advantage

What are we best at? What are our core competencies?

What characteristics of our organization enable us to meet our customer's needs better than our competition can? What are we best at in our market and in the eyes of our customers?

Identify your key competitors and substitute products and do a SWOT analysis on each one.

Use this analysis to determine your competitive advantages and strategies to enhance and strengthen them.

Human Resources

Do you have the capacity and competencies to achieve your goals? Identify the skill sets needed to execute on the opportunities you've identified and to achieve the goals you have established. Do you have the human resources required to execute on your plan?

List your current team members and identify the skills sets you need to hire to achieve your goals. Include a timeline for on boarding.

Operations Plan

Operations are what transform your goals and opportunities into reality. Identify the individual projects that comprise your larger goals and how these projects will be executed. Use project management tools Gantt and PERT charts to detail each initiative. Know when each project will start, what the budgets are, what the critical paths are, and who will lead them and be responsible for execution and completion.

Financial Projections

The financial projections need to align with your aspirations. This is where each element is quantified, budgets created, and timelines established.

Use a financial model spreadsheet and NPV and IRR to assess the potential results for each opportunity you consider pursuing. These are your decision-making tools.

The financial projections map out the tactics in detail. This is the road map to implementation and execution.

Rinse and Repeat

Review and revise your strategic plan during an annual planning session solely dedicated to focusing on this work. Update it regularly as results are gathered and you gain more clarity. You will not achieve the precise goals established in your strategic plan. The art is in making those goals aggressive but achievable. Research shows that you'll come much closer to them versus if you didn't plan at all. Its not about the plan, its about the planning.

Strategy Implementation

Implementation is a crucial component of strategic management. Implementation is taking the results of the plan and creating actionable elements that are infused through the organization.

Implementation is where we turn the plan into practice and performance. It's easy to sit around and dream up great things to do, it is another to roll up the sleeves and get down to the doing.

Decision consistency is a hallmark of strategic implementation. Successful strategic implementation is indicated when an organization exhibits consistent behavior.

Implementation plans prioritize the key areas that create value for an organization. These include how products and services are developed and delivered and what support activities are required.

Implementation is how we make strategy work. This takes buy-in and ownership by all the stakeholders that are ultimately relied upon to affect the strategy.

It is also critical in the implantation phase to consider that for every strategic initiative you attempt to make actionable, you also create pernicious effects on employee behavior. Its human nature to figure out the best way to game a system to one's benefit and you must be on the look out for these unintended consequences.

Strategic Management

Leadership is creating and communicating a vision. Managing is putting that vision into practice and making it a reality. Planning is the link between the two. Proper planning must remain flexible and adapt to new information. The ability to develop effective strategies that account for change needs to be baked into our planning process.

We live in a rapidly changing environment where we set goals, create a plan, implement the plan, and course correct when faced with obstacles and inertia.

The strategies we develop must be adaptive and responsive to change.

"It is not the strongest of the species that survive, nor the most intelligent, but the one most responsive to change."

Charles Darwin

Managers face a turbulent, confusing, and threatening environment. The only constant is change. Decisiveness can be a strategic advantage but decisions are made with imperfect and partial information. Decisions need to be made in the face of governmental policy and regulatory changes, dynamic economic and market forces, demographic trends and lifestyle changes, and technological advances.

Most of these shifting circumstances are not anticipated in planning sessions nor addressed in the strategic plan.

Dealing with rapid, complex, and often discontinuous change in an opportunistic way requires decisive action based on incomplete information.

We need to actively **manage the momentum** of the organization to keep it moving forward and in the right direction. These concerns form the basis of

Strategic Management. It is a practice that resides at the intersection of leadership and management.

Strategic Management is an iterative and adaptive process including the following steps:
- Strategic Thinking
- Strategic Planning
- Business Planning
- Managing Momentum
- Execution of Plan
- Feedback and Measurement
- Iterate (Rinse and Repeat)

The best way to predict the future is to participate in its creation. You know where things are headed, because you are making it happen.

By engaging in activities that make an impact on progress we are in a better position to dictate the direction of change. It is not enough to simply be responsive to changes. You must participate in creating the future.

Leaders must see into the future, create new visions for success, and be prepared to make significant improvements to products, services and their delivery. Anticipate disruptions, convergences, and emerging trends and exploit them.

How We Got Here

Here is some back-story about how these concepts evolved.

Long-Range Planning to Strategic Planning

Long range planning in business became popular after World War II.

After things stabilized in the aftermath of war, Post-WWII economies began rapidly growing, as did the **demand** for many products and services. Long-range **forecasts of demand** enabled manufacturers and managers to develop detailed planning for marketing, distribution, production, human resources, and financial requirements for their growing organizations.

Long-range planning helped them anticipate how much capacity they would need in order to meet the projected demand. Planning became a tool in competing and succeeding.

Business owners and executives began to realize that it wasn't a good idea to do your long range planning at the last minute. They began to become more strategic about planning early and often.

Increased Pace of Change

As the pace of innovation increased and customers became more discriminating, companies began to face more disruptive forces. Industries became more volatile.

Long-range planning operated under the assumption that the organization would continue to produce its present products and services. This only works in a static environment. For a static world matching production capacity to demand was the critical issue.

Long-range planning evolved into strategic planning as a way to adapt to a rapidly changing environment.

In the last decades of the twentieth century strategic planning evolved and expanded into strategic management. This re-conception was an acknowledgment that organizations not only had to totally reinvent themselves on a regular basis, but also that continuously managing and evaluating their strategy was a key to success.

Strategy isn't just an annual exercise that ends with putting the newly minted plan document on the shelf. It is a continuous process that relies on measurement and feedback.

There are many management techniques for measuring, comparing and analyzing results. What gets measured accurately gets managed properly. Some of the more recently refined approaches to business operations measurement are:

- Benchmarking
- Quality improvement

- The learning organization
- Lean Six Sigma
- KPIs
- OKRs

These represent various management processes for setting, communicating and monitoring goals against results in organizations. They are analytic and data driven.

Analytic approaches integrate strategic thinking and planning with managing strategic momentum. They aid in assessing the adoption of the strategy throughout the organization.

They hold managers accountable for implementing the original initiatives. They are also useful for organizational learning and adapting to be responsive in the face of a rapidly evolving and changing external environment so as to course correct in the face of disruptions, competition and threats that were not anticipated in the original plan.

As the great Prussian general Von Moltke said,

"No plan survives contact with the enemy"

Or as adapted by the great boxer Mike Tyson:

"Everybody has a plan until they get punched in the face. "

Strategic management is about identifying and nurturing the strategy that emerges after contact with external forces.

Strategic Managers

Strategic managers develop the ability to evaluate the changing environment, analyze data, question assumptions, and develop new ideas. They are also able to develop and document an action plan aligned with the strategic plan. This is another iteration of strategic planning moving down into the organization.

Strategic Management incorporates strategic thinking, planning and implementation in a coordinated and recursive process.

Managing Strategic Momentum

The only legitimate work in an organization is work that contributes to the accomplishment of the strategic plan. It takes the orchestration of management and leadership to direct an enterprise toward the desired future.

"Leaders are obligated to provide and maintain momentum"

Max DePree CEO of Herman Miller furniture and author numerous management books.

Making Strategy Work

In many cases there is a disconnect between Strategy and Tactics. Strategy is often misconstrued as simply an annual exercise, an event that creates a 'product': the strategic plan document. Strategy should be thought of a process to be used to actually run the business better.

Strategy integrates with tactics and creates a continuous feedback loop. You have your goals and vision, you experiment with ways to implement, and you course correct as you go. Buck up, suck up, and come back when you mess up. That loop needs to be managed to create and sustain forward momentum toward goals.

If the strategy is not actively managed, it will not happen. It will fail. Epically.

The objective is to achieve the organization's goals. It is crucial to keep our Eyes on the Prize. We do that by managing the strategy to achieve the strategic goals of the organization. And we manage the strategy by measuring the effectiveness of what we are doing.

A major objective of management is to maintain strategic momentum. This entails overcoming inertia and doing the actual work to accomplish specific objectives. It is based on aligning decision-making processes and their consequences.

Effective management is a **learning process** that relies on strategic thinking, periodic strategic planning and **evaluating** strategy performance.

A key to managing strategy is the ability to detect emerging patterns and help them take shape.

Rational strategies rarely work out as originally planned. Adapting to the environment and course correcting is a function of recognizing and codifying the strategic imperatives that emerge out of confronting the world.

An organization may end up with a strategy that was quite unexpected as a result of having been swept away by events and circumstance. This is the dynamic of emergent strategy. It entails being opportunistic. The Latin phrase is Carpe Diem: Seize the Day.

The Learning Organization

As an organization moves into an uncertain future there is a sense of feeling our way along and learning. It is a process of Reformulating and Groping. It is not a direct path from here to there. It is zig-zag and sometimes retrograde.

Strategy evolves and emerges during implementation as the organization gains new information and feeds that information back to the formulation process. We modify the strategic initiatives en route.

The external environment is in constant flux and strategists are unable to accurately predict future and even current conditions. The organization will find itself unable to respond appropriately to powerful external forces with the existing strategy. Strategy needs to be flexible and modifiable as it encounters a world that didn't get the memo about how to cooperate with your plan.

Other competitors are operating in the market and implementing their own strategies. Their actions may block a planned strategic initiative of yours. This unanticipated competitive move can force the activation of a contingency plan or a period of groping.

Acknowledge these inevitabilities and prepare to react and be flexible.

Strategic Leadership

Strategic Leadership is the ability to influence others to engage their own decision-making abilities and agency in navigating wiser outcomes that reduce risk and enhance the prospects for an organization's success, while maintaining financial sustainability.

What Strategic Leadership Requires

Adaptive strategic leaders are who will thrive in uncertain environments. The ability of an organization and its leaders to adapt is the key survival skill.

"It is not the strongest of the species that survives, not the most intelligent; it is the one most adaptable to change."

Charles Darwin

Strategic Leaders

Strategic leaders are the motive force of organizational learning. They create an inquisitive environment that challenges and questions the status quo. They search for the lessons in both successful and unsuccessful outcomes by conducting post mortems and after-action reports. They study these events with their team in an open and constructive way to ferret out what to leverage and what to avoid going forward.

PREPARE For Organizational Learning

PREPARE is an acronym for an iterative 7 step process for framing organizational learning and providing a strategic framework for leaders.

PREPARE:
Predict
Reflect
Explain
Pick
Align
Resolve
Educate

528

Let's dig into the details of each step in the process.

Predict

Take time to plan and anticipate what you expect to happen in any given situation. This doesn't mean over analyzing and worrying about what might go wrong and getting into arguments in your head about events that probably won't happen, but having a sober assessment of expected outcomes.

"I've had a lot of worries in my life, most of which never happened."

Mark Twain

Write these down so as to review in an after-action post mortem and see how your expectations aligned with reality. This is a very helpful exercise. When we don't write down what we anticipate we tend to bend our thinking to quickly to what actually went down and that cuts us off from some creative thinking and options.

Most companies focus on what is directly ahead and react or develop tactics to deal. The leaders lack peripheral vision and a sense of the adjacent possible. This leaves an organization vulnerable to competitors who sense and respond to tentative actions. If the sharks smell blood, your blue ocean is going to get red in a hurry.

In order to predict and anticipate effectively: Look for game-changing convergences on the periphery of you market segments. Search beyond the current boundaries of your business seeking disruptive developments. Develop broad external networks to assist scanning the horizon effectively.

Reflect

Think Critically

Question everything. Question the prevailing assumptions. The manager asks how and when; the leader asks what and why. Reframe problems to get to root causes. Challenge current prevailing beliefs, assumptions and mindsets. Especially challenge and question your own. Root out contradictions, sycophancy, and bias in the organizational decision process.

Avoid Groupthink

Gather a diversity of opinions. Create a team of rivals. Use Red Team and devil's advocates to challenge conventional wisdom and undisputed decisions. Employ the dialectic method of thesis, antithesis and synthesis. You cannot passively allow lemming behavior, herd-like belief, and safe opinion if you want your company to maintain or gain competitive advantage.

Critical Thinking Skills

The ability to think critically is a set of skills that help one determine shit from Shinola. It is each of our individual responsibility to cultivate these interactive capabilities that act as a filter set. Cultivate these:

Reasoning
Evaluating
Problem Solving
Decision Making
Analyzing

Explain

This is your ability to recognize and accurately interpret signals from the competitive marketplace. You have to get good at picking signals out of noise.

"The test of a first-rate intelligence is the ability to hole two opposed ideas in mind at the same time, and still retain the ability to function."

F. Scott Fitzgerald

Ambiguity is uncomfortable and our innate tendency is to resolve it quickly. The challenge is to get comfortable with ambiguity while gathering more information from a diversity of viewpoints.

Hold fast and synthesize information from as many sources as you can gather and let your viewpoint develop. You're looking for patterns and trends. Incorporate multiple sources of data. Encourage others in your organization to do the same.

Employ the scientific method and test multiple hypotheses. Iterate and pivot towards good decisions. You need to be action oriented but not hurried. Make hast slowly, or as they say in Latin **Fastina Lente**

Pick

There needs to be a pace and cadence to your decision making process that is action oriented. Don't fall prey to analysis paralysis. Remember you will always be working with partial and incomplete information. Develop a culture and processes that arrive at a good enough position that balances speed and rigor. Perfection is the enemy of good enough. Time to take a stand. Be decisive.

"The price of inaction is far greater than the cost of making a mistake."
> Meister Eckhart

It is important to explain and communicate the rational behind decisions and how they align with strategy. Articulate the decision in a manner that gets to the crux of the matter.

Align

Build support. Try to bring diverse viewpoints into alignment by understanding what drives other people's agendas including what remains hidden.

Discuss tough issues especially when its uncomfortable. Address the elephants in the room and don't allow things to fester.

Resolve

You won't build complete consensus. If you do, go back and review the steps above as it is probably a signal of groupthink or lack of diversity. Foster open dialogue and build trust. Engage key stakeholders and address divergent viewpoints.

Educate

Honest feedback is harder and harder to come by as an organization scales. Cultivate it. This is crucial. Failure is a valuable source of organizational learning. Run a post mortem on all successes and failures. You learn more from failure than success. Be nimble and agile and course correct rapidly in the face of new information. Acknowledge and encourage failures that provide insight and were pursued in the manner of this framework.

Leadership and Management

Tactical thinking is "doing things right," while Strategic thinking is "doing the right things."

Strategic thinking is typically leadership: creating the vision. Whereas Tactical thinking is management: implementing the vision.

Prepare: the 7 Ps

The 7 Ps is a British Army adage for Proper Planning and Preparation Prevents Piss Poor Performance.

You have what it takes

No one is born excelling in all these different skills. The good news is that they are learnable and you can cultivate them with self-awareness and an open mind. Now get to it.

Synopsis of Elements of Strategy

Cognitive science has shown that our brains need to see the big picture before the details.

With that in mind, I am going to reiterate the big picture at the beginning of the book. There is a pedagogical technique I am employing here of: tell them what you are going to say, say it, and tell them what you said. Now that you have gone through the process of thinking about them in detail, they are worth reviewing.

There are three elements of a strategy:
- Objectives
- Scope

- Competitive Advantage

Objectives are the goals that define success. For each objective, the strategy must also establish the **metrics** that will measure and define meeting the goals. The goals need to be measurable and achievable. Perfection is the ideal but is not a practical goal.

"You can't ever reach perfection, but you can believe in an asymptote toward which you are ceaselessly striving."

Paul Kalanithi

Scope defines the boundaries of the organizations potential activities. Scope represents the strategic guardrails or riverbanks. It is the articulation of what the enterprise will and will not do.

Competitive Advantage details why customers buy your products rather than those of competitors. It is essentially the feature set that is superior in the mind of customers to the features of your competitors.

Competitive advantage relates to the tightness of the coupling of Product/Market Fit. Your product or service must satisfy a customer need, address a customer pain point, or provide delight. Your unique value proposition provides the criteria to align the firm's activities and places parameters on future experiments.

This is how you gain clarity about how you will win.

We have been looking at some pretty heady and abstract concepts. Let's close out with something more fun and playful.

Strategic games

Playing games aids in brain development. The brain has neural plasticity. We learn and adapt. Old school board games offer developmental opportunities for mind expansion. We can reap big benefits from play.

Gaming provides a no risk, low stakes environment for gaining intuition around the dynamics of a subject. It takes theory and puts it into practice on a bounded field with rules.

For a fascinating deeper dive into this subject, check out the great treatise on games *Finite and Infinite Games* by James Carse.

Playing strategy games is a great way to gain facility in acting strategically.

Strategy games give us a framework to rehearse and practice thinking, reacting, adapting, and competing. They come with the added bonus of enjoyment. Delight and enjoyment are key components of accelerated learning. If you enjoy the process, you do it more and that is how you get good.

Here are a few classic games of strategy:

Chess

Chess is like a metaphor for strategy. If you search "strategy" lots of chess board images come up.

Everybody should have a chess set. It just looks classic and feels homey like having a piano or fireplace. The rules are easy to learn and the permutations of play are vast. The game is usually divided into three stages: openings, middle game, and end game. There are many opening sequences that have been developed over the years and they are well worth some study. One of my favorites is the Nimzo Indian.

Go

Go is an ancient Asian strategy game for two players. The aim is to surround more territory than the opponent. It is played on a beautiful board with black and white pieces. It also has relatively simple rules and its permutations of play are orders of magnitude more than chess. While chess is rule-based in a way that allowed it to be programmed successfully by computers to out calculate human competitors, Go had to wait for artificial intelligence learning to outstrip human champions.

Risk

Risk is a mid century modernist strategy board game of diplomacy, conflict and conquest. Risk is a political strategy game. Two to six players can play risk. Risk is played on a board that depicts a map of the earth, with territories, which are grouped into continents. Risk is a great party game with friends.

Diplomacy

Diplomacy is another mid century modernist political strategy board. It has game theory elements of Prisoner's Dilemma in that players form alliances and cooperate, or defect and betray each other. It also has negotiation phases.

Summary

Thanks for reading and I hope you found this book and the concepts in it valuable Cultivating the habits of mind that lead to strategic thinking, planning, and implementing is a long term process. Be patient and remain committed. When making any decision, think of the long-term consequences and act accordingly.

Always play the long game.

The End

Thank you for reading!

Dear Reader,

I hope you enjoyed *MBA ASAP* and found it filled with useful and valuable information..

As an author, I love feedback. Candidly, you are the reason that I organize my thoughts, write, and explore these topics. So, tell me what you liked, what was helpful and what could be better explained or left out. You can write me at jjcousins@gmail.com and visit me on the web at www.mba-asap.com.

Finally, I need to ask a favor. If you're so inclined, I'd love a review on Amazon of *MBA ASAP*. I'd really appreciate your feedback.

Reviews can be tough to come by these days. You, the reader, have the power now to make or break a book. If you have the time, here's a link to my author page on Amazon where you can find all of my books: https://www.amazon.com/-/e/B01JVF2XTU or just search for the title and my name on Amazon. A quick review will be immensely appreciated!

Thank you so much for reading *MBA ASAP* and for spending the time and effort with me.

In deep gratitude,

John Cousins

Sign up for my Newsletter and get free books. Sign up at www.mba-asap.com and receive Reading and Understanding Financial Statements absolutely free.

Receive announcements of free and discounted books and courses.

About the Author

John is an author of over 20 books, blogger, podcaster, online course creator, investor, inventor, entrepreneur and musician. John began his career, after graduating from Boston University and MIT with degrees in Media Studies and Electronics, working for one of the great early Silicon Valley tech firms: Ampex. He then spent a decade in Manhattan working for ABC Television as a systems engineer designing and building facilities for the network and managing programs for sports and news; big spectacles like the Olympics and political conventions.

John then received his MBA from Wharton. He has since taken two companies public as CFO and CEO and has had 15 years experience as a public company CFO and ten years experience as a public company CEO. John has been involved in many start up and public company financings and deal making. He has founded numerous startups in alternative energy, life sciences, and technology. His career shifted to teaching at numerous universities in US and internationally in the past ten years. His company MBA ASAP delivers digital content on business topics via eBooks, paperbacks, audiobooks, podcasts and online courses. Visit http://www.mba-asap.com/

FREE EBOOK DOWNLOADS

Go to www.mba-asap.com and click on
the big orange button